INDUSTRY OF NATURE

ANOTHER APPROACH
TO ECOLOGY

Frame Publishers, Amsterdam
Directed by Élodie Ternaux (matériO)

CONTENTS

Aviator George R. White built a foot-propelled flying
machine and patented his version of the ornithopter.

p.125

TO START WITH

BY ÉLODIE TERNAUX

_____ Our daily activity, in the Paris matériO library of emerging materials, is assisting all sorts of creative people – architects, designers, artists, etc. – with their projects and more specifically in their choice of materials. Over a period of a few years, the requests and preoccupations of the people coming to see us have become closely linked to issues of sustainable development, in particular as far as the ecological dimension is concerned. Today there are very few questions on materials which don't involve recyclability parameters, traceable and certified sources, energy-efficient conversion processes, etc. This public awareness, if a key feature and engine for change, is not always on the one hand fully put into action and on the other hand in accordance with an industrial society that has not yet undergone a major revolution. Alas, it must be admitted that some projects seem to be conducted with a good conscience, which then proves to be false and turns out to be mere green-washing. The issues relating to sustainable development are substantial; the parameters are numerous and complex and, without any doubt, navigation in sustainable waters is difficult, arbitrating on the relevant decisions to be taken and making sense without compromising ourselves. As Baron de Coubertin so wisely said, 'The important thing is to participate'. We are in the first stage of a long conquest for the more reasonable and the more sustainable.

_____ At the centre of our ecological questions lies that about the connection we maintain with nature. One of the recurrent questions in choosing a material, for example when a designer is seeking to adopt a more sustainable approach, is: 'Is this material natural?' The eternal debate about natural compared with artificial, a debate which in effect is now in full swing, with the profoundly-anchored conviction that natural materials must exist and that they must, in essence, be 'better' than artificial materials. There goes a sustained prejudice, and a dichotomy which should not exist. Everything is natural, everything is artificial. Man, a product of nature, makes and converts elements from nature. If we consider that a bird's nest, a complex conjunction of thin twigs and delicate leaves, is 'natural', then why not consider that the Olympic Stadium designed by architecture firm Herzog & de Meuron, which opened in 2008 in Beijing, China and christened 'the bird's nest' is itself also perfectly natural? In what way is a wooden chair really more natural than a chair made of plastics material? At least may I consent to accept the idea of a thickness of artificiality as suggested by Ezio Manzini in his famous book *La materia dell'invenzione* (The material of invention). Indeed polymethyl methacrylate is more 'converted' from oil than moulded plywood is from the trunk of a tree but are they not both part of nature?

_____ Mankind has spent some time struggling to get away from this nature, considered to be hostile. This species, endowed with the power of speech, quickly became superior to all and has devoted a lot of energy in its struggle to dominate natural elements. Today, for a short time, mankind almost manages to master them, but the tables are turned by the threat to the very survival of the species that happens to have this mastery. And the movement for reversal, therefore: man gently starts to regain contact with his environment and discovers with astonishment, with curiosity, envy and interest, this nature with which he has completely lost touch. Man realises at last, with humility, that to listen to and observe the living world around us gives us access to an incredible source of information, inspiration and innovation. Nature finally gives us evidence of quite disconcerting 'intelligence' and now seems to be an example of an 'industry', with complete mastery of sustainable development. Whether we simply copy from it, use living organisms in our projects or transfer some of its technologies, nature offers us a fantastic terrain for creativity.

_____ Man knows very well how to imitate: from false fur and floral motifs to imitation leather, nature constitutes a substantial reservoir we use so blithely. Man also uses nature in a particularly important (and worrying) manner by draining its resources. We're not going to stop helping ourselves to these any time soon. Just as any species does, we have to ensure our livelihood by using the available resources. It all depends on the equilibrium of the systems we are endangering more and more, by using a little too much of what nature offers. It is there, among other things obviously, that notions of sustainability come into play in our actions. It is also there that certain boundaries can be crossed, towards the biological use of certain organisms which become simple machines in the service of man and for which we can no longer be guarantors of permanence. The threshold to genetic modifications of certain species for our benefit is then quickly passed.

_____ To really take inspiration from nature on the other hand, from its forms, structures, systems and functions which are optimised under certain conditions, that's when we have quite a few cards to play. This is the approach that current biomimicry* emphasises, led by the American biologist Janine Benyus _read_ p.33, accompanied by others throughout the world, for example Gunter Pauli, Gauthier Chapelle and Emmanuel Delannoy. How obvious to turn to nature with its billions of years of experience, research and development in order for us to advance _see_ p.13.241. How astonishing that the discipline is not more firmly established, when you think that the biomimetics principle has always been there. By going back to take our lessons from nature, as Leonardo da Vinci invited us to do, we have in our hands a way of tackling the questions posed by our complex world and, furthermore, in a sustainable manner. This approach to sustainable development, seems more profound than a lot of 'sticking plaster' solutions adopted today. However, it needs a great capacity for retention, observation, understanding and a real change in our way of thinking. Janine Benyus, observing nature, emphasises the following principles:

Nature relies on one main source of energy: solar energy.

It uses only the amount of energy that it needs.

It matches form to function.

It recycles everything.

It bets on diversity.

It works with local expertise.

It limits its own internal excesses.

It uses constraints as a source of creativity.

_____ Nature is a veritable expert in sustainable development. Victor Papanek, in his book _Design for the Real World: Human Ecology and Social Change_, published in 1971, was already emphasising that in his eyes* biology and its associated disciplines offer the designer very significant potential to reach a new, creative vision of the world. He assured us that a designer must take an interest in ecology* and ethology (the scientific study of animal behaviour) to find equivalents in nature and in biological systems. How can we fail to admire the daily feats of engineering achieved by nature? From the functioning of ourselves *read* p.85.205.207, to that of some frogs to resist freezing *read* p.83, to that of chameleons or stick insects to each camouflage themselves with their individual strategy *read* p.93.97, to that of termites in constructing a thermally-regulated dwelling without electric air-conditioning *read* p.233, to that of trees in drawing their energy from sunlight *read* p.111.113.185, and so on. Diversity, BIOdiversity *see* p.57. There is no doubt that we have to fight effectively to preserve this biodiversity* which is under threat today, not even from an altruistic desire for its preservation but in a sudden burst of selfishness before we see the disappearance of very valuable sources of engineering, design and sustainable development.

_____ With scientific training, I spent rebellious years getting away from these subjects. Yet today I'm happily going back, proof that the old adage 'you go back to your first love' is still true. This is a family book and it makes me very happy, a chance to bring together the scientific expertise of both my parents – my father, research director in the CNRS (*Centre National de la Recherche Scientifique* – the French National Centre for Scientific Research), specialising in neurocybernetics* and my mother, lecturer in biology and geology – with my modest knowledge at the crossroads between science and creativity. The way this book is brought into being is a good example of the multidisciplinary principle which I believe to be very important to the relevance, originality and quality of projects. The team thus consists of two scientists keen on popularisation and education, a committed and talented graphic designer, a typographer and illustrator and his artist mother (it's a real family affair), an experienced female editor in an enlightened publishing house, a thorough translator and the woman at your service, part engineer, part designer.

_____ A project like this one, flirting with science and design, inevitably raises questions on the precision of the scientific content when it is gathered and designed for a non-scientific audience. Where does one draw the line? When does it become too complex, when does it become too simple? There's no doubt that scientists and experts, with this book in hand, will contest its accuracy as we took shortcuts in order to offer easier ways to be part of this amazing complex world. How to (and even whether we should) communicate scientific facts is an eternal debate amongst the scientific community; one that unfortunately divides and sometimes dismisses curious minds who quickly discover they cannot reach and grasp the essence of science, or that one will not grant them the access in order to protect its privileged expertise. Seeing the excitement in children and adults alike when they discover how magical, intriguing and complex natural phenomena are, and seeing how this knowledge explains and enlightens our world, proves how essential scientific education and communication are at any level. It's this very specific excitement that makes biomimicry a field of high interest when it comes to ecology. Contrary to most methods or solutions presented to us – mainly associated with down-cycles, to, let's face it, rather dull-repulsive-serious-implying efforts solutions – the wonders of nature arouse the desire to create in a positive way, call upon our child-like spirit of amazement, and are utterly refreshing and precious.

___ The aim of this book is to open a door to incredible natural diversity, to the fascinating mysteries of living organisms, to the inexhaustible source of inspiration found in nature and to the intense challenge that faces us. The book is a kaleidoscope of information and inspiration, especially, but not exclusively, about the very precise approach offered by the concept of biomimicry. My hope is that this book will stimulate people to take care of their relationship with nature. It consists of several parts, to be read in any order you choose. However, the Janine Benyus interview stands out as a point of reference. Clear and didactic, the biologist knows how to base her approach on evidence that just cannot be ignored. By means of a historic panorama, several interviews, various carefully chosen images, a detailed glossary and bibliography and a selection of strategies adopted by nature and which have or could give rise to applications for mankind, we hope to offer all you designers an inspirational tool which will persuade you to dip into nature, to confront yourselves with its enlightened intelligence, to learn, learn and learn again to be more rational and analytical, while being more innovative.

___ 'Man's engineering can imitate many inventions, thanks to the use of various instruments contributing to the same goal. However, he will never make them more beautiful, more simple or better adapted than those of nature because, in its inventions, nothing is missing and nothing is unnecessary'. Leonardo da Vinci

___ Particularly in these changing times, when values waver and seem on the point of being reassessed, the challenge is there for us to go into battle.

3 SECONDS AGO...

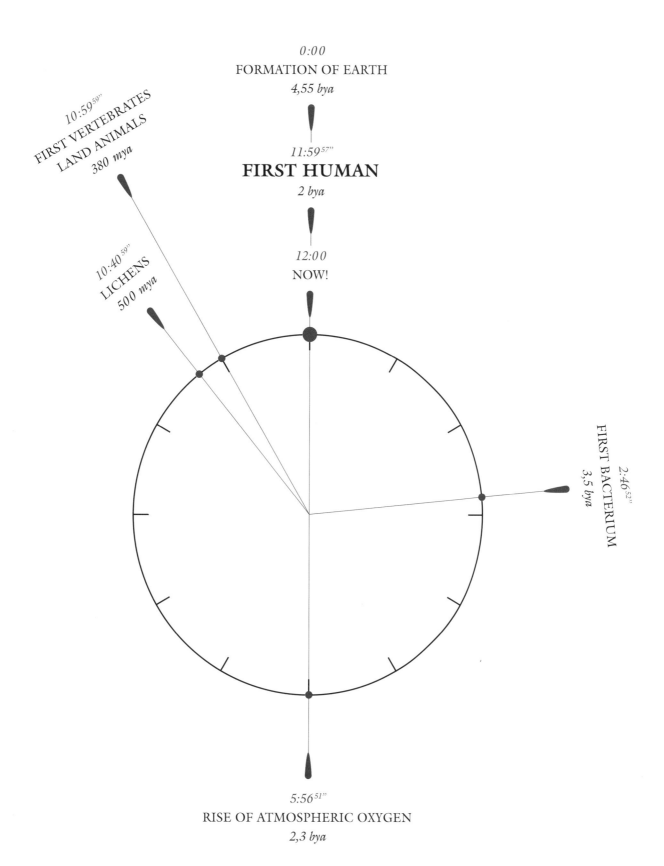

0:00
FORMATION OF EARTH
4,55 bya

10:59⁵⁹"
FIRST VERTEBRATES
LAND ANIMALS
380 mya

11:59⁵⁷"
FIRST HUMAN
2 bya

10:40⁵⁹"
LICHENS
500 mya

12:00
NOW!

2:46⁵²"
FIRST BACTERIUM
3,5 bya

5:56⁵¹"
RISE OF ATMOSPHERIC OXYGEN
2,3 bya

A visual that represents the time of Earth's formation until today as a 12-hour clock – starting at midnight (4.55 billion years ago) – shows that the first human only made an appearance 3 seconds before noon.

NATURE
AS A MODEL

BY JEAN-PIERRE TERNAUX

I.

MIMICRY:
A LIFE-SAVING REFLEX
IN SPECIES

NATURE HAS A LOT TO TEACH US

——————— On planet Earth, our environment has evolved over several billions of years, slowly building a complex nature where living organisms, plants and animals in their land-based, marine or aerial territories have adapted to many variations of environmental conditions over the history of our planet ^{see} p.57.241. Whatever their place on the evolutionary scale, living things have specific anatomical and physiological features. Under these conditions, plant and animal species, including man, are capable of expressing elaborate behaviour, allowing the resolution of complex problems whose main aim is to maintain the survival of the species.

—— Biomimetics* consists of studying species in their natural environment, constructing models existing in nature to understand the functional mechanisms, and studying the possibility of artificially reproducing the shapes, materials or biological processes and their behavioural expression.

—— From the Latin *bio* which means 'life' and *mimesis* 'to imitate', biomimetics is a way of observing and taking inspiration from nature in order to create.

—— This approach interfaces with all scientific disciplines, with basic research and their applications in technology and industry. This quest for knowledge, from observating and understanding the mechanisms which govern the way living things function, has generated contemporary artistic movements inspired by nature and a field of creative innovation in the domain of design and architecture over several decades ^{read} p.33.

MIMICRY: NATURE'S STRATEGY
IN THE SERVICE OF NATURAL SELECTION *
AMONG SPECIES

——————— If biomimetics is one of man's specific methodologies to take inspiration from observing nature in order to create, mimicry is an adaptive strategy which concerns many animal species. The mimicry strategies of animals are many and varied, but they have a common aim: escape from possible predators. To do this, various species are capable of using means to escape from the sight of their predator. One then speaks of camouflage strategy or cryptic mimicry ^{read} p.93.97. These phenomena have been widely copied by mankind for protection against an enemy during armed conflicts. In more sophisticated ways, some species take on morphological attributes of other, inedible or dangerous species, passing themselves off as other species. Mimicry therefore requires the use of a more complex mechanism of co-evolution which comes in three forms: a form serving as a model, an imitative form and a duping form.

—— Two great names are associated with the discovery of the basic principles of mimicry in plant and animal species: those of the British scientist Henry Walter Bates and the German scientist Friedrich Theodor Fritz Müller. At the age of eighteen, Henry Walter Bates (1825–1892), a plant entomologist, published a short article on beetles in the *Zoologist* journal. After reading a book entitled *A Voyage Up The River Amazon* by William Henry Edwards (1822–1909), published in 1847, Bates explored the Amazon valley as far as the border of Peru. Between 1848 and 1859, he collected specimens of 14,712 species, 8,000 of which were previously unknown to science. The majority of the species listed were insects, birds, reptiles, fish and mammals. The results of his exploration were published in a very successful book entitled *The Naturalist on the River Amazon*. As well as discovering new species, Bates corroborated Charles Darwin's theory of evolution by publishing the first article devoted to the theory of mimicry around 1862. The publication about the imitation, by a species, of other life forms or inanimate objects brought tangible scientific arguments about the possibility for a species of Amazonian butterfly in the Dismorphiinae family to evolve and take on colours similar to those of another species belonging to the Heliconiinae sub-family, a species avoided by predatory birds because of its toxicity. Similar examples are also described by Bates among birds and reptiles. This type of mimicry is known as Batesian mimicry. Recent work confirms Bates' observation and theories. Batesian mimicry describes the biological processes brought into play by a given harmless species which adopts the physical appearance, such as patterns and colours, of a noxious species. The aim of this modification of the appearance is to have protection from predators, the latter having learned to avoid genuinely noxious species. In this context, by natural selection, the survival and continuance of the mimicking species is assured.

_____ In the same era, the German biologist Fritz Müller (1821–1897), carried out brilliant research into the evolution of various species such as crayfish, jellyfish, annelids (ringed worms such as the familiar earthworms), flat worms, bees, termites and the pollination of flowers such as orchids. Being a talented artist, Müller drew relevant, detailed illustrations to accompany his observations on nature. Müller was the first to highlight the symbiotic relationships between the *Cecropia* genus of trees and ants _read_ p.225. The insects protect the trees against parasites and climbing plants, while the trees offer the ants shelter and access to nutritional resources named, after their discoverer, 'Müller bodies'. As a biologist, Müller published a single book in his career called *Für Darwin* (For Darwin) in 1864. This includes a large amount of data, obtained in particular from crayfish, which confirmed Darwin's theory of evolution by natural selection, which had been published some years previously. In 1878, as an ardent defender of Darwinian evolution, Müller also provided convincing explanations relating to a certain type of mimicry which until then was not understood. His observations in the field allowed him to show that two different venomous or toxic species were capable of adopting the same warning livery in relation to their predators. This similar appearance allows them to benefit from repulsion of their respective predator, and vice versa, thus improving the effectiveness

Henry Walter Bates

of their defence mechanism. This particular form of mimicry is known as Müllerian mimicry and is not limited to fauna. Many plants with similar flowers obtain mutual benefit from attracting the same pollinating insects.

_____ Apart from these types of mimicry, plants and animals are capable of automimicry*. Numerous species of butterflies or freshwater fish have some sort of spot simulating the presence of an eye*. The aim of the latter is to produce a surprising effect for the predator or, depending on the orientation of the mimicking sign, to mislead a predator's perception ability. These evolutionary changes allow the prey to very quickly adopt escape behaviour.

_____ Camouflage is also a strategy used by many species to escape their predators. This evolutionary development is different from mimicry as it consists of imitation of motionless objects in the environment. This is the case for the stonefish, for example, or stick insects whose morphological characteristics are similar to those of leaves, twigs or animal droppings. Species of a larger size don't imitate any particular object but their morphological features and colours make them blend into their environment. Some species in tropical rainforests, such as chameleons or geckos in Madagascar or marine species such as squid, cuttlefish or octopus, have the ability to change their colour to blend into their environment. This quite distinctive strategy can be used just as well in aggressive behaviour as for defence.

_____ All of these mimicry strategies, both in the plant and animal kingdoms, whether changes of shape, colour, odour, taste or even sound, give these 'mime artists' characteristics resembling those of target species which have limited interest as food for a predator. An insectivorous bird will ignore a stick insect which looks like a twig, cuttlefish will avoid predators by blending with a sea floor. A target mimic can also present a risk for the predator, some flies resemble wasps, some non-venomous snakes are capable of imitating the sound of a rattlesnake, several species of butterflies have markings resembling the eyes of much bigger animals. Some mimic species can also present a food interest for their prey, which is the case, for example, with carnivorous plants which give off an odour of putrefying flesh to attract the flies they feed on _read_ p.117. Mimicry is sometimes also involved in behavioural recognition of or by fellow creatures. This is the case among the social insects such as ants. By continuous chemical exchanges, each individual is capable of imitating the respective odours of other ants. This builds a characteristic colony odour, an indispensable key to being recognised as belonging to the colony.

BEHAVIOURAL MIMICRY:
BY THE INDIVIDUAL TOWARDS SOCIETY

_____ At the behavioural level, mimicry is a fundamental mechanism for learning. By watching a fellow creature, a perception of the utility and interest of the thing being done can be acquired. It's also in this context of observer and imitator that the rules to be followed to reproduce an action are acquired. By reproducing an action, the difficulties of its execution are discovered and the chain of basic actions, both conscious and muscular, which shape its optimal accomplishment are memorised. The reproduction of an action is at the very root of memorisation of a technique. Behavioural mimicry is not the prerogative of the human species but concerns all animal species. It is particularly important among the vertebrates, in particular during postnatal development, a key period for the acquisition of knowledge by the newborn. For a mammal, behavioural mimicry occurs in many learning scenarios in acquiring the principles of using its body in its own space, of using tools, of various techniques, of language or the development of the mental abilities allowing the expression of deductive reasoning or the resolution of complex problems. The processes of imitation initiated during development are all grouped under the term behavioural mimicry and make a major contribution to the development of adult behaviour. Behavioural mimicry can be considered as a cultural factor capable of shaping the specific behavioural patterns of a given species. In parallel with the genetic factors which characterise innate behaviour, an epigenetic factor* comes into play and this is partly responsible for acquired characteristics.

_____ The influence of behavioural mimicry is not limited to an individual of a given species, but concerns groups and the mass dynamic as well. The process of imitation has now been studied for several decades, in particular in great-ape and human societies. In our con-

Fritz Müller

temporary societies it contributes information and communication to produce models which govern the behaviour and appearance of populations and individuals. Events induce collective emotions carried on currents of imitation which construct homogeneous social groups propagating the same sensation or the same opinion throughout.

_____ Gilles Deleuze (1925–1995), a French philosopher; René Girard (born in 1923) a philosopher and anthropologist of violence and religion, a member of the Académie Française since 2005 and an inventor of the mimetic theory; and Gabriel Tarde (1843–1904), a sociologist and philosopher, have all shown that certain emotions, certain fantasies and certain fears are typical of social groups. Emotional, happy or angry sensations, or again those of anxiety induced by events, are communicated to individuals and are propagated via the mass media channels. Newspapers, magazines, radio, television and the internet are all involved in this propagation. Individuals all thus become linked by collective stress, the same emotion, a single sensation they all share. Social groups are thus animated by a wave of imitation of the collective sensation. These actually shared perceptions can lead to affective disorders which are collective and make people feel as if they exist as a united people. In this context, behavioural mimicry can also be examined from the angle of its consequences for society. From the sociopsychological point of view, it is the same source of group phenomena or crowd behaviour which can lead to excesses, collective blindness, ranging from conformism to collective hysteria. Even more dangerous, behavioural mimicry can result in manipulation in the context of propaganda or under the domination of a guru.

BIOMIMETICS: FROM NATURE TO CREATION

_____ While mimicry concerns phenomena of imitation between different species or between individuals of the same species, biomimetics* involves only the human species. It consists of artificial reproduction of the properties of one or more biological system. Biomimicry* is a genuine methodology taking inspiration from living organisms, or more generally from the world around us, eventually including not only biological components from our environment but also some relating to the mineral world.

_____ The use of biomimetics methodology is above all a methodology concerned with scientific research, the aim of which is to facilitate the study of natural systems by laboratory reproduction of phenomena hidden in the complexity of real organisms. This scientific approach, even though generally reductionist, allows progress in gaining knowledge of the intimate mechanisms which govern the functioning of living organisms. This methodology is generally used in the domain of biophysics to obtain access to the principles of functioning in molecular complexes. By extension, it also allows access to new structures in living organisms, to identify and reproduce molecular interfaces in the laboratory so that their specific functions and their role in a complete living organism can be studied.

_____ Apart from its interest in advancing knowledge relating to living organisms, the biomimetics approach offers the possibility of developing innovative therapeutic applications. In this context, current research concerns the development of nanoprobes* and intelligent nanovectors* and control systems to allow drugs to be transported within an organism to target specific cells. Applications of biomimetics methodology also concern improvement of diagnostic techniques by the development of high-quality molecular imaging, the production of biomaterials for restorative surgery, the development of new man/environment interfaces or the development of new virtual-reality and augmented-reality technologies in the service of both the health and pathology of mankind.

_____ Just like mimicry which concerns not only the individuals of a species but also their relatives and their social organisations, biomimetics* today takes inspiration from knowledge acquired in the domain of ecosystem* organisation <u>read</u> p.167, or more generally from the functioning of living organisms, to better integrate organisational principles and human technologies in the societal domain. The exploitation of natural mechanisms, to apply them in different technological domains, is today described as bionics*.

_____ In the course of the last three decades the uses of biomimetics methodology, at first limited to the domain of research in functional biology and its applications, also went on to be disseminated and are going to penetrate into the milieus of creation, where they can play a major role in a movement of innovation inspired by nature.

II.

MAN AND NATURE: EXPLOITATION, BIOMIMETICS AND SYNTHETIC BIOLOGY

BIOMIMETICS: FUNDAMENTAL AND APPLIED RESEARCH

_____ In most cases, biomimetics methodology consists of the re-creation of microscopic biological systems by using basic cellular elements such as molecules*, membranes, nucleic acids, etc. with a view to reproducing all or part of a cell or tissue system (assembly of cells) and studying its functional properties. Cellular and molecular models can be built from previously isolated and purified molecules, such as carbohydrates*, protides, lipids* and nucleotides*, which are the basic elements of cell construction. Artificial saline* solutions, with the same composition as intra- and extra-cellular milieus may also be used in these molecular models. The development of artificial systems can be tracked by means of specific markers such as fluorescent molecules <u>read</u> p.169. The most commonly used today are proteins* extracted from jellyfish, capable of binding to certain basic molecules, which then fluoresce when illuminated with light of a specific wavelength. The architecture of biomimetics models can also include surfaces treated to be hydrophilic* or hydrophobic* <u>read</u> p.203.217.237.239 and inorganic components capable of influencing the shape of the cell elements being studied.

_____ Taking into account the extreme complexity of the molecular and cellular systems in living organisms, the relevance of biomimetics models (*in vitro** approach) is limited in some cases and the results obtained under these conditions always have to be verified and confirmed by experiments conducted on equivalent real systems (*in vivo** approach).

_____ In the field of biophysics, biomimetics models have allowed characterisation of the physical properties of molecules which play a major role in cell rigidity and motility*. The construction of artificial membranes by using lipid bilayers on a specific substrate, allows the mechanisms for transporting ions and molecules through the membranes to be studied, for example in nerve cells the molecular mechanisms involved in the transmission of nerve messages <u>read</u> p.159.

BIOMIMETICS: THE BEGINNINGS OF A SYNTHETIC BIOLOGY

Synthetic biology relies on the principles of biomimetics. This relatively new scientific field combines research in the fields of biology with engineering principles, aimed to design and construct (synthesise) new biological forms and systems with controllable functions. Synthetic biology is still in its infancy, as the understanding of the principles of biological functions and their development is still far from complete. In this field, the use of the principles of biological engineering, such as *in vitro** models, standardisation, normalisation, automation and computer-aided design, all contribute to simpler, faster, less expensive processes to modify living organisms.

The concept of synthetic biology arose in the 1900s, inspired by the work of Darwin on evolution and that of Gregor Mendel (1882–1884) relating to the laws of heredity. The movement was launched by several biologists, lead by Hugo Marie de Vries (1848–1935), a Dutch botanist who put forward the possibility of studying and controlling the evolutionary mechanisms of species in the laboratory, to create new life forms with particular novel properties. In his book *La biologie synthétique*, the French biologist Stéphane Leduc (1853–1939), maintained that biology must be successively descriptive, analytical and synthetic. Jacques Loeb (1859–1924), a German physiologist living in the United States, would, without any doubt, be considered as the leading promoter of a technology specific to biology.

Charles Robert Darwin
© Natural History Museum, London

Synthetic biology really came out into the open in the last three decades of the 20th century. The use of recombinant DNA* techniques by Stanley Cohen and Herbert Boyer, co-recipients of the Nobel Prize in Physiology or Medicine in 1996, the discovery of restriction enzymes* and their application in molecular engineering by Werner Arber, Daniel Nathans and Hamilton O. Smith, co-recipients of the Nobel Prize in Physiology or Medicine in 1978, and the invention in 1984 of polymerase chain reaction techniques, a molecular biology method for 'amplification' of DNA *in vitro*, would allow gene analysis and description, construction of new genetic configurations and evaluation of their functional properties.

Synthetic biology gained a new impetus at the start of the 21st century with the work of Tom Knight in the Massachusetts Institute of Technology (MIT) with his introduction of the 'BioBricks' concept, which allowed standardised construction of systems using biological components for various functions. At the same time, Roger Brent, Robert Carlson, Drew Endy and Adam Arkin in the University of California were going to advocate a different approach, closer to engineering, which they called 'intentional' or 'constructive' biology. In opposition to genetic engineering, which they considered unperfected and random, their approach was more rational, inspired by engineering sciences. Their methodology seemed more mature and robust, allowing the construction of biological systems with predictable functions. They nevertheless rejoined the synthetic biology camp, in particular during the 'Synthetic Biology 1.0' conference organised in 2004 at MIT. This scientific event marked the real beginnings of synthetic biology.

At the end of the 1990s, geneticists selected a bacterium* called *Mycoplasma genitalium* which could easily be cultivated and multiplied *in vitro*, under conditions providing it with the essential nutrients for its metabolism*. This bacterium possesses the smallest known genome* in the animal world, with only 482 genes coding for the proteins making up this organism. Analysis shows that only 28% of the genome codes for proteins with essential functions. In 2007, the bacterium *Mycoplasma laboratorium* was constructed from *Mycoplasma genitalium*, becoming the first so-called synthetic bacterium, built entirely from a synthetic chromosome* by genetic engineering. In the absence of stress, this laboratory *Mycoplasma* reproduces freely *in vitro*.

In 2010, work by biologist John Craig Venter's team, published in the scientific journal *Science*, described for the first time the possibility of manufacturing a complete living organism from a synthetic genome with 1,078 oligonucleotides* and consisting of 1,077,947 base-pairs, assembled in a circular genome called 'JCVI-syn1.0'. The synthetic bacterium thus created results from a strain of *Mycoplasma capricolum*, whose genome has been replaced by the synthetic construction described above. Under these conditions a new strain of the bacterium was created, *Mycoplasma mycoides JCVI-syn1.0*, for which Venter registered a patent.

*Organisms create
what they need.
There is a notion
of sufficiency.
It is one of life's
principles that we call
'optimising rather than
maximising'.*

Janine Benyus

There is no doubt that synthetic biology is going to develop in a big way over the coming decades. The protagonists in this field, biotechnology* specialists, see in synthetic biology a wide redefinition and extension of biotechnologies and genetic engineering. The main aim is to design biological systems under standardised and stable conditions, which are capable of processing information and producing various potentially useful molecules* to construct new polymers, medicines or foods. Yet again, innovative biological systems could be new energy sources, allow manipulation of various chemical elements and the genesis of a new synthetic chemistry. The development of synthetic biology is likely to lead to improvements in our environment.

BIOLOGY AT THE HEART OF DESIGN AND INNOVATION

The development of biology in the second half of the 20th century led to a new look at nature, beyond the frontiers of scientific disciplines. The birth of ecological movements with a primary aim of protecting nature, allowed the spread, through all the strata of society, of principles likely to contribute to the protection of natural resources and the rise of a new methodology, taking account in particular of the long-term possibilities of reducing fossil energy resources. This sphere of influence was increased by the first oil crisis in 1973, giving the ecological movements additional arguments in favour of an industry and an economy showing more respect for the natural heritage of planet Earth.

In the industrial and economic world, this period has been beneficial in causing active reflection on the means to be used to invent new technical solutions, inspired by nature, for the manufacture of consumer products. In this domain, bio-design is an innovative conceptual trend in industrial design which, by its curvilinear architecture, responds to the imperatives of ergonomic efficiency and optimisation of forms. This methodology, initiated by Luigi Colani in the 1960s, harmoniously associates form with product efficiency, integration with the environment and economies in materials and energy. The 'father' of bio-design, Colani, a German designer with an Italian father and a Polish mother, studied sculpture and

Janine Benyus

painting at the School of Fine Arts and Architecture in Berlin and then studied aerodynamics* at the Sorbonne in Paris from 1949 to 1952. This twin-track training allowed him to very quickly express his talents in the automobile industry, in the design of bodywork inspired by biological forms and allowing significant fuel economy. He worked successively with various manufacturers including Fiat, Alfa Romeo, Lancia, Volkswagen, Ferrari, Lada, BMW and Volvo and also in the aeronautics industry (Rockwell, Boeing). In the 1960s he designed many objects produced by well-known manufacturers and showed a talent and a particularly fruitful eclecticism: furniture, spectacles, pens, television set cases, trains, lorry bodywork, aircraft, built-in kitchen units, a piano, etc. His magnum opus was definitely the Canon T-90, the first camera to be ergonomically designed as an object with a man/machine interface. His research and his work, inspired by a deep affection for nature and for optimum relations between man, object and environment, have contributed to him being described as the 'Leonardo da Vinci of the 20th century' and 'design messiah' in Eastern countries.

THE BIOMIMETICS APPROACH FOR ECOSYSTEMS

We are in a period when climate change, anthropisation*, increasing greenhouse gas emissions, loss of biodiversity* and exhaustion of fossil fuel* resources are being called into question by public opinion, scientists, decision makers and citizens, with the result that protection and preservation of the environment, research on 'clean' energy sources and the development of 'green' chemistry *read* p.141 constitute the major focal points for the 21st century. In a globalised economic system where profit flaunts itself as the single common objective, present day societies now seem to have a new regard for nature and build new technological approaches more reliant on the use of natural, less-polluting resources and based on a better understanding of the functioning of the biosphere*. This approach, although on the rise in our societies and heavily promoted in the media, is not without difficulty when account is taken of the multiplicity of factors which govern equilibrium and the development of the different ecosystems on our planet. The successful outcome of such an approach involves the opening up of scientific disciplines and the application of a policy of interdisciplinary research. In this context, worldwide scientific research is still only taking its first steps. Yet again, this approach inspired by nature cannot content itself with global and single solutions, but needs to take account of local environmental characteristics.

_____ The emergence of biomimicry* is credited to Janine Benyus, who published the book *Biomimicry: Innovation Inspired by Nature* in 1990. This American biologist who is president of the Biomimicry Institute, proposes a real industrial revolution, totally constructed on natural properties and contributions *read* p.33. Benyus outlines several major principles in nature and invites us to take inspiration from them: solar energy as the main energy source and energy consumption which is self-limiting to requirements; adaptation of form to a desired function in relation to the construction of objects and setting up of services or optimisation of organisations. This set of principles applies not only to organic material recycling processes but also to the products of chemical engineering, allowing a quasi-total use of all the molecules* produced naturally and artificially. Biomimicry also banks on biodiversity by structuring its exploitation by mankind and preserving in it ecological niches for each species used. This approach also involves the setting up of conditions for an effective social dialogue allowing the construction of enlightened action plans using local expertise. Finally, the ecosystems biomimetics approach, subject to the difficulties and constraints of complex biological systems, must show itself to be an innovative source of creativity. Biomimicry thus opens up a new route in the design field and, more generally, in the field of creativity.

_____ The applications of such an approach are many and research carried out in this domain is already bearing fruit for the wider public or arousing interest in the industrial world and the creative milieu. The development of hydrogen and electricity production imitating photosynthetic* processes *read* p.111.113.185, research carried out to produce ultra-pure water filters constructed on the principle of membranes and proteins* imitating systems used in nature, Velcro® modelled on the fruit of the burdock (a variety of thistle) *read* p.63, turbojets constructed on the form and principle of the functioning of the nautilus *read* p.197, self-cleaning window panels inspired by studies of the biophysics of the 'lotus effect' *read* p.203, the pantographs (overhead-line current collectors) of the Japanese high-speed train modelled on owl wings to re-

duce nuisance noise *read* p.181, eco-buildings taking inspiration from termite-mound air conditioning *see* p.233, micro robots capable of walking on water by exploiting the physical principles of surface tension*, as pond skaters (water striders) do in nature *see* p.237, so many examples which are mentioned in this book, showing the extent of interest in the progress of biomimicry.

III.

NATURE AND CREATIVITY: A LONG HISTORY AT THE HEART OF HUMANITY

DESIGN, CREATIVITY, INNOVATION AND BIOMIMETICS

_____ Design can be considered as a discipline whose objectives aim to physically represent a thought, a concept, an intention or an achievement. These objectives have to take account of various constraints, which may be functional, structural, aesthetic, educational, symbolic, technical, productive or environmental. All of these perceptions relating to design have a social, economic and cultural context. Design is also at the crossroads between creativity, the arts, sciences and technologies and today constitutes an interface of innovation between sciences, technologies, the artistic milieu, the creative world, industry and the economy.

_____ The root of the word design is to be found in the Italian word *disegno* which, in the Renaissance, constituted one of the major concepts of the theory of art. Its meaning encompasses both design and drawing. This dual concept was preserved in 17th century France as *dessein*, bringing together the notions of 'idea' and its 'implementation'. In Anglo-Saxon culture, this duality is introduced into the theory of art in the terms 'drawing' and 'design', meaning a plan and its graphics (philosopher Earl of Shaftesbury, 1712). The double sense of design disappeared in the 1750s to leave two different semantic fields, that of design in its practical form and that of design in its concept of an idea, recalling the material/spirit duality expounded by René Descartes.

It was at the start of the 20th century, in the boom years of industrial society, that design with its initial meaning of *designo* came to be adopted internationally to designate the processes of designing and shaping.

The meaning of the word design changes according to periods, cultures and individuals. It can be conceived of as applied art, creative execution, or as an autonomous discipline both in its practices and in its theories. For Anglo-Saxons, design is considered more as a conception, an idea, an intention or an action plan. In French, it will often be translated as a search for harmony between the form and function of an object. In Italian and German, the use of the word design is more for craft and industrial traditions. These different meanings didn't stop crossing over throughout the 20th century. This situation is going to generate certain ambiguities as to understanding of what the issues of design disciplines are in a wide field where creativity becomes the general rule. The designer differs from the craftsman in not being a specialist in a particular material, wood, metal or plastics. He is no longer a technician or an engineer, as he is not a specialist in a given technique or a particular sector of engineering. He establishes himself as a veritable leader of an orchestra navigating across all the domains of knowledge and aspects of global organisations, creating indispensable links between thought and practice. This designer's approach can be compared with that of the complex philosophic thought as well as scientific approaches to systematism (the practice of classifying). Its role is to create logical links between objects, flows of information, images and symbols which are part of our environment today ^{read} p.261.

Undeniably, the observation of nature and understanding the mechanisms which govern biological functions have been an influence throughout human history on all creative movements, whether they be art, architecture, scientific research or industrial innovation. Design that one can qualify as a discipline in the service of a function, a true process of resolution of problems relating to use, form and technique, has now appropriated the methods of biomimetics, and in this way brings new solutions to the major environmental questions of our contemporary societies. It's not a matter here of a simple imitation of nature but a veritable process successively involving observation, creation and application ^{read} p.251.255.

Robert Boyle
Published in Britain's Heritage
of Science, London, 1917
(from a painting by F. Kerseboom)

MASTERY OF MATERIAL: AN ESSENTIAL KEY TO THE PROCESSES INVOLVED IN DEVELOPMENT AND CREATIVITY

The construction of our civilisations and their development over the course of history are, to a great extent, linked to the acquisition of techniques allowing mastery of materials and exploitation of nature, to provide the energy necessary for the conversion of these materials. This technical deployment, at the origin of the chemical sciences, started with the first prehistoric civilisations and the discovery of fire, the first energy source used by man. Using fire as a source of light, heat, cooking of food, etc. would allow the improvement of daily life. Mastery of fire very quickly allowed the first conversions of materials, in particular the fabrication of glass, ceramics and metal alloys. Many archaeological excavations over the whole of the planet bear witness to early activities marking the birth of a scientific discipline with universal principles.

In effect, chemistry and the modern chemical sciences are fundamentally linked to man's desire to understand his own functioning, his environment and nature in general in its widest dimension, from his territory to the universe and to characterise the properties of matter whether of mineral or organic origin. And then again, chemistry, with its concepts, theories and the investigative tools it has helped to develop, allows us to understand the mechanisms which govern the conversion of matter. With the Industrial Revolution, this quest for knowledge about changes in the states of matter led to the development of a very wide field of innovation whose zenith is certainly still a long way away today. Thus from far back in history, chemistry would be punctuated by many attempts to develop coherent theories on the structure of matter, among which the atomic theories and theories of the elements proposed respectively by Democritus and Aristotle, or again those initiated around the alchemy of the Middle Ages, would remain the most popular. Chemistry would only distance itself from these more or less archaic principles in the 17th century, with the experiences and scientific method used by Robert Boyle. His famous book *Sceptical Chymist*, published in 1661, marked the real beginning of modern chemistry. The work of Antoine Lavoisier, dedicated to the laws of conservation of mass, made a similar contribution to making chemistry a real science. Today, chemistry has become multidisciplinary, undeniably connected to almost all scientific domains, such as physics, mathematics, engineering sciences (chemistry of materials and energy), biology (biochemistry, pharmacology), the sciences of the universe and the Earth (astrochemistry, geochemistry), ecology* and the environment (green chemistry), and also the sciences of man and society.

     This synopsis of the history of the discipline with its characteristic keywords, which are the result of a much more extensive field of investigation beyond the limits of the chemistry domain, are a relevant illustration of the way in which chemistry and its applications have made an essential contribution to modern society. To understand nature and transform matter in the service of man actually gets its whole measure here, even if history also bears witness to deleterious social consequences whose traces are still having some effect. Chemistry and material sciences today make a major contribution to the design and implementation of objects, procedures and innovation in the bio-inspired systems sector.

THE UNIVERSALITY
OF THE BIOMIMETICS APPROACH

     The idea of constructing machines capable of 'aping' man is certainly embedded in our genetic heritage. This dream, which is still a dream today, marks out our civilisations and throughout history will not cease to mobilise many designers, philosophers, scholars, technicians and engineers. Artificial reproduction of human behaviour, by constructing anthropomimetic machines, originates from a movement imitating the organs and functions of the human species, where the brain and the hand are the key parts in the construction of a functional mimetic entity. In this field, automata certainly represent the oldest tradition, from those made in antiquity up to modern industrial machines, now capable of automatic assembly of cars, television sets and computers among other things. This tradition, initiated by the Greeks and then passed on to the Arabs, is still with us. The Italian engineers of the Quattrocento period (in the 15th century) were the heirs before these automata became the basis of the machines of the Industrial Revolution.

Jacques de Vaucanson
Portrait by Joseph Boze

     Initially used as salon objects for entertainment purposes, automata rapidly became technical objects which were the first in the mechanical age to imitate the limbs and hand of a man. The automaton went on to imitate the functions of the sense organs, giving rise to the audiovisual age; it then went on to become an extension of human intelligence in the era of cybernetics. This latter period was to mark the dawn of bionics*, with its applications in the field of artificial intelligence, robotics inspired by nature (robot swimmers inspired by fish, robotic insects *read* p.65.89.179.183.237, etc.), the design of hydrodynamic* clothing (inspired by shark skin *read* p.155) and aerodynamic* clothing (inspired by a duck profile) or again the design of helmets to match the morphology and structure of the human head. Bionics will also open up new routes for exploration in the field of prostheses, allowing possibilities of replacement of a limb or a failed organ by a machine capable of restoring a vital function (artificial heart, renal dialysis machine) *read* p.105.

     In line with the mechanistic theories of Descartes and Leibniz, Jacques de Vaucanson (1709–1782), a French inventor and artist with a mechanical background, went on to invent automata whose successes would prove to be limited by the fact that their principles were ahead of their time. The first Vaucanson automaton was constructed in 1738, representing a seated shepherd playing a flute. This was animated with arm, lip and finger movements. The success of this android quickly aroused suspicion among the public and Vaucanson struggled to demonstrate that the sounds emitted by the automaton came from a flute and were not generated by something called a bird organ (a device used to encourage caged birds to sing) hidden in the stand, but actually a quite refined imitation of a flute being played by an automaton.

     In 1741, while medicine and knowledge of the human anatomy were making significant progress, Vaucanson presented to society in Lyon a design for an artificial man which could be used to simulate human movements and serve as a model for courses in anatomy and surgery. Things got complicated when he produced his duck automaton. A bird automaton would normally have flapping wings, but Vaucanson added imitation of chewing food and digesting it. The duck would eat grain, digest it and produce excrement (it would be learned later that the digestion was in fact just a deception). In 2007, Belgian artist Vim Delvoye succeeded in a similar project with his machine called 'Cloaca', which was actually capable of the digestion of food and producing excrement.

_____ The automata of the 18th century, capable of making programmed movements, were going to open up an insatiable desire for engineering products in the 19th century's Industrial Revolution. Automata left the salons and machines entered the factories.

_____ Vaucanson's ideas and convictions about the possibility of imitating living beings and creating machines capable of reproducing any human behaviour are still with us today. In the 20th century this universal quest, so characteristic of human nature, benefited from the enormous growth in knowledge in many, or even all, scientific disciplines. For example, we could cite the fundamental advances in our understanding of cellular and molecular mechanisms controlling the transmission of nerve messages in the neuron* and cerebral networks, and the birth of new disciplines such as neurocybernetics*, opening up pathways in computing and robotics and generating applications in terms of mimetic machines in the service of man.

_____ After Sir John Eccles (1903–1997), winner of the Nobel Prize in Physiology or Medicine in 1963 for his work on nerve-message transmission in neurons, Warren Sturgis McCulloch (1898–1969) a neurobiologist and Walter Pitts (1923–1969), John von Neumann (1903–1957) and Alan Turing (1912–1954), all three of them mathematicians, were going to be pioneers in the creation of computer sciences. Their work, based on some neurobiological data obtained by Eccles, was going to lead to the 'formal neuron'* model and to the construction of the first computer by Franck Rosenblatt (1928–1971) in 1957. The Perceptron, a network of artificial neurons, was capable of performing mathematical operations using a 'learning' algorithm.

_____ Closer still to the observations and analysis of the functioning of living organisms, there is the incessant progress in genetic engineering, biotechnology* and synthetic biology. It is now possible to envisage the eventual standardised construction of living organisms from elementary building blocks of organic material. Very far from dying out, progress in biomimetics is today opening up an immense field of innovation and creativity.

D'Arcy Wentworth Thompson
Image ref. ms50125-1. Courtesy of the University of St Andrews Library

NATURE: FORM AND FUNCTION

_____ For the novice, observation of nature can arouse sensations of chaos: many plant and animal species with very different forms cohabit in different milieus ^{see} p.57. Without any prior knowledge of biology, nothing could lead one to imagine any close links between an earthworm, a grasshopper and a rat, or again between an alga, a fern and an oak tree. Nevertheless, a biodiversity* that man has exploited and domesticated from antiquity to meet his needs for energy and food, is to use it for the hardest farming tasks or for its therapeutic properties.

_____ The work of Georges-Louis Leclerc, Comte de Buffon (1707–1788), Jean-Baptiste Lamarck (1744–1829) and Georges Cuvier (1769–1832), all French naturalists, allowed the different known species to be listed and classified as a function of their morphological characteristics.

_____ Species with similar forms make up homogeneous groups in a growing hierarchy where the forms are more and more complex, with man putting himself right at the top of this classification. Efforts made to classify species would contribute significantly to the development of the theory of evolution set out in 1859 by Darwin in his book *On the Origin Of Species*.

_____ As well as highlighting the principles of natural selection*, the classification of species allowed a demonstration of the close relations existing between the physiological forms and the functions which characterise them. This relationship between form and function applies both to whole organisms and also to the form of cells, tissues and organs within them. The genetic revolution in the middle of the 20th century brought evidence that the form of living organisms is dependent on the expression of specific genes. Mutations of these genes, induced generally by environmental conditions, give rise to new morphological characteristics and new forms better adapted to the environment: a principle of optimisation and adaptation which characterises all living organisms.

_____ Not only are biological forms in a close relationship with the functions and behaviour of each species within its ecosystem*, but the latter are also subject to the rules of physics, mechanics and mathematics. D'Arcy Wentworth Thompson (1860–1948), in the first printed edition of his book *On Growth and Form*, published in

1917, was the first mathematician to explore the degree to which differences in the forms of related animals could be described by means of relatively simple mathematical transformations. His book, inspired to a large degree by the work of Darwin on natural selection and enhanced by many illustrations, has enthused and influenced generations of biologists, architects, artists and mathematicians. Thompson's research found a number of examples of correlation between biological forms and mechanical phenomena. He showed, for example, a similarity between the shapes of jellyfish and the shapes of drops of liquid falling into a viscous fluid, and between the structures of hollow bones in birds and the design of structural timberwork in architecture *read* p.175.211. This work integrates the dynamics of the physical and mechanical phenomena which govern the development of forms in living organisms in the course of embryonic development and gives rise to important notions about the involvement of generic physical laws in the biological mechanisms controlling the form and the growth of different species.

_____ Once again, the data accumulated by Thompson result from observation of nature and the use of an approach quite close to biomimetics*. As far as the form of living organisms is concerned, one finds here the preoccupations of our distant ancestors, like Leonardo da Vinci who wondered about and took an interest in the resemblance between trees and blood* vessels (1508), and much later the assertions of Nicolas Steno (1636–1686), a Danish scientist pioneering in the fields of anatomy and geology, who pondered over the branching patterns of silver deposits in mine samples compared with the structure of snowflakes.

_____ These questions of similarity between natural forms, and by extension between natural and artificial forms, are far from being abandoned and are still topical today. The search for common physical laws governing these phenomena is still mobilising the scientific community in all disciplines. The branching structures of plants, rivers, certain minerals, snow and ice crystals, organs such as bronchial tubes or vessels, neurons*, bacteria*, artificial crystals and certain fluids surely have a construction plan involving common mechanisms? If the numerous arguments converge in favour of this assumption, the domain to a large extent, still remains unexplored, allowing

Louis Sullivan
Historic photograph, Courtesy of the Richard Nickel Committee and Archive, Chicago, Illinois

anticipation of a huge field of fundamental research, but also an almost endless source of creativity.

_____ In the living world, the form of species is adapted to their milieu and the organs responsible for physiological functions have specific and suitably adapted forms in the majority of cases, likely to provide vital functions at the optimum cost in energy *read* p.73.197. This adaptation and optimisation of functions occurs at different scales, going from the molecule* to the whole organism, via the morphological organisation of cells, tissues and the organs involved. For example, the shape of the cells constituting muscles, that of nerve cells, that of cells in the vessel walls or in the respiratory organs 'branchia' in marine species and lungs in vertebrates, is different. Although every living cell has common intrinsic properties, their forms confer on them physical and metabolic properties which meet the requirements of the functions they support. Also for example, the elastic and contractile nature of the cells which constitute muscle fibres, the large exchange services developed by the cells constituting branchia, bronchi and bronchioles are the basis of the biological mechanisms which provide motility* and respiration. This functionalism in nature, gradually built up throughout evolution, incontrovertibly highlights relationships between form and function and constitutes a major concept, the fundamentals of which have been applied widely in the design field and especially in the architectural sector.

_____ At the start of the 20th century, the American architect Louis Sullivan (1856–1924), a great master in the Chicago School of Architecture and pioneer in the construction of the first generation of American skyscrapers, was celebrated for taking up the first principle of functionalism in a single phrase: 'form follows function'. These few words summarise his vision of architecture, according to which the size of the building, its mass, its spatial language and all the other characteristics of its appearance must derive solely from its function. Thus, this proposition means that if all the functional elements are taken into account rigorously, architectural beauty will naturally and necessarily follow. This architectural movement was opposed to the eclectic and academic styles of the 19th century, which avoided putting decoration on structures. This came back to the designs of Austrian architect Adolf

*Go, take your lessons
from nature,
that's where
our future lies*

Leonardo da Vinci

Loos (1870–1933), an enthusiast for the plainness of modern architecture, who published a work entitled *Ornament und Verbrechen* (Ornamentation and Crime) in which he forcefully went against ornamentation and was biased towards clear reading of function in the form of a building.

_____ Sullivan's functionalism was going to be the origin of modern architecture and the concept was meticulously taken up by Charles Edouard Jeanneret-Gris (1887–1965), a French architect of Swiss origin, better known under his pseudonym Le Corbusier, and by the German Ludwig Mies van der Rohe (1886–1969), both enthusiasts for concrete, steel and glass. Their buildings simplified preceding styles. In his book *Vers une architecture* (Towards an Architecture), published in 1923, Le Corbusier referred to houses as 'machines for living in'. His Villa Savoye at Poissy and his Cité Radieuse at Marseille are two emblematic and obvious examples of functionalism, integrating man and his relationships with the concept of construction.

_____ For the last 50 years or so, Sullivan's functionalism has been widely criticised, giving rise to a post-modern architecture where constructions no longer take on functional responsibility but have to be considered as works of art. Thus, as Ieoh Ming Pei the celebrated American architect of Chinese origin emphasises, 'Art cannot lay itself open to criticism'. The position of the American architect Peter Eisenman, a great theoretician of the post-modern era and hostile with regard to the user, is yet more radical, 'I don't do function'. This castigation of the theories of functionalism and the movements for 'deconstruction' started a few decades ago and is credited to both Peter Blake, an American architect of German origin (1920–2006), and the American Charles Jencks, leaders and promoters of the post-modernist movement. With his book *Form Follows Fiasco*, published in 1977, Peter Blake was going to wipe out Sullivan's functionalism.

_____ The environmental questions which society poses today, i.e. climate change, a looming energy crisis, protection of the environment, reduction of greenhouse gases, etc., have given rise to thoughts on the designing and implementation of an ecological architecture, or at least a sustainable architecture, more respectful towards the environment. This vigorous movement no doubt takes inspiration from the properties of living things and their optimised abilities allowing effective expression of vital functions with the least cost in energy. This new type of architectural engineering is developing in multi-faceted forms, taking account of diverse criteria linked to technology, management, our health and respect for nature. So there are several guidelines tracing the progress of a sustainable architecture: the choice of natural materials meeting the requirements for our health; the availability of energy-saving items; the reduction in energy requirements; and the choice of energy sources and the context of environmental life _read_ p.163.223.233. Although based on concepts that are praiseworthy in terms of human comfort and protection of the environment, sustainable architecture is now widely criticised, instead of being a movement propped up by media pressure and society's questioning about the future of the planet. One finds in it the ideas and concepts of the ecological movements of the 1960s, a sort of revival of marginal movements which will perhaps not lead to a comeback for a recognised architectural style, even if certain ecologist architects update organic forms, as stated most strongly by the protesting ecologist movements.

Leonardo da Vinci
Self-portrait

NATURE AND AESTHETICS

_____ Throughout history the beauty of nature anywhere in the world, whether or not populated by animals and vegetation, has never ceased to inspire artists, painters, sculptors, photographers and film directors. The observation of life in its environment always has been and still is a source of artistic creation, even if, as Paul Gaugin said, 'The artist must not copy nature, but take elements from nature and create new elements'. In the artistic field, this quotation expressly translates the basic principles of the biomimetics* approach: observe to create and construct.

_____ The 16th-century Italian painter and naturalist Arcimboldo (1527–1593), known for his portraits made entirely from fruits, flowers or even species of marine animals, was perhaps one of the first to have used a biomimetics approach in his pictures. His portraits, consisting exclusively of natural elements, do not translate as an oeuvre which is only to be derided. Art historians consider him a master, scientists a true zoologist. This painter didn't just copy designs taken from naturalist treatises of the period. Even if he probably took inspiration from *L'histoire entière des poissons* (The complete history of fishes), published by Guillaume Rondelet in 1554, more than half of the species represented in his picture *Aqua* (Water) produced in 1566, do not appear in that bible of ichthyology. The painter didn't content himself with immortalising a bestiary (a type of book popular in the Middle Ages, describing real and mythical animals), but introduced a precocious doctrine of evolution into his compositions. The most archaic animals are at the top of the picture but the whole takes into account an evolved organism: man.

    Ernst Haeckel (1834–1919), a German zoologist in the evolutionist tradition, is known as a staunch Darwinist and a pioneer in research on marine fauna, but beyond that his work marked an era in the domain of culture and the history of ideas because of the relationship he established between science and art and his monistic philosophy*. In 1899, Haeckel wrote in his publication *Kunstformen der Natur* (Art forms of Nature), 'Nature produces in its bosom an inexhaustible mass of wondrous forms which, in their beauty and variety, surpass anything man can create as an artistic form'. In this publication, which includes a hundred accurate drawings of marine invertebrates produced during his scientific research, Haeckel wanted to enable a non-specialist public to have access to the wonders of nature spread across the ocean floor, or visible through a microscope. In this context, Haeckel also expounded his aesthetic theory of monism, which considered nature and the cosmos as a single entity. Haeckel postulates the priority of the beauty of natural forms over artistic forms, thus bringing a biological foundation to art.

    This aesthetic evolutionist theory went on to acquire notoriety and popularity in different publications like *The enigma of the world,* published in 1899, or *Nature's marvels,* published in 1904. For Haeckel, forms from nature were transformed into artistic forms but in reality remained natural forms, even when idealised or stylised. This pantheistic philosophical conception of a 'nature god' and of nature as the seat of a universal soul lead the author to true veneration of nature, where contemplation is essential. The interest that man shows in

Ernst Haeckel
Photograph by Nicola Perscheid

relation to the forms of nature as artistic forms, which for millennia have allowed him to imitate originals to create secondaries, lies for the most part in their beauty, that is to say in the pleasurable sensation aroused by their contemplation.

    In his search for the foundations and laws which govern the development of forms, Haeckel highlighted the unity of forms in all living things, and in doing so reduced the infinite variety of plants and animals to a few classes of elementary forms. Drawn essentially to the aesthetic features of species, his research work was focused on the study of the lower marine organisms: radiolaria*, jellyfish, diatoms and physalia *read* p.141. He was fascinated by the aesthetic qualities of their forms. His illustrated atlas and his analytical monographs on the species he studied, as well as those of his publications intended to popularise science, rapidly aroused a response among the secular public. His original drawings of radiolaria with their symmetrical radial forms, polyps, jellyfish or coral which were reproduced in his atlas by the lithographer Adolf Giltsch (1852–1911), were soon used as models by many artists, craftsmen, sculptors, designers and architects for ornamental forms. His biological publications made a profound mark on the Art Nouveau artistic movement which, in that period, was already moving away from a floral style to take new inspiration, allowing new artistic criteria linking form and content. His influence would bear fruit in numerous architectural works or ornamental objects using varied artistic techniques. The Haeckel monographs devoted to radiolaria certainly had a great influence on the French architect René Binet (1866–1911) with whom he exchanged long letters. Binet's monumental gate, installed in the Place de la Concorde in Paris for the Universal Exhibition of 1900, was an elegantly stylised radiolarian in cast-iron, illustrating the architectural transposition of an artistic form from nature in a masterful and imposing manor.

    Today, progress in biology, marked by the development of genetics and molecular biology and their applications in genetic engineering and biotechnologies, have generated new art forms, described as biotech art or transgenic art. A transgenic fluorescent green rabbit called Alba acquired iconic status all over the world. Fifteen years were sufficient for a new artistic trend to develop, hence finding inspiration from all fields of biology and all the knowledge accumulated in relation to the functioning of various species and the relationships between species and with their ecosystems*. Transgenesis*, tissue culture, animal or vegetable selection/hybridisation*, tissue transplantation, synthesis of artificial DNA* sequences, electrophysiological* experiments and techniques for viewing molecular biology are biologists' tools that the artist has appropriated. He has left his studio to enter the laboratory, deliberately contravening procedures of perceptions and metaphors to go into the act of direct manipulation of the living entity. For the artist, biotechnologies become real tools allowing the fabrication of fluorescent green animals, the designing of organic objects with the aid of cell cultures, the implementing of sculptures with micrometric dimensions which take shape in bioreactors and under the microscope or even use DNA as an artistic medium.

——— 'Take it and make use of it' one might say. The strategy of these artistic movements, faced with a new cult of the possible, which brings a real opportunity for creation of new living organisms and, as envisaged by Vaucanson in the 17th century, creation of a genuine artificial man capable of imitating all of our behaviour, is to infiltrate the milieus where the knowledge and the techniques are to be found today. This art is disturbing, because it touches on our fears and reflects our contradictions about technological revolution: Utopia or reality?

——— This new form of artistic production is therefore arising in close collaboration between artists and scientists such as that initiated in the SymbioticA art-science collaboration in the department of anatomy at the University of Western Australia in Perth, where artists and researchers work with each other. The TC&A (Tissue Culture and Art) project uses cell culture as visual art. Their living productions, illustrated for example by their beating 'Pig Wings' obtained from pig-cell cultures, show an irony regarding the commercialisation of living things, for which the prospects should be fabulous, according to some experts. In the project 'Disembodied Kitchen', the banal normality of factory farming is put to the test in the production of edible, semi-living 'sculptures' cultivated from a muscle biopsy carried out on a frog, which is continuing to live next to its growing frog steak. These steaks pick up the thread of research carried out in the 1960s, dedicated to fabrication of 'petroleum steak' as a cheap protein* substitute, a project abandoned at the time of the first oil crisis in 1973.

——— This art nouveau of life has seen several artists setting up in the field of biodiversity*. George Gessert abandoned his paintbrushes to devote himself to the techniques of plant hybridisation and construction of aesthetic installations which conceal a profound reflection on the use of genetic engineering and eugenics. Brandon Ballengee tries to recreate a species of extinct African frog from related species, while Marta de Menezes in collaboration with a university laboratory in the Netherlands makes unique species of butterflies by injecting a chrysalis to obtain controlled patterning on the adult's wings.

——— Andy Warhol cloned Leonardo da Vinci's *Mona Lisa* in 1963 and today Edouardo Kac plays with concepts of genetics in his work *Genesis*. In genuinely transgenic bacteria*, the metaphorical encoding of a biblical phrase and founder of our conception of mankind is subject to mutations. Kac made these bacteria mutate by using ultraviolet radiation. The powdered DNA of the mutated bacteria is enclosed in a small flask, an ornate relic of a 'protein' engraved in solid 24-carat gold, rendering the intangible tangible. Even though they are effective in the mainstream of 21st-century biological engineering and the philosophical and ethical questions they give rise to, these artistic movements nevertheless remain quite marginal. As Jens Hauser, the contemporary art critic and Franco-German writer recently emphasised, 'While we only consider biotech artists through their choice of tools, they will be expected to turn on us'.

CONCLUSION

'NATURE'S WORKS ARE MUCH MORE DIFFICULT TO UNDERSTAND THAN A BOOK OF POETRY' Leonardo da Vinci

——— Biodiversity and evolution in nature are without doubt sources for creativity and innovation. The last 2 years concluded with the Charles Darwin commemorations in 2009 and the World Year Of Biodiversity proclaimed by the United Nations in 2010. Tangible evidence of the developments in the fields of biology and the environmental sciences in our societies.

As has often been repeated in preceding paragraphs, the preservation of our planet is now one of the major issues today. Increasing demographic pressure, the reduction in stocks of fossil fuels*, the extinction of some species and increasing anthropisation*, responsible for the exponential growth of greenhouse gas emissions linked to global warming*, all constitute alarm bells for the preservation of our natural milieus and their native species. This assessment means we have to change our ways of thinking and our position to create conditions for a change shared by all humanity.

We must encourage creativity and innovation to produce sustainable solutions to meet the objectives we need to aim at within a relatively urgent deadline. The task will be arduous and not without pitfalls, but perhaps it is not too late to initiate change. Within itself, nature has immense adaptive capacities from which we must take inspiration. This search for solutions goes via the use of new approaches encouraging the emergence of an increased creativity, taking account of all the parameters which govern equilibrium in ecosystems*, whether they are physical, chemical or biological parameters or factors relating to man's place in nature or to his social organisations. In this context, it seems today that one approach to the challenges we have to face would be to follow nature's example: build a world more in keeping with our environment, with a carefully considered policy of sustainable development. This approach would be very relevant in our present circumstances. Biomimetics*, the theoretical aspects of which have recently been expounded by Janine Benyus, seems at this point to be a particularly promising route to take. This approach consists of generating innovation by taking inspiration from the effective and sustainable solutions developed over millions of years by various species of plants and animals in the service of the biosphere* *see* p.13.241. Here it's a matter of studying and analysing the processes of natural selection* in nature and their underlying laws: cooperation, symbiosis*, adaptation, stress, evolution and processing of waste. There must be a collaborative approach between scientists, engineers, technicians, designers and all creative people in the wider sense of the term.

The fields of application of this approach are many, generating innovation in the sectors of eco-design and industrial ecology*, but also in the domain of information and communication systems organisations.

Nature is still very far from being totally explored and the complexity of living organisms will still necessitate many years of research to accurately reveal the major laws which govern its functioning. To be effective, the biomimetics approach must be based on fundamental interdisciplinary research and on the setting up of active and innovative interfaces with the protagonists of innovation in all fields. The effectiveness of the biomimetics approach will only reach its optimum level if the knowledge-based society (Lisbon Treaty with this aim was signed by the countries of the European Union in 2000) finally finds the means to build itself. This issue, like that of sustainable development, constitutes the challenge to be taken up for future generations.

LET'S DISCUSS IT WITH

JANINE BENYUS

NATURAL SCIENCES WRITER,
INNOVATION CONSULTANT AND FOUNDER
OF THE BIOMIMICRY INSTITUTE

How did the story of biomimicry begin?

_____ Primarily in very obscure journals, I found examples of people studying leaves to not just understand *about* photosynthesis*, but to learn *from* photosynthesis and try to create a solar cell* that worked the way a leaf does. It grew from a trickle of papers to a flood of papers, and I began to collect. I realised that there was a new discipline developing, a new field that covers many different arenas. Everywhere I looked in human endeavor – in material science, in energy, in health, in computing, in sensors, in business, in agriculture – I began to find people who were consciously trying to emulate life's genius. And yet at that point in time this emulation did not have a single name, so people involved in material science would call it biomimetics*, people in agriculture who were studying prairies as a model were calling it Natural Systems Agriculture*, people who were following primates around the jungle to see how they self-medicated were calling it Zoopharmacognosy*, and in Germany it was being called bionics*. There were all these different terms, but there wasn't a single term that encompassed all the different ways of looking at the natural world for advice.

_____ That was a tremendous opportunity for me, as a writer, to be able to notice this growing pattern and to name it. Having to name it began in having to write something on the tab of the folder where I was collecting the papers. I gave it the name biomimicry*, and that was many years ago. My first book *Biomimicry: Innovation Inspired by Nature* was published in 1997 and at that point I began to write my next book. I knew that *Biomimicry* was an important book and hoped it would highlight and help to fund the research, because I thought it was really valuable. I had no idea what was going to happen next. Companies and innovators started asking me to bring biologists to their design table. In the book *Biomimicry*, I reported on long-term research efforts, but companies reminded me that they are inventing every day. Preferably, biological inspiration should be there at the moment of creation, and that means having a biologist shoulder to shoulder with a designer as they are scoping and creating. That was the beginning of biologists being at the design table. It literally started with creative professionals who realised that they had perhaps been looking for sustainability in all the wrong places. People had basically been in an echo chamber of their own at, trying to look at what other engineers were doing, or what other designers were doing, but it was all very self-referential. Then some people realised that what was needed was to really break out of their own design approaches and to recognise that they were surrounded by incredibly sophisticated designs – technologies that had been in research and development not for 10 or 15 years, but for up to 3.8 billion years. ^{see} p.13.241. Having been trained in engineering, architecture or design, many people had never taken a biology course in their professional training, but they realised that there were 30 million species with amazing adaptations that they knew very little about ^{see} p.57. So they needed to bring in another person, a biologist. It was very similar to when designers pulled up a chair to the design table for a psychologist or an ergonomics or human factors specialist. Pulling up another chair, that's how it began.

How would you define biomimicry?

_____ I would define it as an emerging discipline. I think biomimicry is also a movement, a solution-seeking methodology, a philosophy, and an approach to design. But more than simply being a philosophy or a framework, biomimicry is very practical in that it is the process of learning from and then emulating nature's designs, recipes and system-wide strategies in order to create designs that are life-enhancing. That is the key. Biomimicry can be practiced without any sustainability ethic but our particular approach to biomimicry – meaning the Biomimicry Guild and the Biomimicry Institute – is to use nature's advice and wisdom to make inventions more lifelike, to have them fit in here on earth, to hae them follow life's design principles. The ultimate result is that human beings get to fit in here on Earth. In order to do that 'story of stuff' has to be re-written and the essential question 'how shall we live?' has to be re-imagined. The models for how to live gracefully on this Earth are all around. Biomimicry simply makes emulation a conscious act.

The technologies seen in the natural world have the same characteristics that people are looking for right now

_____ At the beginning of a design project, one of the first questions is: 'How would nature do what I'm trying to do here?' It's a very simple question but it is profound in its answers, in that the way organisms have solved design challenges is usually very different from how humans have solved them. Julian Vincent, a wonderful biomimic from the United Kingdom who just retired from the University of Bath, did an interesting study. He used TRIZ data, an analysis of the worldwide patent database, to answer the question: 'When humans were confronted with a particular challenge, how have they solved the challenge through history?' There is actually a pretty small subset of invented principles that people use again and again. When Vincent looked into the biological literature about how life would solve the exact same physical or chemical problems, he thought that the answers would be very similar, but in fact they weren't. There was only a 12% overlap between the way humans and the rest of the natural world solved certain problems. This means that 88% of the time there is a surprise. That novelty, I think, is bringing a lot of creative professionals toward biomimicry. There are those moments of saying, 'Oh my goodness, that's so elegant, why didn't we think of that?' There is a real delight in that. Beyond the novelty, there is also inherent sustainability, because organisms have a budget – an economic budget, an energy budget – that they cannot blow. They have to do what they do with a minimum amount of energy. They have to be judicious with material use. A bird has to make an amazingly lightweight bone structure in order to fly and yet be strong *read* p.125, an Abalone has to manufacture its hard ceramic shell *read* p.213.215 and a spider it's silk *read* p.217. Because the manufacturing processes occur in or near their own body they can't use high pressure, toxins nor heat, beat and treat processes, but they have to find benign chemical formulas and manufacturing processes. Inherently, the technologies in the natural world have the very same characteristics that sustainability designers are looking for right now. Today's designers are looking to use materials in new ways that minimise material use while maximising function. They are looking for ways to manufacture at the beginning of the life cycle in ways that are benign, and they are thinking about those materials being recaptured at the end of their life cycle, which is what has to happen in any ecosystem* – that's the rule of cyclic processes. People are looking for ways to do everything with less energy, and they want to use energy that is closer to current sunlight than it is to ancient photosynthesis, or fossil fuels*. It's interesting that the current design brief, our ideal, is the same design brief that organisms have. Organisms don't have the ability to go to the Middle East and fight a war for oil. They don't have the ability to mine the Earth for large amounts of metal. They find other ways to meet their needs. This is why I think we have seen, in the last 20 years, such an enormous multiplying of patents and interest in nature-inspired innovations, both in academia but, even more importantly, in private research and development labs, companies and architecture studios. There is really good reason that people are now finally turning to the natural world. It is because the design brief leads us there naturally.

Is every artefact that humans make natural?

_____ I would completely agree with that. I think that cars, cell phones, aeroplanes and houses are natural. Humans are biological organisms and create houses the same way as a shellfish creates its shell or a bird creates its nest. The question, for a biologist, is not whether an artifact created by humans is natural. The real question is: a biologist, is that the question is not whether it is natural or not, the question is: 'Is it well adapted or is it maladapted?' From a biological standpoint, the bird's nest must pass muster, it must pass one simple test. How will the chicks fare in this nest? Will they be healthy? If the nest is made with toxic fibres that the bird picked up somewhere and the chicks die as a result, then natural selection * basically says that the bird's approach to nest building was not very well-adapted. Now the same thing is happening with human technologies. Natural selection is judging whether the technologies are well-adapted or maladapted and this is far more important than what the market has to say. In the long term, if a house is poisoning its inhabitants or diminishing its owner's sperm count, natural selection is saying it's not very well-adapted.

_____ Well-adapted means fitting into the habitat, it means that people and their offspring especially, are able to survive in that habitat 10,000+ generations from now. So, well-adapted means: 'Will life continue over long periods of time?' Therefore the question should be, how well-adapted are our technologies to life on Earth over the long term. Unfortunately, right now they are not very well-adapted. Then the question becomes: 'What is well-adapted?' Can a set of design principles be gathered that leads towards increasingly better adapted products? That is also what biomimicry does. We work a lot with clients and help them invent a particular technology, but perhaps even more importantly, we give them a framework called 'life's principles'. Think of it as nature's eco-design check list. We, as scientists, have looked through scientific literature for any traits or design principles that all organisms have in common. Not an individual octopus or a bison but something that the bison and the octopus have in common. What is the code of conduct in the natural world that is non-negotiable? We list these and call them 'life's principles' and designers now use those to scope out a project. They are principles like life practices benign manufacturing or life uses a small subset of the periodic table * instead of every element in the periodic table. Life does its chemistry in water instead of toxic solvents, life uses current sunlight, or life maintains itself through turnover or self-healing. Then a designer takes these principles to create a wish list: the design should be self-healing and resilient; it should be able to learn and adapt to local conditions; it should be locally attuned and responsive; it should be manufactured in benign temperatures and in water. Then during the design process the list is also used, and finally, it's consulted again during the evaluation process.

_____ This design approach has been extremely powerful because it represents a list of best practices that comes not from human cleverness but from time-tested, well-burnished wisdom in the natural world. Artefacts in the natural world are not created in a vacuum, they are not

Humans are biological organisms and create houses the same way as a shellfish creates its shell or a bird creates its nest

created for a market, they are very context sensitive, they are created for a particular habitat and under a very strict set of criteria. Those principles, those biological truths, could be applied to everything people do. It is quite a high bar to consult nature as model, measure and mentor, but I think that's where biomimicry is going. I think it is more than merely a set of technologies that is going to come out of biomimicry. I think it's a paradigm shift, a mindset shift that says: 'We are a biological species, this is our home planet, we want to stay here, we want to fit in here and if we're going to fit in here we have to play by Earth's. The first step is to learn Earth's rules, to become apprentices of the organisms that have lived here longer than humans. The people who design our world must become nature's apprentices in order to understand the real rules by which the real economy works – the real economy being Earth's economy.

People have to become apprentices of organisms that have lived here longer than man

————— Biomimicry began with mimicking nature to create cool technologies, but what it's evolving into is not just bio-inspired products but a bio-inspired culture. When we go to the companies we work with – huge corporations like Coca-Cola, Colgate-Palmolive, General Electric, The Boeing Company, Herman Miller, Interface and Nike – we go there to solve a particular challenge for them. What invariably happens is that the managers come to us and ask how nature would design a company? How can the firm become more resilient? And suddenly we are talking about 'resilience science' * and they are not trying to green just a product but they are trying to green their whole company. This move from biomimicry as a product design methodology to biomimicry as a cultural framework is a really interesting one.

Is there progress in the natural world?

————— Organisms create what they need. There is a notion of sufficiency. It is one of the life's principles that we call 'optimising rather than maximising'. Optimising is to do only what is necessary to meet needs. An elk, for example, grows its antlers to a certain size and that size has to be large enough to interest females, it has to be strong enough to be able to have territorial fights with other males but if it is too large, if those antlers are maximised beyond a certain point, the elk won't be able to walk through the forest. There is a penalty for maximising. There is continual progress in the natural world; life as a whole is much more innovative than any human culture. Every single organism is a brand new combination of genetic material never seen before. But, interestingly, life carries from one generation to the next only that which works. So while there are lots of new ideas, there is also a very strong selection process. There is variation, there is mutation, there is sexual recombination of genetic materials and there are all these new ideas, new kinds of proteins * leading to physical and behavioral differences in each individual. In the end there is a rigorous selection process that bases its selection on whether a certain trait increases an individual's survival chances, and the survival chances of its offspring in the long term. And that's all that matters. The new technologies that evolve are also put through the same filter every single generation and that's why natural selection * is a very powerful thing. What makes the cut are brand new amazing technologies that are good for life, and life always keeps what works. What works gets carried on.

There is continual progress in the natural world, life is much more innovative than any human culture

————— Rather than growth for growth's sake, there is optimization and development in the natural world. Things become increasingly complex and elegant, more fitting. The goal for any organism is to fit into its habitat and to fit in with its co-evolutionary partners in an ever closer match. This creates progress in the natural world, a progression towards a closer fit with habitat conditions. Now, hopefully, human technologies will be growing towards a closer fit with the biological reality of living on this planet, this is what I think should be the goal. Pumping up technologies to increase market share is important for profitability but there are now all these other characteristics by which rightness of innovations is judged, and a very important part of them these days is whether it is life-friendly, safe, healthy and neces-sary. Today, designers are asking themselves whether they even need to create a certain product – a really good question! The question is just as important as whether it is beautiful and whether someone will love it. We recently gave an architect the following brief to build our house: 'Make it too beautiful to ever tear it down'. In the United States this is a very rare design brief. The architect followed the brief and people will love this house for a long time. Those new kinds of questions being posed are se-lection questions. We act as agents of the natural selection and this creates a different role for designers.

I think that the most durable things in the world are those that were so well-made that no one wants to throw them away

As a biologist, are you still amazed by nature's wonders?

_____ I think that wonder is like the universe, it is continually expanding. When I get up in the morning, the first thing I do is look through the scientific literature headlines. Read-ing articles is my greatest joy because just when I think I cannot be more amazed, something comes up that people finally realise, finally understand. Scientists who are profoundly involved in the material will tell you that they know nothing. There is so much to know and we are now only beginning to grasp some things. For instance, there is this new idea that the reason that photosynthesis is so effective may be because it is a quantum phenomenon. That brings it to a whole new level. Here is nature, working at the level of quantum physics, trying out every single possible molecular orientation in order to transfer an electron* through a membrane and finally collapsing to the most effective state.

_____ I'm just amazed when I begin to compare human technologies to nature's. The leaf for instance, it's self-assembled at room temperature on a tree, it's made from carbon dioxide* essentially, it tilts to follow the sun throughout the day, if the wind comes it curls up into a Fibonacci shape and creates the best flow structure for the wind to go through so that it doesn't get ripped off the tree *read* p.197. It protects itself, when an insect chews on a leaf on one part of the tree the leaves on the other part of the tree get the signal and begin to beef up their defenses, it radiates heat, it's a plumbing device moving sugar down to the roots and water upwards. The branching structures within its veins are optimised to be a mathemati-cally perfect way to distribute fluid *read* p.129. At the end of its life it is completely recycled and up-cycled into other products on the forest floor, as well as being a quantum device* that is 98% quantum efficient in terms of gathering solar energy and turning it into fuel, into chemistry – the leaf is a sophisticated, silent manufacturing plant *read* p.111.113.185. It's re-ally an amazing thing, and when I look at solar cells, which are created with incredibly toxic manufacturing processes and can't go back into the soil at the end of their life, I think to myself, 'We've got a long way to go!'

_____ Our apprenticeship to nature begins now, but it is a life-long process for every de-signer. There is so much to learn from the natural world! Part of the joy of my job is to watch people be amazed, to fall in love, to realise that the universe is absolutely magical; it's way beyond anybody's science fiction fantasy, it's better than that.

How would nature do what I'm trying to do here?

Janine Benyus

Could you describe nature as an industry?

_____ One of the things that makes biomimicry possible, is to dissolve the myth that says that humans are not nature, to dissolve the myth that says that humans are the only ones that do technology. When I look at a leaf, I think that it embodies the most amazing technology, the most amazing engineering, the most amazing chemistry. I don't have any problem looking at it in that way because I think humans have more in common with these organisms than we think. However, when someone says they are going to take the genes from a spider and put them into a goat through transgenic engineering and expect the goat to become their factory milking out the proteins* of spider silk for them (an ill-fated scheme by a now-defunct company called Nexia), I think this is the voice of a coloniser *read* p.217. Seeing nature as a machine, or a factory is actually how industrial agriculture is seen, how some forestry processes are seen and how some people see natural resources. They see nature as a warehouse or a work horse. To me that is to lose sight of the fact that a tree is more than just amazing technology, it is a living thing that responds, it's alive, evolving and adapting. That is the difference between machines and life. Seeing a living organism as a slave or a machine lacks respect, and at the heart of biomimicry there's an increasingly keen respect for these organisms. Not for what can be extracted from them, or what can made into products or become domesticated, but rather for what these organisms can teach.

_____ Seeing an organism as a teacher or mentor, completely changes your relationship with that organism. If you think of any mentor you've had in your life, someone who taught you something essential, you'll see why. If you were to see that person humiliated or degraded in some way, you would be the first to stand up and protest. In the same way, I see biomimics become ardent conservationists when they take nature as mentor. This is a very key and transformational part of biomimicry. Becoming a student rather than being a conqueror or a coloniser, changes your relationship with the rest of the natural world. The idea of why biodiversity* is important becomes self-evident. When I address an audience and give them 15 amazing case studies of how organisms work and what we've learned from them, I pause to ask, 'Do you understand why conserving biodiversity is important?' People in the audience spontaneously burst into laughter, which says: 'Well, of course, now we will never be able to look at biodiversity in the same way again'. Long ago, the relationship between mankind and nature was that humans were very afraid, being in awe. It switched to one of humans as master and nature as slave, humans having the illusion that it was their right to control and exploit nature – thinking it was put there for their use. Lately, among many people who understand what's happening on the planet, there's been a relationship of guilt, of humans feeling pity for organisms. Pity, though it may trigger an annual donation to a conservation organization, is not a very powerful emotion. Respect is much more powerful than pity. Biomimicry is a rich spring of amazing, sustainable innovations, guide posts that teach us how to design for this Earth. But it's much more than that. To me the most important thing about biomimicry is that it changes humans' relationship with nature from one of domination to one of appreciation. That's a very big step!

_____ Another thing I find important to remember about biomimicry comes from a field of study called social group reference theory. This is the theory that who we compare ourselves to is key to our behavior, and the fastest way to change is to change who you admire. For example, say a designer or an architect, while growing up, compares himself with Donald Trump and wants to be a real estate mogul like him. When he then meets someone who has started a local food bank in the city, collecting food for home-

Biomimicry changes a human's relationship with nature from one of domination to one of appreciation

less people, he suddenly begins to compare himself with that person instead. That's the fastest way for personal change to happen. What we're doing in biomimicry, instead of comparing our technologies with one another, is comparing them with nature's technologies and realizing that we're falling short of our new ideal. That's when change happens and the desire arises to be more like this hawk, this flower or this butterfly or to have a building becoming as self-sufficient as a tree. Suddenly, that new metaphor is very powerful, realizing that we're falling short of our new ideal. Then a biologist can actually teach the designer how that tree works and how the water system in the building could be changed, how energy could be gathered and how the water could be filtered. It's that comparison that is actually so powerful.

At a certain point you need to use the tree, right?

_____ There are three kinds of 'bio': 'bio-utilisation'* for example, is using wood in the home. My entire house is made from local wood. People will always use products from the natural world. There is a way to over-harvest and there is a way to harvest sustainably, so hopefully people will harvest sustainably and locally. The second is 'bio-assisted technologies'*. This could be keeping a cow to produce milk, keeping bees to produce honey or using bacteria* to clean waste water or using yeast to make bread and beer. This bio-assistance is actually a very old technology, and there is a sustainable and non-sustainable way to domesticate an organism. The sustainable way, is through natural breeding of those organisms. When people start to put an organism in a tube and think of it as a little machine that they can switch on and off, they often begin to tinker with that organism's genetic code to get it to produce faster or do more. To me, this transgenic engineering is where the line is crossed into a domestication* which is dangerous. I think bio-assisted technologies are great as long as they are done without transgenic engineering. The third kind of 'bio' is true biomimicry*. Take the abalone shell for example. It has been studied at length for its ceramic properties because it is twice as tough as our high-tech ceramics. Abalones could be harvested to bio-utilise the shells or they could be domestically farmed to make shells for us. Another option however would be to learn the recipe by which they make their shells and to manufacture this ceramic ourselves. So, in brief: bio-utilisation is the process of harvesting the product, bio-assisted or domestication is the process of breeding the producer, and biomimicking is the process of becoming the producer.

Bio-utilisation is the process of harvesting the product, bio-assisted or domestication is the process of breeding the producer, and biomimicking is the process of becoming the producer

_____ Another example; and one of the most interesting biomimetic* ideas these days, is how to use carbon dioxide as a raw material for building materials. There is a company called Calera that borrows the coral's recipe for making it's reef – it uses dissolved CO_2 as one of the ingredients! Calera does is take the CO_2 out of the smokestack and combine it with a slurry of minerals that you would find in seawater. Automatically, the material combines and precipitates out into a substitute for Portland cement, which releases 6-8% of all CO2 emissions in the world. This basically comes down to making tonnes of building material out of CO_2 and sequestering it for long periods of time. Instead of using corals organisms to make reef, they are actually biomimicking the process. I think that's very important. This is in contrast to a bio-assisted approach to plastic, namely, taking the gene from bacteria (some bacteria actually make a biopolymer), inserting it into a tobacco plant, planting it in the ground and having the plant make the plastic for us. Another way this could be done is by putting the gene – bacteria make plastic, basically they make a biopolymer – into a tobacco plant, planting it in the ground and have the tobacco plant make the plastic. Then the tobacco plant uses CO_2 to make a biodegradable plastic. Instead, Geoffrey Coates of Novomer has found a way to take CO_2 and make the biodegradable plastic in a low temperature lab process, which saves energy, agricultural pesticides and loss of soil fertility. If someone gets a plant to make plastic, they're basically mining the fertility from that ground while they should really be at the level of learning the chemistry and mimicking it. I'm not against bio-assisted or bio-utilised technologies, but I do think that because people are so used to harvesting or domesticating, they tend to get into this rut. When I hear that people are going to be using plants to make plastic, I think that's the wrong way to go! To me, that's a shortcut which is disrespectful of the organisms, but even more than that, it's intellectually lazy. People know how to make all kinds of things that have never been on earth before, like 80,000 synthetic chemicals on the market. People know how to make stuff. But chemists are never asked to make stuff in new ways, stuff that is locally sourced, biodegradable, and self-assembled without heat, beat, or treat. Nature shows us that it can be done, it is a matter of will.

How can creative professionals take part in this?

_____ We have a Professional Pathways programme where we are training biomimicry-certified professionals. It provides various courses, from an hour-long course on the web all the way to a 2-year Master's programme. This is an opportunity to be able to get a certification in biomimicry, to know how to work with biologists and to do biomimicry. The courses are offered by Biomimicry 3.8, which is our larger organisation that encompasses both the Institute and the Guild. Our institute is for academic research and focuses on the work with universities, while our Guild is a consulting firm working with corporations. Our next big project is to create a global membership network that biomimicry professionals can subscribe to. Our job will be to nurture this growing network with tools, resources, information databases, teaching materials, and a social platform. Spreading and localizing the DNA of biomimicry through a thriving, supported network is the most biomimetic thing we can do.

JANINE BENYUS

Janine Benyus is a natural sciences writer, innovation consultant, and author of several books, including *Biomimicry: Innovation Inspired by Nature*, published in 1997. Benyus has received several awards including the 2009 Champion of the Earth award in Science & Innovation from the United Nations Environmental Programme and has been honoured as one of *TIME International's* Heroes of the Environment. In 1998, Benyus co-founded the innovation consultancy called Biomimicry Guild. The Biomimicry Guild is the only innovation company in the world to use a deep knowledge of biological adaptations to help designers, engineers, architects, and business leaders solve design and engineering challenges sustainably. Benyus also co-founded the non-profit Biomimicry Institute and currently serves as president on its board. The Biomimicry Institute is a not-for-profit organisation whose mission is to naturalise biomimicry in the culture by promoting the transfer of ideas, designs, and strategies from biology to sustainable human systems design. Benyus and the staff of the Biomimicry Institute recently launched asknature.org, a public database of biological literature organised by design function.

LET'S DISCUSS IT WITH

CATHERINE LARRÈRE

PROFESSOR OF PHILOSOPHY, WRITER OF SEVERAL
BOOKS ON ENVIRONMENTAL ETHICS

What sort of relationship does man have with nature?

_____ Ever since the 17th century, people thought that technology would allow them to tear themselves away from nature. Francis Bacon (1561–1626), the English philosopher, who contributed a great deal to this type of thinking, proposed that a technological thing was all the better if it didn't have an equivalent in nature, if it was completely new. He said, 'To conquer nature is man's most noble task' and René Descartes proclaimed the idea that man should become 'master and possessor of nature'. Both of them reduced nature to an undefined thing, something inert which people could do with as they pleased. There will probably always be people who have this point of view. There will always be attempts to patent living things, patent DNA* sequences and genes, etc. People will defend these patents by claiming that it's living matter, therefore it's only matter which can simply be sliced up. This domination always used to be more of a pretention than a reality. It's only since recently that humans actually have the means to be rulers over nature. There are new technologies and masses of people on this planet, which is a tangible force. Mankind has become the master and possessor of nature but is not very pleased about it.

Mankind has become the master and possessor of nature but is not very pleased about it

_____ In Bacon's Utopian novel *New Atlantis* or other works of this genre, there is an inquisitive anticipation, right up to cloning. This shows that basically technical projects are old fantasies. Bacon wasn't a genius who foresaw things for which he hadn't the means to see – biology wasn't a science at that time. Fundamentally, technology seems to be the execution of ideas that have been around for a long time. It's certain that today's problems, such as erosion of biodiversity*, extinction of species, climatic changes and water problems, are the result of industrial changes which started at the beginning of the 19th century. Beyond any doubt though, these industrial changes have been thought out before.

_____ Following the industrial changes in the 19th century, geographers and naturalists began to study and demonstrate the lasting impact that human beings are having on the Earth. In 1864, George Perkins Marsh wrote a book entitled *Man and Nature*, a wide-ranging study of planet Earth and the lasting human effects on the environment, from the Pyramids and the work of the Pharaohs to all the work on the dykes that the Dutch carried out. This book shows that man has been making its mark on the environment for a very long time.

_____ Today, there are tendencies emerging which show that instead of getting as far away as possible from nature, people actually never get away from it. In towns, people shelter from cold and from snow – escaping from nature and becoming independent from it – but at the same time they contribute to global warming* which makes them become even more dependant. That triggers the thought that it's perhaps necessary to look at ways to fit in more harmoniously with nature. Today, it's a matter of imitating nature rather than producing an invention that's distanced from it.

What would be a 'good' use of nature?

_____ Certainly not domination or conquest! It would sooner be what is sometimes called 'ways of piloting it'. A relationship with nature which is modelled on a ship's helmsman, someone who works with natural elements and directs them. The helmsman of a ship manoeuvres with the wind and currents to get to his destination, using nature's power to his advantage.

Among the manifestations of man's imprint on nature, would it really be problematic if biodiversity* is endangered?

_____ Species are mortal, just like individuals, even though they last for millions of years longer, but in the end they also disappear. Almost all species that have existed since the beginning of life on Earth, have disappeared. There is therefore a 'regular' disappearance of species ^{see} p.57. They live, they die and others are born, therefore there is replacement. What is almost certain today is that there is a loss rate which is much greater than generally accepted. There have already been phases of great extinctions, everybody knows about the disappearance of the dinosaurs, but that took almost a million years. Where man is involved, this process is evolving extremely quickly. It's increasing because species don't have time to adapt, they are in situations which force them to disappear. This is, of course, awkward for those species. It's also awkward for humans and for all the living things associated with humans in one way or another. Naturalists have shown that everything is closely linked. The possibility of reproduction in migratory birds depends on the fact that they should be in a certain area at the time when a certain type of flower is blooming, but if this blooming is out of step with them, then they can't reproduce. It's less awkward for the biosphere * in general, that will more or less be able to cope with it. There are enthusiasts for the Gaia hypothesis * who state that the Earth is 'alive' and that Gaia has coped with worse things, that it's sturdy and will survive.

Your first book, *Les philosophies de l'environnement*, describes various philosophies, particularly Anglo-Saxon philosophies. Can you describe these?

_____ For widely cultural, complex reasons these philosophies are developed in Anglophone countries, especially in former British colonies, namely North America and Australia, not India or countries that were already populated. In these countries there had been a very rapid occupation of more or less deserted lands. The colonists seized territory that they'd practically destroyed. Those people have had the pride of colonists in being confronted with what they call 'wilderness', a wild expanse, and dominating it. At the same time however, there was a sense of shame of the massive destruction to which they subjected the territories that they occupied. It's from there that thoughts of morality developed which, as in all philosophical work, go beyond their cultural era. The moral reflection that developed on the relationships between man and nature does not really have an equivalent in continental Europe or in Third World countries. It's a trend, or even several trends in contact with each other, of

Problems relating to nature have arisen because people have had a purely instrumental relationship with nature

quite sophisticated moral thought. The idea in fact is that problems relating to nature have arisen because people have had a purely instrumental relationship with nature. They considered nature solely as an available resource and as a great big rubbish bin. If people consider that there are values in nature and that different natural entities have worth in themselves, then people will see things differently and have more respect for nature. It therefore takes a major effort to imagine on what basis people might tell themselves that it's not only human beings who have dignity or intrinsic worth*.

_____ In the 1970s a lot of fundamental articles appeared on environmental ethics – the philosophy of an ethical relationship with the natural environment. In 1973, Arne Naess wrote a paper in which he made a distinction between the 'deep' and the 'shallow' ecological movement. The shallow ecology focuses on combating pollution and resource depletion, whilst the Deep Ecology* consists of an holistic approach with intrinsic relationships that recognise the inherent worth of all living things. In 1975, an Australian philosopher Peter Singer published the book *Animal Liberation* in which he argued that animals should have rights based on their ability to feel suffering and not based on their intelligence. And then there are more interesting theories by philosophers such as Holmes Rolston, J. Baird Callicott and Bryan G. Norton. Aldo Leopold (1887) can be considered the founding father of these ethics. He studied at Yale Forest School that had recently been founded and offered the first post-graduate forestry programme in the United States. He then became a forestry worker. Leopold participated in the extinction of wolves, with the idea that it could produce more game, more deer and other ungulates (hoofed animals) for winter hunters. The extermination of the wolves resulted in a proliferation of ungulates, with major environmental damage and his realisation that he'd made a mistake. Because he was such an energetic campaigner in the very active wilderness organisations at that time, especially for conservation of wild nature, he left active service and took a chair at the University of Madison in Wisconsin. He bought a cabin there to go hunting and fishing. In 1948, while helping a neighbour fight a fire, he died of a heart attack. This happened just before his book *A Sand County Almanac* was published. In the very active literary tradition in the United States, this work is known as 'nature writing' *, of which Henry David Thoreau, with his *Walden; or, Life in the Woods,* is one of the founders. The term almanac indicates that the work follows the seasons, with little stories telling how Leopold saw animals. Endearing stories, but Leopold remained a scientist and eventually proposed a 'land ethic', which was the first formulation of an ethic or a morality for the relationship between man and nature. His regularly cited concept is, 'A thing is right when it tends to preserve the integrity, stability, and beauty of the biotic community. It is wrong when it tends otherwise'. It is said that in hotels in the Rockies in the United States, one is just as likely to find the work of Aldo Leopold as one would find the *Bible*.

Can you tell us more about Deep Ecology?

_____ The Norwegian who introduced Deep Ecology, Arne Naess (1912–2009), had quite an interesting life. He was attracted by philosophy, a type of study that wasn't easy to carry out in Norway at that time. Therefore, in the 1930s he first went to Paris and then he went on to study in Vienna. The city held a leading position in philosophy because the famous Vienna Circle was located there. Naess participated in the Vienna Circle, but finally preferred metaphysics in work on language as well as psychology, and went on to produce a thesis on psychology in California, where he worked on animals. He returned to Norway, to be perhaps one of the first teachers of philosophy in the country and founded the Oslo philosophy

*The question is not
'making use of technology
or not using technology'
but rather
which technology to use?*

Catherine Larrère

department. There he wrote a philosophical work in Norwegian and English. Having been involved in resistance activities during the war, he not only became a Norwegian hero but an interesting resistance fighter because he was inspired by Ghandi's non-violence. So he wasn't a resistance activist that planted bombs, but an effective resistance fighter with more durable achievements.

_____ Rather belatedly, when he was about 50 years old, he took an interest in environmental questions and resigned from the university. In 1973 he published *The Shallow and the Deep Long Range Ecology Movement,* one of the foundation articles mentioned earlier. Various books had rung alarm bells before, like biologist and writer Rachel Carson's *Silent Spring* on DDT or *The Limits to Growth* by Donella H. Meadows, Dennis L. Meadows, Jørgen Randers and William W. Behrens III. Naess, however, made a distinction in superficial ecology*, that the policies in place can fit in without problems as well as a more radical ecology which obliges redefinition of the existing reports. He set up a platform, which takes account of living things, as also intrinsic value theoreticians do. He postulated that all living things have an equal right to exist and also took account of the relationship with the Third World, which people had not talked about much.

_____ Naess then wrote a book entitled *Ecology, Community and Lifestyle: Outline of an Ecosophy*, first published in Norwegian and translated into English by David Rothenberg in the 1980s. It was notably because of the English version that he became famous. The term 'ecosophy'*, which was introduced by Naess, means an integrated philosophy of ecological harmony. Americans have a tendency to say that ecology as a science provides almost everything needed to guide people ethically. Naess didn't think science is enough and in his book, he explained the relevance of philosophy to the problems of environmental degradation. Looking at his work clearly shows that he brought several dimensions into account (political, economical, technological) and tried to reflect on it with a policy of non-violence. He didn't take up a radical position. He was also not hostile to technology, but simply thought that technology is linked to culture and, like the philosopher and theologian Ivan Illich, he made a distinction between soft (low-impact on ecosystem*) and hard technology (high impact on ecosystem).

_____ The impression that people have of Naess, especially in France, is partly based on his popularity in the United States. Through militants in environmental movements like Earth First!, Deep Ecology* is moving to the forefront. It was appropriated by the most radical environmentalists in a profoundly misanthropic way, something Naess certainly did not do. It was very good that his book was translated into French a few years ago. People finally realised that Naess was not the fundamentalist defender of nature, which is the impression given by the Americans.

Intrinsic worth* seems to be a recurring term, can you shed some more light on this?

_____ Here are two examples to allow full understanding of this notion. The first is the 'Last Man' scenario by Australian philosopher Richard Routley who suggests that one should consider the following scenario: 'Imagine that there is only one man left on Earth, all other conscious beings have disappeared and so, this man is going to die. Before dying, he endeavours to destroy everything with him'. The question arises: do his actions qualify as good or evil? When thinking about it, in the moral sense of the term, there is only good or bad in the things that people can do to one another. In the above scenario, there is nothing bad done to anyone and therefore it is not bad. At the same time, intuitively, people feel that what he is doing is not good. The idea of intrinsic worth is to ask oneself if each living creature isn't a good thing in itself, quite independently of the use people are going to make of it.

_____ The other example is that of biologist E.P. Pister, an employee of the American wildlife services, who is interested in a small fish whose common name is the Devil's Hole pupfish. A fish which lives in marshes and other watery areas. Its life is threatened by urban

Arne Naess postulated that all living things have an equal right to exist

sprawl, which drains and destroys its environment and its habitat. Pister decided to save this little fish and do it the American way, via a judicial route. He went to the Supreme Court and won, although it did take a long time. He explained his actions to many people. They always asked him: 'But this little fish, what's it good for? Is it good to eat? No. Pretty? No. Does it contain something which could cure illnesses? No. Can you use it against …? No.' After a while, because he was tired of explaining why he was fighting for this little fish, he looked at the people and said to them: 'And you, what are you good for?' People know they don't have to be good at something to be good. If people recognise their right to exist and respect, without having the need to justify their use, why shouldn't it be the same for a little fish? This is the notion of intrinsic worth.

_____ I'm not fanatical about intrinsic worth, as it has quite a few drawbacks, among other things, on a practical plane. It takes individuals into account while operations on nature take account of populations and, moreover, can cause individuals to be sacrificed. The notion of intrinsic worth is difficult to apply because, if people have respect for everything, they can't live normal lives – which include walking on the street and stepping on an ant, for example. The notion mainly applies to wilderness, it's another way of saying: 'don't interfere with nature when it can function on its own'.

What do you think about environmental action today?

_____ There are lots of reasons to be pessimistic. The failure of international conferences, feeble efforts, gas emissions and erosion of biodiversity* are some examples, but at the same time what strikes me, is that there have been tremendous changes. People's attitudes have changed enormously. Twenty years ago, Luc Ferry regarded the Anglo-Saxon theoreticians as fascists in his book *The New Ecological Order*. Now no one would say that, even he would no longer write it. From that point of view, there was a suspicion and today it's no longer in our thoughts. The ineffectiveness of political decisions that are being made are a cause for concern, but there is also a real change in mentalities and that is important. The next step is to translate this into reality.

_____ There is still plenty of ignorance, but above all it's a problem of intervention levels. The small things are actually a bit of a laugh. I don't want to say that you shouldn't put the light out when leaving a room, but it's at the overall level that the important decisions are made. Ignorance could make people think that little gestures are enough. This is also shockingly evident in Al Gore's film *An Inconvenient Truth*, it tends to focus on little gestures only, there are no other references. At the overall level it's evidently complex. The right level at which to intervene has to be found. This level is not necessarily that of the state, which seems the most obvious. There can perhaps be regional or trans-regional forces which are more significant.

What does biomimetics* mean to you?

_____ There's no single solution to environmental problems. Focusing on only one solution is never a good thing, people should consider a diversity of options. Biomimicry* is one solution to environmental issues. It's ambition is to look at nature much deeper than just on a purely technological level. Nature is more complex than the technology people can come up with, it continuously reveals surprises. However, it's a little disturbing to say that nature is an extremely efficient industry. This plays in two senses, it's good that technology does not give itself, as with Bacon, the single objective of being as far away from nature as possible, but when you think of nature purely as a technology, that's to say according to human technological efficiency criteria, there is perhaps something which gets lost between times as there is much more to nature. People certainly have to avoid being anthropomorphic about nature, which can be destructive. So, it's good to have a technological ambition but it should involve seeing nature, not in a very functionalistic and industrial form, but in its complexity that consists of living organisms. The question is not 'making use of technology or not using technology' but rather which technology to use?

Nature is more complex than the technology people can come up with, it continuously reveals surprises

CATHERINE LARRÈRE

As a Professor of Philosophy at the University of Paris 1 Panthéon – Sorbonne, Catherine Larrère teaches political philosophy and applied ethics, focusing on environmental ethics (ethics of the relationship between humans and nature). Larrère has been working on environmental issues since 1992, the year she met American environmental ethics specialists at a conference of the Rio Earth summit in Brazil. Her husband Raphaël Larrère is a trained agronomist and former researcher at the INRA (National Institute of Agronomic Research) and together they published a book, on the good use of nature, *Du bon usage de la nature* (Paris, Aubier: Collection Alto, 1997), a reflection of how people's vision of nature can guide environmental policies. Together, they have also published many articles on environmental ethics and are currently working on another book. In 1997, Larrère also published a book on environmental philosophies, entitled *Les Philosophies de l'environnement* (Paris: PUF, Collection Philosophies).

LET'S DISCUSS IT WITH

HERVÉ NAILLON

MARKETING AND INNOVATION CONSULTANT, INVENTOR OF THE CONCEPT OF ETHICAL MARKETING

What has changed in the field of sustainability?

——————— Thanks to natural global warming* 14,000 years ago, the ice-age ended and the role of humans changed from 'hunter-gatherer' to 'farmer'. People were able to stay in one place to plant and harvest. Wandering tribes settled and cities were created. Since people produced more than they needed for their personal consumption they could sell their products. Others were no longer working in the fields but were making pottery for storage, and thus commerce was created. The main structures of this 14,000-year-old model have for a long time relied on servile manual labour but now rely on virtual labour. Energy and climate consultant Jean-Marc Jancovici translates the kilowatt-hours that are extracted from fossil fuel* into 'slave equivalents'. For example, the power of a tractor working in the field equals the work of 1,000 to 1,200 men. But it seems that, at a given moment the tractor will no longer be able to run on those 'slave equivalents' and that's when the problems start. We are at a major turning point in human history once more. But this time the global warming will be one of our own making.

—————— Man's relationship to time and space changed drastically in the 20th century. Until then, there was the time of the seasons, the time of vigils before religious festivals, the belfry and church time, but everything occurred in a single space. Up to the First World War, the majority of French people, who were peasants, on average had not been more than 5 km away from their village. It was a major expedition to go to the local fair, perhaps 10 km (6 miles) away! Today, everything's a snapshot. The press covers a spectacular event that occurs in some corner of the world and a week later it's overtaken by another event. At the same time, people are in a manifold space: working in Paris, talking to a Swedish agency via Skype and having correspondents in New Zealand.

—————— What also changed in the 20th century was the discovery that the Earth is finite. An old atlas of the Western world, dating back to 1920, shows Africa as having a blank in the middle. At that time it was still unknown. It was an infinite world that could be explored and discovered. But in his acceptance speech in 1960, John F. Kennedy spoke of 'new frontiers' because the old quest to push back the frontier was finished. Admittedly, there are still many things to discover: the bottom of the oceans, or what's under the Earth's crust. However on the human scale, because man doesn't go to the bottom of the oceans nor can he go under the Earth's crust, people have been more or less everywhere. In 1968, the Apollo 8 mission took the famous photo of the Earth and then people truly had a complete picture.

Being aware of the Earth's finiteness helps people better understand the question of limited resources

—————— Being aware of the Earth's finiteness helps people better understand the question of limited resources. Oil is not the only resource that is limited. There are 17 chemical elements in the periodic table* that make up what is called rare earth elements*. These mineral reserves are needed for new technologies such as lasers, camera lenses, fluorescent lamps, X-ray tubes and much more. The demand is increasing rapidly and therefore access to all the rare earth elements has become the subject of a conflict in the WTO between China on the one hand, currently the predominant supplier, and Europe and the United States on the other.

_____ Resources, however, aren't the only things that are limited. The former president of Madagascar, Marc Ravalomanana, was brought down following a scandal about the lease of arable land to Daewoo. Being a large corn importer, the South Korean consortium planned to cultivate the land, thereby cutting its dependence on other exporting countries to feed its population. The deal was cancelled by Madagascar's new president, Andry Rajoelina. Other countries are doing the same. The Chinese, for example, are buying land in Africa for food security. The Earth is finite.

People have forgotten this notion of interdependence but are becoming aware of it again

_____ Although there is this realisation, which is important, there is also the notion of interdependence. The problem is that people turn their thoughts to biodiversity* on the one day and the next day they talk about global warming. They see a meeting on the Australian mining resources and then a meeting on climate change in Japan. These elements are all linked. People generally have a linear approach: they extract, convert and throw away. The cyclic notion is the natural one though, everything goes round in a circle, with interdependence. A tree grows and its leaves fall to its roots, but they are not going to feed it directly. A complete chain comes into play to turn the leaf material into compost. People have forgotten this notion of interdependence but are becoming aware of it again.

_____ There are now 6.9 billion people on earth, 20% of whom are using 80% of the resources and are responsible for 80% of the greenhouse gases. It's important to realise that there is global warming which brings about millions of global-warming refugees. The people in the African Sahel region for example, plagued by extreme droughts, have no other choice than to move into towns and take the first low-paid job they can get. They render unemployed the people who used to do the work for higher wages, who in turn, try their luck in the Western economy, and subsequently are sent back on greenhouse gas-emitting charter flights, while they should be welcomed. Last year, there were 45 million climate refugees*. France is responsible for 1.2% of the global annual CO_2 emissions. Therefore, mathematically speaking, France should take in 540,000 refugees.

_____ And then there is globalisation*, which relies on two key points: the exchange of merchandise across the world; and financial exchanges. Transport of this merchandise relies for 96% on cheap oil (trains, boats, lorries, etc.). Now we are confronted by a real problem: cheap oil is finished. We're not running out of oil yet but we are running out of low-priced, easily refinable and convertible oil. The economy is going to depend on expensive oil. There are substantial quantities of it in the Canadian tar sands, for example, but it's very expensive and very polluting. If the carbon emission reduction on exploiting this oil is built in, it will be even dearer. If it's not, it accelerates global warming, but in all other respects it will have consequences for globalisation and exchanges and perhaps will allow a certain re-localisation of the economy. This can already be seen with certain products, heavy goods and those with a small margin, for example carpet tiles. Carpet tile manufacturers have factories in Europe, as it is financially disadvantageous to have them made in China and shipped to Europe.

Can people combat this individually?

_____ That is extremely complicated as people don't have access to all the necessary information. As a society we are not materialistic enough. This may sound strange because it is understood that today's society is a materialistic one, but in a strict sense it is a completely non-materialistic society, it's an 'object' society. Every object is an entity unto itself. All links with materials are severed. Nobody is capable of saying what's in the iPhone for example, in terms of materials. Where does it come from, how is it mined or refined, what is its impact, its carbon footprint*, its impact on water, is it involved in the eutrophication* – cause of excessive plant growth by addition of nutrients – of water resources, the disappearance of some species or other? It's impossible to say, because people are not in touch with the materials any more. As a result it becomes very complicated, when contemplating the choice criteria. When there's a relevant health dimension in the hygiene, beauty and food sectors, the information is available because it is mandatory, but traceability in food is not even really guaranteed. People might know a certain cake is organic, but where does the wheat come from? That is simply not traceable anymore. There is a lack of reliable sources of information or training and above all there is a flood of disinformation. Every day publicity messages are coming in from those who benefit from an object and who do everything to make everyone forget that for every object it's the material that has the impact. For a pair of tennis shoes, the materials and the conversion of these materials into a pair of sports shoes represent a 5% value, while marketing represents up to 25%. Buying certain shoes means buying marketing. Publicity is a worldwide business, second only to arms sales. Turnover of advertising agencies with more than 10 employees reached 456 billion dollars in 2009, so including all the freelancers and all the internal publicity budgets of companies, spending on publicity will surely be close to the 1,200 billion dollars for arms sales! This creates a constant disinformation. Companies make a living out of the frustration that they continuously generate, what's more, they have every interest in generating frustration to provoke sales. This is what's important today; it's not so much the object as the act of buying in itself. It would be good to go back just a bit to materialism and to regain contact not only with nature, which I find a bit simplistic, but to regain contact with the materials. To understand where they come from, what's needed for their conversion and what the damage is in negative spillovers that no one pays for, such as greenhouse gases.

> *Companies make a living out of the frustration that they continuously generate*

What about man's relationship with nature?

_____ For millennia man has perceived nature as hostile. Indeed, the Great Plague that killed around 100,000 people in 1665 was quite hostile. In the 21st century we're getting to a point where it's man who is becoming hostile to nature. This can be considered rather gratifying, as we've won. The desire for domination over nature is fulfilled and nature now fears man. The biggest dangers from nature are conquered. There is still a small margin, like the natural catastrophes such as floods, earthquakes and hurricanes, which have major effects, but the struggle against nature that's hostile every day is won by mankind ^{read} p.43.

_____ Whence the impact on biodiversity. Nowadays people are talking about mass extinction, where a great number of species rapidly become extinct, which is serious ^{see} p.57. The question remains whether man is capable of living outside nature, outside the existing ecosystem* and equilibrium. There are very localised examples of man modifying his biotope*. In the 19th century for example, the English who colonised Australia introduced new species including rabbits. Being able to breed all year long in the mild climate, they multiplied rapidly and became a real menace to farming. Ever since, Australia has tried to reduce the rabbit population as their effect on the country's ecology* is devastating. Another example is the introduction of bovine animals by the colonists, as there were no pre-existing Australian cattle. Once introduced, the presence of cattle lead to the arrival of dung flies which multiplied and now there are hordes of flies pestering the population. This might seem insignificant but these local phenomena make people's lives unbearable. If this would be done on a grand scale, the consequences would be even more serious. Each species has its own place and function. Taking one element out of an ecosystem changes everything radically, with no possibility of recovery.

_____ If the bees that pollinate flowers in the orchards in California would disappear, the trees in the orchards would bear no more fruit. Human beings could do the pollination with a fine paintbrush, but studies show that that would cost about USD 14 billion per year.

How does biomimetics fit in this picture?

_____ It is important that there is an awareness that man is also a natural element, and that there should be an exchange in order to create harmony between humans and nature. Man's part of the bargain is to restore the ecosystem* and there are already manufacturers who are doing this. Lafarge Eco Systems is specialised in the rehabilitation of closed quarries. Before mining activities even begin they have a rehabilitation master plan in place. Through landscaping, planting and attracting suitable wildlife they put back an ecosystem where otherwise only bare ground would exist. This ecosystem is then maintained and opened to the public for educational and revenue purposes.

_____ An exchange works both ways. We should also look at everything that nature gives us, by studying it and investigating the way in which we can copy or work intelligently with it. Phytoremediation* – using plants to treat environmental problems – is an example of working in harmony with nature. Certain plants have the ability to absorb toxins from soil, water or air and to store it without having to dispose of it. These plants can be used to clean up polluted soil in a 'green' way. This is literally using the tools that nature gives us.

_____ The issues that arise here are twofold. The first question is whether it is sufficient to simply use or imitate without thoroughly investigating the total functioning with a systemic approach <u>read</u> p.167.225. Secondly, there is an ethical issue: the notion of patents. Dealing with biomimetics* very quickly turns into a question of patenting a living entity. Patenting the fact of having discovered a super molecule in a plant is one step, but what's the next step? It's a gift to mankind, hence the whole idea that biomimetics must go via an open-source approach. If one is going to patent what nature provides and which would resolve major environmental issues, then it is only reserved for those who have the means. In the end, Earth is only one planet and we're all living on it. This applies to all new environmental technologies. For instance, if Europe develops biofuels* from algae and patents it all to ensure that the Chinese and the Indians don't have access to it, these countries will continue to use the coal they have, instead of changing to biomass power stations. Europe can then have beautiful biomass power stations for its own personal use, while others spew out CO_2, each one more than the other. The climatic disturbance will affect everyone. Therefore there must be an approach of interdependence and cooperation, or inspiration and cooperation without patenting or limiting access, even though this goes against the dominant way of thinking.

Biomimetics must go via an open-source approach

_____ It's also important to remain cautious about the scale of how to look at things. There is the risk of depriving one of a benefit by relying on certain applications too soon. Technology must be made open-source via the internet, accessible to the whole world and subsequently adapted to meet local criteria. Natural adaptation occurs in the context of any given ecosystem. There's going to be local development, with local energy to adapt. There are no unique solutions. Marketing services prefer unique solutions and products worldwide, but that is just a fantasy. Even a bottle of Coca Cola is different in every country.

Is there a place for designers?

_____ I think there's a form of collective intelligence which should be set up. These would be rather creative groups in which a designer, an engineer and a marketeer work together, in synergy. That's collective intelligence, just like the wonderful examples of collective intelligence that nature gives us, like termites *read* p.233, ants and bees *read* p.79.171. This would ensure a greater creativity than that which an individual designer is capable of imagining. In order to achieve this, there must be a certain humility and acceptance of the idea of passing things on. To take something, giving it the maximum spirit, intelligence and know-how within the limits of one's abilities and then to pass it on to someone else, so that in the end the result is optimal.

HERVÉ NAILLON

Having a background in geopolitics, history and philosophy, Hervé Naillon applies a systematic approach to sustainable development, a topic he has specialised in during the last 11 years. During his geopolitics study course he wrote a dissertation on the transfer of dangerous waste between the United States and Haiti, and after doing voluntary work for Max Havelaar he started carrying out social and environmental company analyses for American pension funds, which had ethical criteria. Naillon realised that these issues could be tackled beforehand, rather than being marked at the end of the process and decided to join a marketing and innovation consultancy in 1999, saying that the great marketing innovation of the 21st century would be 'ethical marketing' (he invented the term), promoting the commitment to sustainable development. Later, he wrote the book entitled *Le marketing éthique* (World Village, 2002) co-authored by Elisabeth Pastore-Reiss. He also met Thierry Kazazian, the founder of O2 France and author of the book *Il y aura l'âge des choses légères* (Victoires Editions, 2003). He worked for this eco-design agency for 3 years as the director of development. Today, he works as an independent consultant in ethical marketing.

BIO-
DIVERSITY

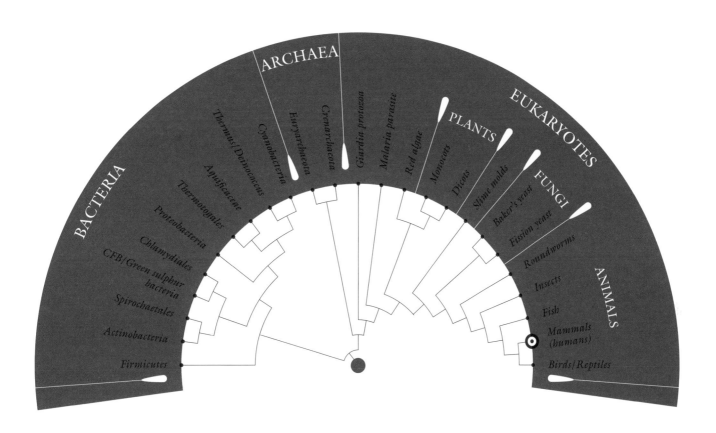

In 1990, the American microbiologist Carl Woese introduced the three-domain system, a biological classification that divides cellular life forms. The three domains are archaea, bacteria* and eukaryotes. The red dot in the centre represents the most ancient organism from which all organisms now living on Earth descend, and the lines springing from it illustrate how all the different species are related.

THE WAY
NATURE
WORKS

_____ The following pages describe 75 'strategies' of nature, examples of how nature handles various situations.

_____ Compared to the extraordinary reservoir of problems solved by all species on our planet on a daily basis, this limited selection provides a tiny glimpse of nature's ability to offer various efficient solutions to certain needs.

_____ Each strategy is presented in a scheme: the question raised, the living organism concerned, a short description of the solution given by the living organism and examples of existing or potential applications, showing how humans, inspired by natural phenomena, convert their gained knowledge into effective solutions. Photographs of these applications are included.

_____ Each strategy thus featured is accompanied by an illustration especially drawn for this book, the result of impressive teamwork by Benjamin Gomez and Myriam Hathout of Dépli Design Studio. Images speak a thousand words and even though wildlife photography often captures all the raw emotion of nature, here the combination of paintings and explanatory drawings feels more personal, efficient and strong.

_____ This chapter, without a doubt, is the core of the book and the strategies were the reason to embark on this project. Amazed by all this display of intelligence, precision, efficiency and _à propos_ we felt it needed to be shared more widely, and especially among the community in the creative industry.

_____ Welcome to the world of biomimicry*!

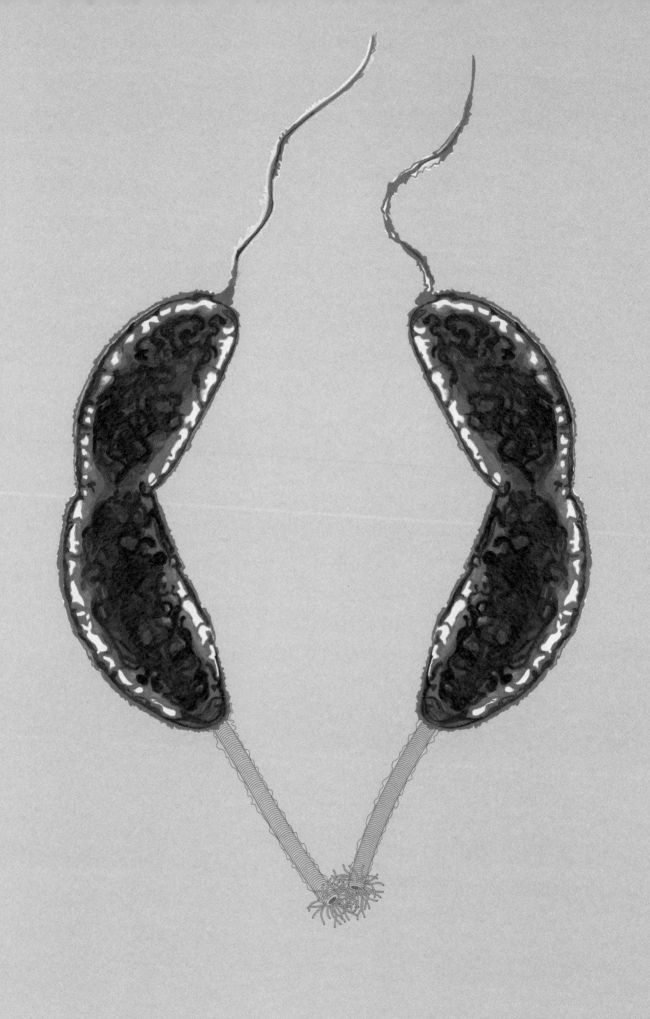

Adhesion
BACTERIA

read p.63.65.69.71

Caulobacter crescentus is a harmless bacterium which lives in aquatic environments low in nutrients, such as lakes, rivers and drinking-water pipes. It has an unusual feature: it fixes itself to solid objects such as rocks or water pipes using a real adhesive. It is found even in some bottles of water or in tap water, depending on the amount of chlorine added to the water and this 'bacterial super-adhesive' is even resistant to saltwater, which normally tends to destroy commercial adhesives.

The adhesive power of this bacterium is provided by its long and thin tail (pedicle), the end of which contains polysaccharides* – polymers – which are extremely adhesive. Its fixative properties have been tested by researchers and found to have much better performance than the commercial 'super glues'. In effect, to scale, the *Caulobacter crescentus* bacterium is capable of resisting a strain or 'pull' of 70 N/mm^2 (10,000 lb/in^2), while industrial adhesives can claim a resistance to strain of a maximum 28 N/mm^2 (4,000 lb/in^2). Jay Tang of Brown University, Rhode Island, found that a 1 cm^2 (0.15 in^2) area of this substance could support a weight of 800 kg (1,760 lb). Or again, that a 25-cent US coin, 24 mm (0.95 in) in diameter, covered with this substance could support a tension of 4,000 kg (8,800 lb), namely the weight of an adult elephant.

Apart from its great strength, this natural adhesive is water resistant and adheres to wet surfaces. It is also biodegradable*.

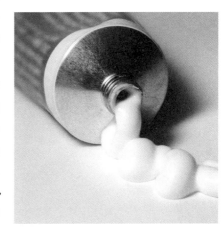

APPLICATION

This exceptional adhesive promises to have numerous applications, especially in the medical field, as it is resistant to saltwater and therefore our bodily fluids. It could replace suture stitches for example or hold dental prostheses in place. It could also serve in the nautical domain, for the repair of boat hulls. Obtained by synthesis or recovered directly from productive bacteria*, it should be available soon. *see* Photo © Makuba

Adhesion
BURDOCKS

read   p.61.65.69.71

______ There are various species of burdocks (members of the Asteraceae family). All burdocks have a two-year growth cycle and in that time they reach a height between 0.4 and 2.5 m (1.3 and 8.2 ft). The plant's natural habitat is mostly in Europe and Asia. In the latter, the root of the plant is commonly eaten as a vegetable. Many people think that the plant also possesses certain medicinal properties, for example, it is used as a blood* purifying agent.

____ Children and adults alike know the plant well for its characteristic flower heads that stick to clothing when thrown from a distance. The flower heads of a burdock (burrs), a specific type of inflorescence* (the arrangement of flowers on a plant stem), are equipped with tiny curved hooks which catch very efficiently onto anything that brushes past them, fabrics, hair, clothing, etc. Furthermore, these hooks are so flexible that they deform when they are pulled away, regaining their shape and their ability to hook on again immediately after.

APPLICATION

In the 1940s, Georges de Mestral, a Swiss engineer, studied the irritating ability of burdock flower heads of hooking into the hair of his dog. He suddenly realised that by reproducing and imitating their hooks, he could devise a new closure principle. Thus in 1948 Velcro® was invented. Its name is quite simply made up from 'vel' for the velours part and 'cro' for the hooks part (*crochet*). It was originally a registered trade mark, but has become a generic name. It consists of two strips, one covered with velours and the other with hooks, which hook and unhook indefinitely. The system has since had numerous imitations and has given rise to a lot of variations. Today there are hydrophobic*, nano-Velcro® and conductive Velcro® systems, etc. _____^*see* Photos © Laurent Hamels / Xuejun Li

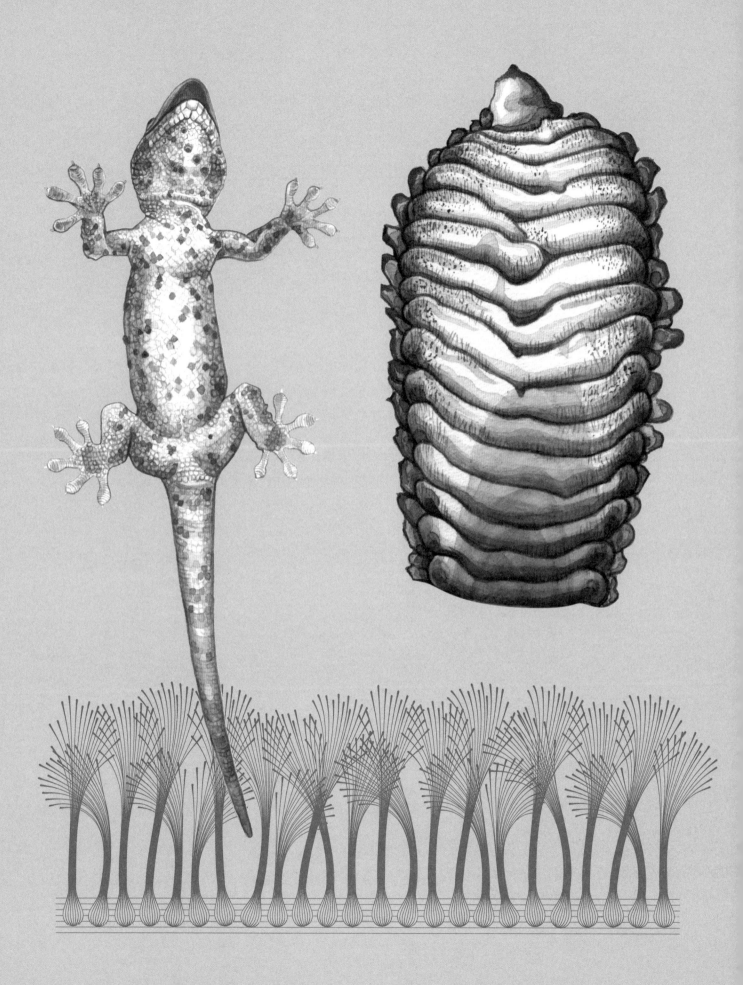

Adhesion
GECKOS

read ——— p.61.63.69.71.237

——— Geckos are mainly tropical lizards that vary widely in size and colour and inhabit countries with warm climatic conditions. They are nocturnal animals which hide in trees and bushes or under rocks during the day. They're also often found in houses which they clear of insects – the main item on their menu.

—— Most geckos (except the 27 species in the Eublepharinae sub-family also called eyelid geckos that live on the ground), are capable of walking upside down on a ceiling or running across vertical surfaces, such as walls. The secret of their astonishing ability to adhere to smooth surfaces lies in their toes. Their toes terminate in millions of keratin* hairs, called *setae* (Latin plural of *seta* 'bristle'). These hairs have a base diameter of a few tens of microns and split up at the end into yet finer hairs which resemble a nano-spatula. These spatulas come into contact with a surface at molecular level, having the effect of maximising the Van der Waals* attractive forces (low-intensity electromagnetic force* of a quantal origin), hence the remarkable adhesive properties of gecko toes. Researchers call this 'dry' adhesion.

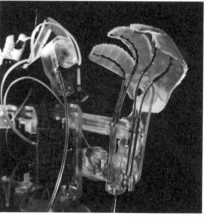

APPLICATIONS

Inspired by the structure of gecko feet, German fastening systems manufacturer Gottlieb Binder developed an adhesive silicone product called Gecko® tape. With 29,000 nanoscopic 'hairs' per cm² (as shown in this scanning tunnelling microscope image) it sticks easily to smooth surfaces without leaving any residue. *see* ——— Image top © Pascal Goetgheluck

Engineers at Stanford University in California have created a robot called Stickybot which can climb up glass by using the gecko-toe technique. 'Microwedges', 20 μm wide at the base and about 80 μm tall (20 μim and 80 μim) on top of an angled suspension layer give the robot its ability to adhere to smooth surfaces. Their sharp tips touch the surface and when pulled sideways – as in climbing – they bend over and stick. *see* ———
Photos bottom and p.66 © Mark Cutkosky, Stanford University

A real Spiderman costume for wall-walkers could be designed using this technique.

read p.65

read p.69

Adhesion
MUSSELS

read   p.61.63.65.71

The blue mussel (*Mytilus edulis*) is a bivalve filter mollusc, much appreciated by lovers of seafood. It is protected by two thin, but firm, hinged halves of external skin that are held together by the animal's muscles. The shell is dark blue on the outside and nacreous* on the inside.

Fertilisation of a mollusc happens outside of the body, resulting in a larva that is swept up by the current and floats in the sea. Its shell starts to develop when a mussel larva is 1 month old, at first translucent and having a yellowish colour, in time the shell turns dark. As the shell gets heavier during growth, there comes a time when the larva loses its floating ability and sinks to the bottom. This is an important moment in a mussel's life as the place where it lands determines its chances for survival, it won't be able to cover large distances anymore. An ideal situation would be to land on a hard surface to which the mussel can attach itself.

The mussel has great powers of adhesion to submerged objects and stays in place even in stormy seas, adhering to any suitable object (rock, jetty support, boat hull), held there by a system of flexible adhesive filaments, known as the byssus* (Greek *byssos* 'fine cloth') which it secretes. A mussel byssus has between 50 and 100 filaments. Each filament consists of collagen*, a structural protein* common in animal tissues. Grouped in bundles, they are held by a cuticle, i.e. an external layer a few microns thick. The cuticle is a complex material with zones of varying density*, making the byssus both wear-resistant and elastic.

APPLICATION

Dr Li, a professor at the School of Silviculture at Oregon State University, discovered that proteins* in soya can be modified to be as efficient as those of byssus* filaments. One can then obtain not only great adhesive ability but also high water resistance. This discovery has allowed Columbia Forest Products to develop PureBond®, a hardwood plywood without the normally used urea-formaldehyde*. Instead, a non-toxic soy-based adhesive is used, inspired by the way mussels adhere to rocks or other objects. *see*   Photos above and p.67 © Columbia Forest Products

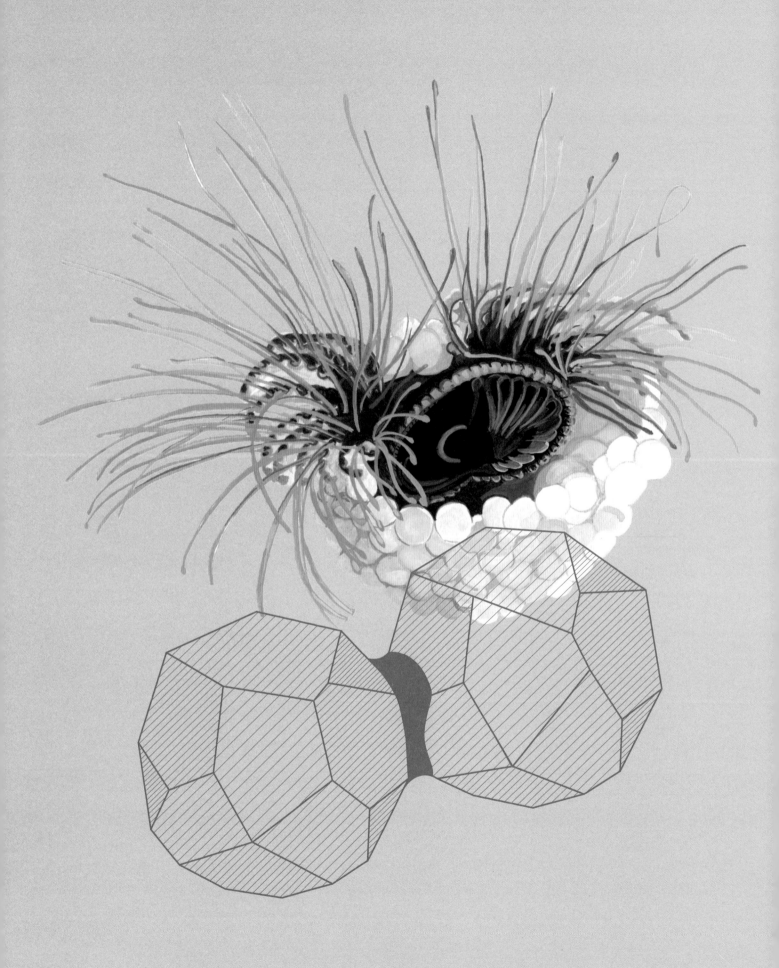

Adhesion
SANDCASTLE WORM

read p.61.63.65.69

Phragmatopoma californica, in the family Sabellarididae, has a soft body. Its common name is sandcastle worm. It has a dark brown colour, measures a little less than 10 cm (4 in) and is common along the Californian coasts.

The sandcastle worm has a special feature: for its protection, it hides in a tubular shelter built from sand particles and pieces of broken shells. When the tide goes out and the water level drops, uncovering its shelter, the worm closes off its tube with a dark _setae operculum_. When underwater though, it sticks its tentacles out of the tube, catching grains of sand and food. The worms live in colonies of compartments, a multitude of small sand tubes resembling submarine sandcastles, hence its common name. These colonies can be quite large, forming a reef of up to 2 m wide (6.6 ft).

To make these constructions, the worm secretes an adhesive substance which allows it to bind particles of the material it finds. This very special adhesive must obviously be resistant to water. It consists of negatively and positively charged proteins*. Synthesised in a special gland, the adhesive is kept in a liquid state by the worm in an acid milieu (in its body). As soon as this adhesive is excreted by the animal, contact with seawater, which has an alkaline pH*, solidifies it. A foam forms very quickly and in a few hours will become a material that is a solid, flexible, high-performance adhesive.

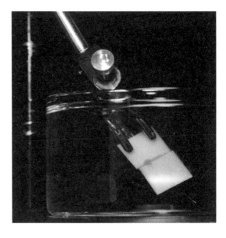

APPLICATION

Researchers at the University of Utah have studied marine animals and succeeded in devising an artificial adhesive inspired by the one produced by the sandcastle worm. The adhesive obtained has the capacity to glue together elements such as bone fragments in a wet milieu or immersed in water. The adhesive is also non-toxic and biodegradable*. Applications in the medical field are anticipated, to assist in the repair of broken bones in the case of complex and multiple fractures, where many bone fragments have to be held together. The photo above shows two pieces of human femur glued together, completely underwater. The synthetic glue is visible between the two bone segments. _see_ Photo © Russell Stewart

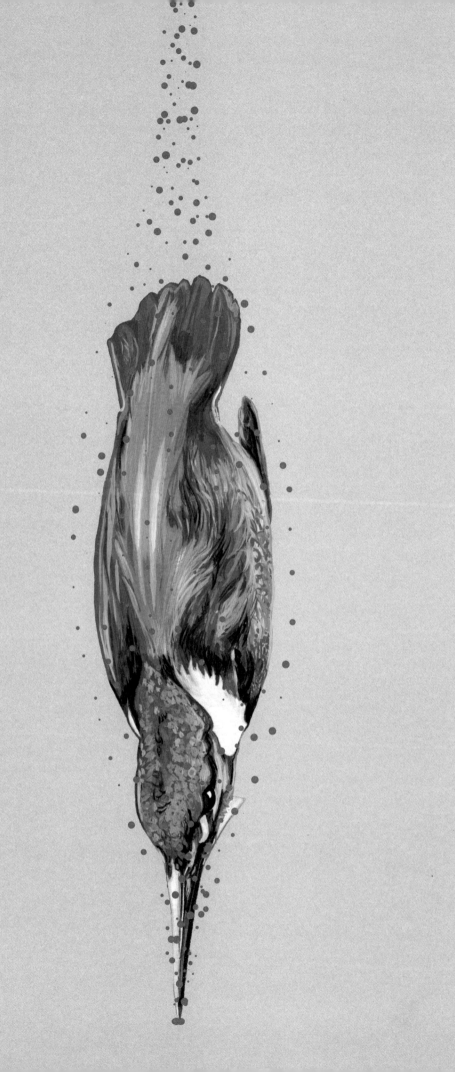

Aerodynamics
KINGFISHERS

read p.125.149.153.155.181

The kingfisher is a member of the Alcedinidae family of birds. There are many different kingfisher species, ranging in size from 10 cm to 45 cm (3.9 to 17.7 in), with different colour variations. The Common Kingfisher is a dazzling bird in flight, a jewel with an iridescent* blue back, orange-chestnut underneath and a beak like a dagger. It has a short tail, short wings and a short neck with a relatively large head.

It feeds on small fish and other aquatic animal life, hunting over ponds, lakes and rivers, where it spends its time going between air and water searching for its prey. The bird has a preference for clear streaming waters with lots of little fish. A shady area makes it easier to hunt as there is no reflection of the sun on the water's surface, making it easier to spot prey from its lookout point which is usually a branch hanging 1 to 3 m (3.3 to 9.8 ft) above the water. Its visual acuity is remarkable since it locates its prey precisely, unaffected by refraction* caused by the two different media, air and water.

When flying horizontally, often over the water's surface, it can reach speeds of up to 80 km/h (49.7 miles/h). Its precision and speed in catching fish, its ability to go with ease to and fro between air and water are quite astounding. It dives without splash or effort, even though water offers more resistance than air, and returns to the surface in a flash, fish in beak.

APPLICATION

The Shinkansen, the Japanese high-speed train, reaches 300 km/h (186 miles/h) running inter-city. On its journeys it has to pass through many tunnels. The entries into and exits from these tunnels cause severe pressure changes, with associated noise and vibration for trackside residents and passengers alike. Taking inspiration from the kingfisher beak, engineers have succeeded in designing a locomotive nose to reduce this nuisance (and power consumption by 15%), while increasing the train speed by 10%. *see*   Photos above and p.76 © David Pursehouse

Anti-bacterial
SHARKS

<u>*read*</u>   p.155.207

_____ As a type of fish, sharks belong to the superorder of Selachimorpha. There are over 440 shark species. Other large, slow-swimming animals that share the seas with sharks are whales. It may be noted that whales are often covered in algae and barnacles that stick to their skin. Somewhat surprisingly, sharks are always completely free of these companions.

_____ The skin of a shark is not smooth, as might be imagined, but instead it is very rough. It is covered by scales known as dermal denticles, rather like small teeth or tiny fins, arranged in rows parallel to the water flow as the animal swims. This specialised surface structure appears under the microscope as a landscape of bumps and hollows of the order of 200 to 300 variations per mm^2 (0.002 in^2) of skin. A terrain too undulating, it seems, to be a suitable location for other organisms and even bacteria*. This topography makes too heavy an energy demand and they prefer to move to more welcoming locations.

APPLICATION

Inspired by the form and patterns of sharkskin surfaces, the antibacterial polymer film Sharklet SafeTouch™ prevents bacteria* such as the golden *Staphylococcus** from developing on its surface. Developed by Sharklet Technologies Inc., following research carried out by the US Navy to find a solution to the proliferation of algal growth on ship hulls, the technology is based on a special microscopic texture (very useful in public places, on door and other handles, etc.). It is the world's first technology to inhibit bacterial growth through a texture alone. The interest lies in the avoidance of using chemical agents: the anti-bacterial properties are due to the film structure itself. As far as algae are concerned, tests show that this type of micro-structure on a surface brings an 85% reduction in the ability of green algae to adhere to a given surface. $\overset{see}{\rule{1cm}{0.4pt}}$ Photo © Pascal Goetgheluck

read p.73

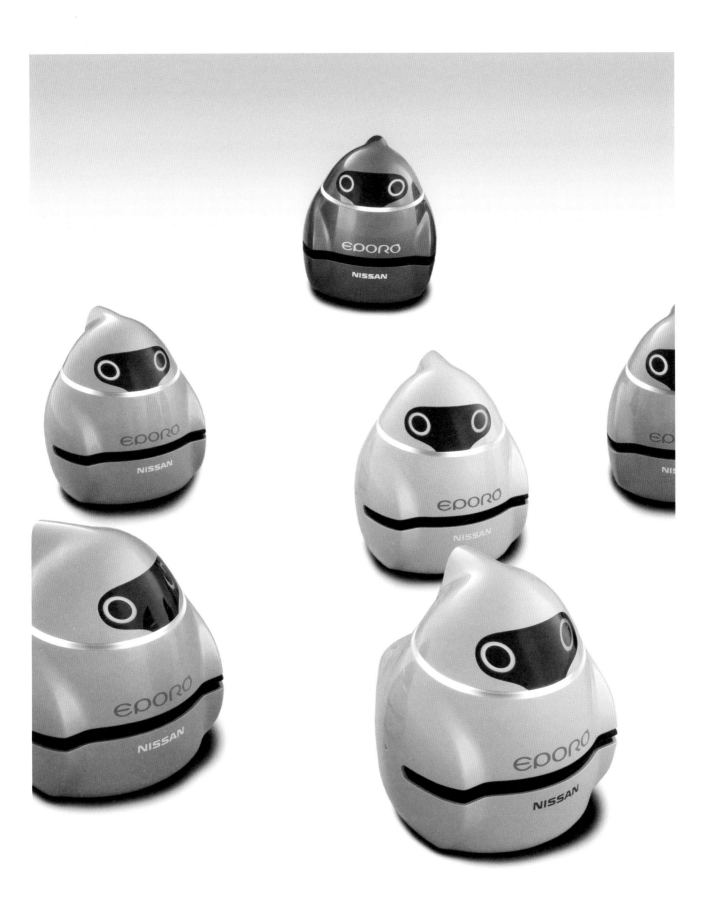

read p.79

Anti-collision
BEES

read p.81.87.89.171.235

After a larva has undergone pupation it becomes a young worker bee, tasked with cleaning the hive and feeding the new larvae. Later its job is to build comb cells. The bees that fly around from one flowering plant to another, are in fact bees being redeployed. In effect, hive organisation demands that once worker bees have finished their many tasks in the hive, they become pollen collectors at the end of their short life. They then have the right to go out to collect pollen from flowers for the hive, where it is used as a source of protein* required during brood rearing. Bees are mostly fuzzy and carry an electrostatic charge which helps them to collect the pollen. In flight, their front wings connect to the rear wings by means of a temporary hook-up system to provide better lift*. The pairs of wings become detached again on landing. Bees generally fly at an average speed of 25 to 30 km/h (15 to 18 miles/h) and can travel up to 800 km (500 miles) in the course of their lives. They are capable of carrying the equivalent of their own weight in pollen and make up to 15 journeys per day, over a radius of 1 to 3 km (0.6 to 1.8 miles) around the hive.

A bee is able to fly without interruption and without colliding, thanks to its complex, high-performance eyes* which cover more than 300°. There is an oval virtual zone around the bee in which it can evaluate its surroundings, making it possible for it to anticipate obstacles and avoid them by deviating from its flight path for a fraction of a second.

APPLICATION

BR23C is a biomimetic* car robot drive that was developed in 2008 by Nissan Motor Co., Ltd, the Research Center for Advanced Science and Technology at the University of Tokyo and its Kanzaki/Takahashi Lab. It demonstrates a crash avoidance system, mimicking the bees' ability to avoid obstacles during flight. For this vehicle, the engineers developed a laser range finder which can detect obstacles in front of the vehicle up to a distance of 2 m (6.5 ft) over a radius of 180°. Once the distance of the obstacle has been evaluated and the information sent to an onboard microprocessor, the vehicle can change direction by turning its wheels. In 2009, Nissan presented a new robot car concept, EPORO*1, designed to travel in a group of vehicles, mimicking the behavioural patterns of a school of fish. The manufacturer's aim is that its vehicles attain at least a half collision rate by 2015 compared to the 1995 rate.

see Photos above and p.77 © Nissan Motor Co., Ltd

Anti-collision
GRASSHOPPERS

read   p.79.89

The grasshopper is an insect of the sub-order Caelifera. It has three pairs of legs, of which the strong hind legs make it possible for the insect to jump and cover a distance 20 times its body length. This leaping is not just accomplished by the jumping muscles but by a catapulting system, located in its knees which propels the grasshopper into the air.

It seems quite incredible to see large numbers of grasshoppers jumping, side-by-side, seemingly quite chaotically, in their search for food, but without ever bumping into each other. Scientists have noted that African grasshoppers which move in swarms have a unique internal radar: a large neuron*, acting as a giant movement detector, is located behind the eyes*. This neuron is called the Locust Giant Movement Detector (LGMD). If the insect is about to collide, the corresponding visual information triggers an action potential*, which means that energy is delivered via the LGMD. This energy is transmitted instantaneously to nerve cells in the wings of the insect, without, it seems, even passing through the head 'capsule' in the brain, to change the flight trajectory. The operation in its entirety takes only 45 ms. As insects see many more images per second than humans do, they are therefore able to react in time even if obstacles approach very quickly. What's more, they concentrate visually on any possible obstacles in their path and ignore any other movements around them.

APPLICATION

It was Dr Claire Rind of Newcastle University in England who first drew the parallel between the astonishing abilities of grasshoppers and the need to develop safety systems for road travel. Safety researchers at Volvo Car Corporation have developed this further. The Volvo S60 features a pedestrian detection system, inspired by the grasshopper's ability to avoid collisions. Radar and a camera-based system detect pedestrians walking in front of the car and warn the driver or apply full auto-breaking power if the driver doesn't respond in time.
see   Photo © Volvo Car Corporation

Antifreeze
FROGS AND ARCTIC FISH

read p.131.193

Freezing diffuses water from cells by osmosis*: cell walls break and release their contents. Moreover, most cells can't tolerate the presence of ice crystals. The cell organelles and tissues break-up, in short the cell dies. However, certain living creatures are capable of surviving freezing conditions.

Some species of frog convert glycogen* in their liver to glucose*, to prevent cells freezing, but allows the formation of ice in extracellular spaces. When the body contains 60 to 65% ice, the heart stops beating, respiration ceases and the frog survives by means of its aerobic metabolism*. If the temperature drops below -7 °C (17 °F), the animal dies. A covering of snow is therefore important for its survival.

Some species of cod and flounder have proteins* which lower the freezing point of their blood* by approximately 1 to 1.5 °C (0.9 °F) below the temperature at which seawater freezes. When ice crystals start to form in the blood, antifreeze proteins cling to its surface, with the result that water finds it difficult to adhere to the crystals: the crystals remain tiny and do no damage to the cells. One species of flounder has this antifreeze in too small a quantity to enable it to withstand temperatures lower than 1.5 °C. However, there is another much more active antifreeze protein in its blood: if a given quantity of normal commercial antifreeze reduces freezing point by 0.1 °C (0.2 °F), the same quantity in this particular flounder reduces the freezing point by 1.1 °C (2 °F). Therefore, with just a small amount of antifreeze, the blood remains liquid.

APPLICATIONS

In order to improve the texture of its ice creams, Unilever is introducing an 'antifreeze' into its production process. This protein – from the bacterium *Marinomonas protea*, recently discovered in the Antarctic – prevents the formation of large ice crystals, making the texture seem softer. This antifreeze could be incorporated into other frozen foods. Unilever is now seeking to commercialise production of this protein.
see Photo © Anna K.

These antifreeze substances are of interest to the food processing industry: they allow the freezing point of certain products to be reduced.

Research also gives hope that 'green' antifreeze products may appear.

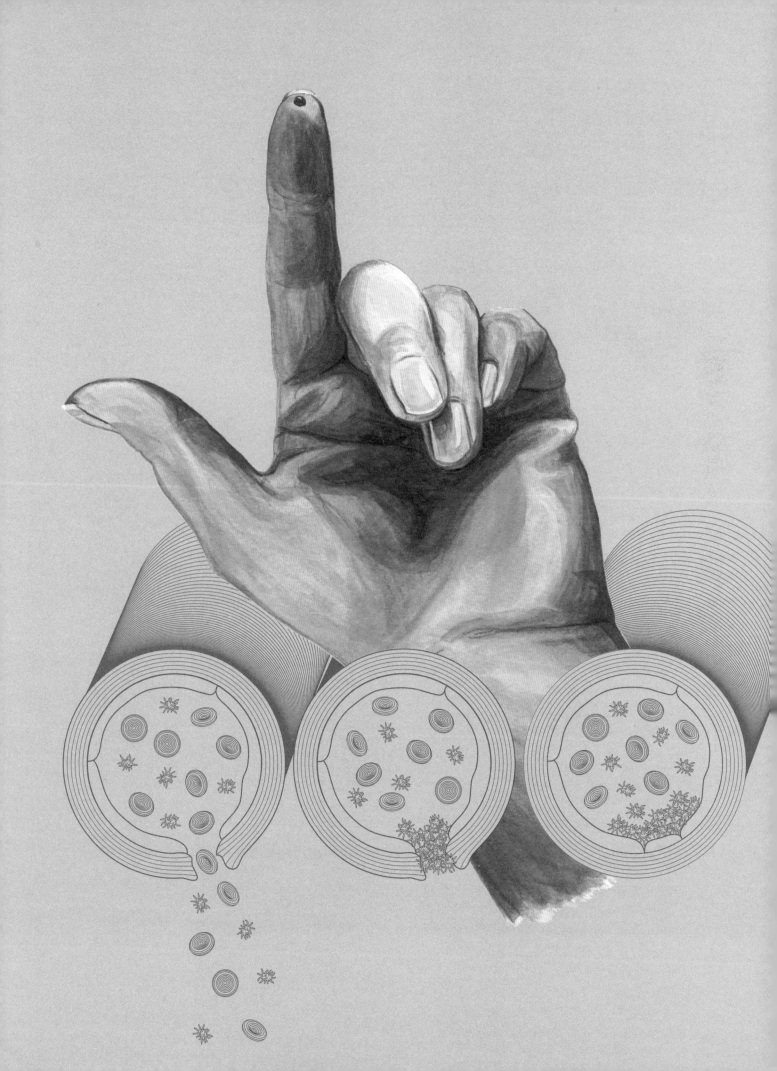

Anti-leak
BLOOD

read p.143.205.207

The average human adult has a blood* volume of 4 to 6 litres. This bodily fluid has many functions which include the transportation of oxygen*, hormones and nutrients through the body, heat regulation and defense against intruders. Blood basically consists of three different types of cells: red blood cells that are mainly responsible for the oxygen transportation, white blood cells that are part of the body's immune system helping to resist infections and parasites, and the platelets that take care of the blood coagulation.

When blood loss occurs, several mechanisms come into play to avoid haemorrhage. First, the blood vessels involved contract, this is called vasoconstriction*. Next, platelets in the blood bind together and form a plug called a platelet clot. Tightly bound by fibres constructed by fibrin* protein*, the accumulation of platelets forms a clot which stops the bleeding.

If the platelet count in the blood is too low then this can result in excessive blood loss because the blood does not coagulate. But if there are too many platelets, blood vessels can become obstructed by blood clots (thromboses) and result in a stroke or other adverse medical conditions.

People suffering from haemophilia (haemophiliacs) have a blood-clotting disorder. This blood coagulation abnormality may have severe consequences even for minor injuries.

APPLICATION

Following the example of blood coagulation ensured by platelets, there are now some oil pipelines which have polymer platelets capable of forming petroleum platelets to block a leak temporarily. Each polymer 'platelet' is marked electronically to allow maintainers to localise the fault and to take corrective action. This technology is called Advanced Technology for Leak Location and Sealing System (ATLLAS™) and could be used in the chemical industry or for water pipes. The Brinker company has now commercialised Platelet Technology™ and has proved its effectiveness.

Anti-reflection
MOTHS

read p.79.89.189

A moth (sub-order Heterocera) is an insect in the order Lepidoptera. Most moths are active during the night and rest during the day on a tree or on the forest floor. Their brownish colouring provides them with a camouflage, leaving them less exposed to predators when they're inactive. There are also day-flying moths that are brightly coloured, thereby communicating that they are toxic.

The eyes* of moths have evolved to prevent daylight being reflected by them to avoid being located, in fact the eyes of moths are almost completely anti-reflective. The cornea of the moth's eye is covered by an even layer of small conical protuberances 200 to 300 nanometres high, with similar dimensions between them. This unusual surface structure reduces light reflection by creating continuity between the refractive index of air and that of the eye. In effect, the speed of the light changes more gradually between the air and the eye and the normally sharp change in the refractive index as the light strikes the surface of the lens, is smoothed out. This reduces the reflectance of the lens, allowing it to capture more light and therefore reflect less light. There is very little reflection to betray the presence of the flying or resting moth and its visual acuity is also increased at night.

APPLICATIONS

Anti-reflective surface treatments are now being designed, particularly in the domain of photovoltaic* panels of silicon solar cells*. Silicon is naturally reflective, obviously in direct opposition to a panel's objective, which is to capture maximum incident light energy.

Today anti-reflective films which have been inspired by the eyes* of the moth, are available to cover flat TV and computer screens.

Autopilot
FLIES

read p.79.81.87.101.171.235

Flies don't have the sensors of modern aeronautics to fly and to control their altitude. Their sensory-motor skills result from data processing in a tiny brain consisting of a hundred thousand to one million neurons* (50 to 100 thousand million in a human brain). When an insect flies above the ground, the image of the latter scrolls from front to back in the centre of its visual field. This constitutes an 'optical flux', a combination of the contrasting ground scenes scrolling past and the observation of height relative the ground. If an insect changes speed, its 'automation' constrains height change to keep the speed/height ratio constant. If flying into a strong headwind, it will make a forced landing, but at zero vertical speed.

After having shown that the electrical signals from the compound eye* of the fly excite the neurons that activate the wings to allow the insect to adjust its flight and avoid crashes, Nicolas Franceschini's biorobotics team demonstrated that these neurons are also involved in a kind of 'autopilot', controlling the lift* force. Researchers modelled the insect's navigation from experience obtained with a flying micro robot called OCTAVE which reproduces insect behaviour. The proposed flight-control pattern takes account of observations made over several years on flying insects. In particular, it explains that insects go downwards in a headwind and rise in a tailwind. The insect's 'cockpit' has movement-detecting neurons which act as 'optical flux' sensors. The electrical activity in these neurons has been studied and analysed and their operating principles have been used in the design of a micro-electronics circuit inserted into a micro-helicopter.

APPLICATIONS

Inspired by the flight-control mechanisms of flies, the micro robot OCTAVE, weighing 100 grams, manages to follow a sloping terrain at a speed of three metres per second, taking off and landing automatically and displaying reactions to head and tailwinds. Underlying these abilities is a stunning performance 'autopilot' inspired by the eye* of a fly. Installed on a UAV (unmanned aerial vehicle) or aircraft, this autopilot could replace many of the heavy and expensive traditional sensors. OCTAVE was designed and built by Nicolas Franceschini and Franck Ruffier of the Biorobotics Department at CNRS and the University of Aix-Marseille in France. *see* Photo © CNRS Photothèque - RAGUET Hubert / UMR6152 - Mouvement et perception - Marseille

Interest is going both ways between biology and engineering. The method consists of using robotic reconstructions to test and validate biological theories. In this way it is possible to decode hidden principles underlying animal behaviour and also to envisage applications inspired by biology. In this specific case, the results obtained open up perspectives for innovation in the aerospace domain and in particular in the control of the crucial phrases where aerial vehicles and space modules fly close to the ground.

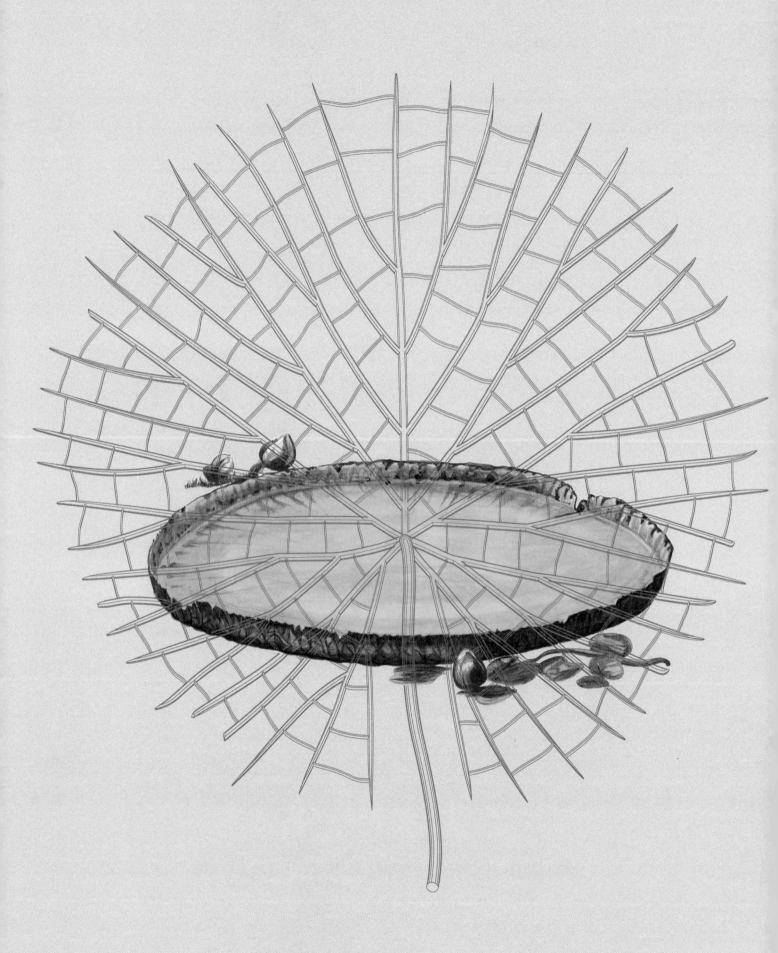

Buoyancy and rigidity
GIANT WATER LILY

read   p.203.211.223

_____ The *Victoria amazonica* is a giant water lily (in fact *the* largest water lily) remarkable for its ability to deploy leaves extending to 3 m (10 ft) in diameter and strong enough for a human to sit on. A member of the Nymphaeaceae family, this astonishing plant is indigenous to South America.

_____ The flowers that the plant produces are also larger than average, spanning a diameter of 40 cm (1.3 ft). The giant water lily is a night bloomer. Each flower blooms only two nights in a row; the first night a white flower shows itself and the second night, after a transformation, a pink flower appears. Then the flower submerges so that its seeds can ripen underwater. A water lily can produce several flowers but they never bloom simultaneously.

_____ The leaves have a vertical edge which allows them to meet other leaves without overlapping. The growth of the plant is very rapid, the leaves expanding by half a square metre (roughly 5 ft^2) per day and each plant can produce 50 of them in one growing season. Examination of the underside of the giant leaves reveals an elaborate network of very pronounced ribs. Rigid radial ribs are interwoven with fine transverse ribs, creating a solid grid which traps air and keeps the leaf afloat.

APPLICATIONS

Joseph Paxton, a 19th century gardener and architect, was inspired by the very special structure of the leaves of the giant lily, to first of all build a glasshouse, the Great Conservatory at Chatsworth, and then the cast iron and glass structure of the Crystal Palace in London's Hyde Park. The latter was built for the Great Exhibition of 1851. *see* _____ Image top

In 2008 the architect Vincent Callebaut, inspired by the same biology, produced a design for a real, autonomous floating city which could house more than 50,000 inhabitants. A response to forecasts of problems caused by rising sea levels and the demand for accommodation for climate refugees. *see* _____ Images bottom and p.94 © Vincent Callebaut Architectures

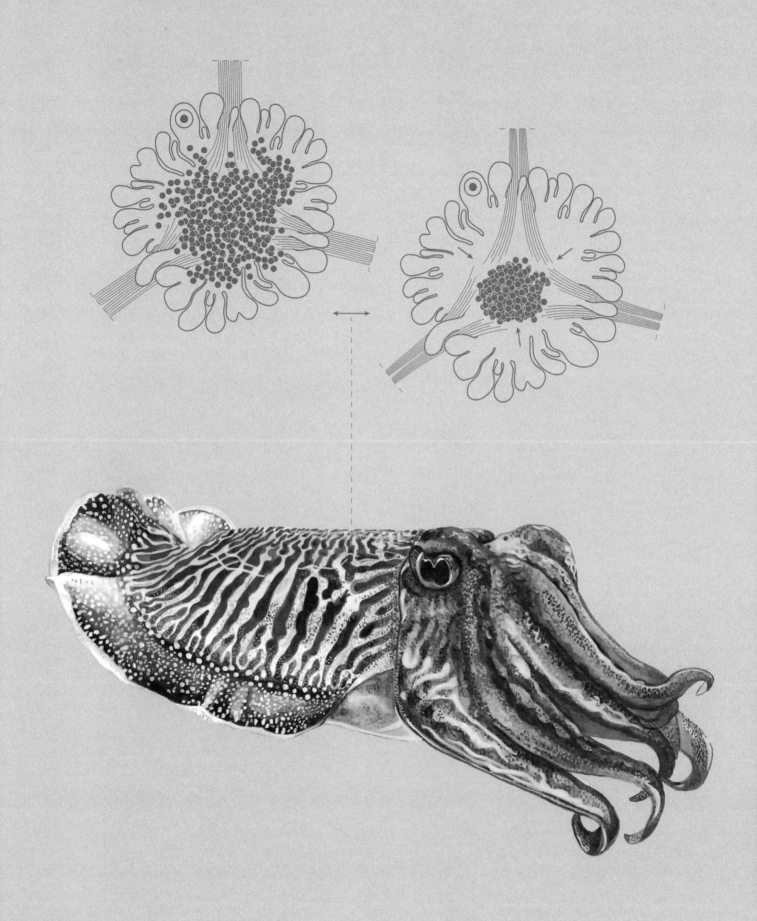

Camouflage
CUTTLEFISH

read p.97.117

Cuttlefish are masters of camouflage, capable of going from visible to invisible and back again in less than 2 seconds. They can use this subterfuge to blend with any background. Resting on a sandy seabed, a cuttlefish's skin may have a pattern of white and brown areas which resemble grains of sand. In the blink of an eye, this pattern can be replaced by another one.

Cuttlefish owe their mastery of disguise to their chromatophores* – cells in their skin containing red, yellow or brown pigments made visible (or invisible) by the muscles surrounding them. These muscles are under the direct control of neurons* located in the motor area of the brain, which explains why these animals can so quickly melt into their background. Cuttlefish can also change the texture of their skin, which contains bundles of muscles (papillae). This is quite useful when they hide close to a rock encrusted with barnacles. The cuttlefish's arsenal of camouflage tricks is completed by leucophores* and iridophores*, pigment cells located under the other chrematophores. Leucophores react to a wide spectrum of wavelengths, which allows them to reflect almost all types of incident light: for example, white light at the water surface and blue light in the depths. Iridophores use a stack of platelets consisting of a protein* called reflectin to produce iridescent* reflections similar to those from butterfly wings. Cuttlefish can activate or deactivate these reflectors in an instant, while controlling the spacing of the platelets in order to select a colour. They can also combine these iridescent colours with those generated by the chromatophores in order to create shimmering shades of purple and orange.

APPLICATIONS

The extraordinary abilities of cuttlefish are of interest to the military: these abilities would be extremely useful for military camouflage. In 2006, defence experts Adam Shohet and Chris Lawrence published an article on mollusc camouflage in the UK *Journal of Defence Science*. In this article they emphasised the ability of cuttlefish to create kinetic patterns, waves of colour running the length of their body to confuse predators.

MIT researchers (Professor Edwin Thomas and co-workers) took inspiration from cuttlefish camouflage to design a pixel with a full-colour spectrum. They used block-copolymer photonic gels with a lamellar structure that reflect light when stimulated by, for example, electric signals. In this case, the colour of the pixel is determined by the level of applied voltage, changing from red to green and blue. This discovery could lead to the development of energy efficient screens.

read   p.91

read   p.97

Camouflage
INSECTS

read p.93.117

_____ Many insects use their shape and colour to imitate the surface they rest on. If homotypy* (form resemblance) is added to homochromy* (colour resemblance), very effective concealment is achieved. It is possible to have almost perfect imitation of bark, branches, leaves or flowers.

_____ Stick insects have enlongated bodies, extended even more by their antennae and legs. The body is gnarled and greenish brown and can even change colour according to the season. When motionless on a branch, they appear to be its small offshoots. The Phylliidae family of leaf insects (Greek *phullon* 'leaf') have wide 'leaf' bodies as well as wings and some even have small 'leaves' on their legs. Everything about them is leaf-like and green.

_____ For their part the mantises, insects of the order Mantodea, have mastered the art of being taken for flowers. Possibly the best known of this order is the praying mantis, *Mantis religiosa*. In the mantis genus *Gongylus*, the whole of the lower part of the body of one species resembles a bunch of dead leaves. From this arises a long stalk, at the end of which there is a splendid petal whose edges shine in azure blue. The insect balances as if at the mercy of the wind, thus hoping to attract the prey it feeds on. If the latter arrives, the flower-mantis relaxes into a trap.

_____ Some species of butterflies go beyond mimicry, to pass themselves off as a dangerous or poisonous creature: some of the butterflies of the *Caligo* genus show large eye-spots on the underside of their wings, leading a predator to mistake them for the eyes* of an owl.

APPLICATIONS

Desiree Palmen uses camouflage techniques in her works of art. By manipulating people's clothing she lets them blend in with their environment, making them difficult to distinguish.
see _____ Photo above: *Interior Camouflage – Floor*, analogue photograph 180 x 100 cm (ed 3), 1999 © Desiree Palmen – all rights reserved, Marres Maastricht, thanks to Risk Hazekamp and p.95: *Interior Camouflage – For Artist in studio during open house*, analogue photograph 135 x 100 cm (ed 5), 2004 © Desiree Palmen – all rights reserved, Duende Studios Rotterdam, thanks to Risk Hazekamp

Several research groups are closely studying the various camouflage strategies which, among other things, may inspire applications for the armed forces. One could think of camouflage for military equipments and sites.

Controlled fall
MAPLE SAMARAS
AND HUMMINGBIRDS

read p.121.125.127

_____ Maples produce characteristic fruits known by different names such as samaras or maple keys. They are commonly known to children as 'helicopters' or 'whirly-birds' in a reference to the way they rotate as they fall, like the wings (rotor blades) of a helicopter. It is astonishing that, on close inspection, their fall can be seen to occur at a constant speed despite gravitational force. Forces of aerodynamic* origin due to air resistance compensate for acceleration due to gravity. It can be noted that the frequency of rotation of a samara is 15 to 30 rpm. The shape of this unique wing, its weight and the attitude of the seed in the air create a mini vortex* during the fall. The vortex tends to 'empty' the air above it, thus creating a small depression which tends to produce an upward force on the samara. While the samara is falling, it is constantly pulled back in the opposite direction, which explains its controlled fall. However, for the samara to rotate while falling, certain conditions must be met, namely the presence of a vertical draught and a slight inclination of the wing in relation to the horizontal. The slow descent allows the samara to be carried far from the tree, enabling wide dissemination of its seeds.

_____ Some birds such as hummingbirds, are capable of hovering flight. By continuously beating their wings they maintain their position in space. They also benefit from turbulence* which develops above their wings, keeping them in the air.

APPLICATIONS

The gyrocopter, first built by the Spanish engineer Juan de la Cierva in 1923, is a device inspired by samaras. It has a similar form, but is a hundred times larger. Somewhere between a fixed-wing aircraft and rotary-wing aircraft (commonly known as a helicopter), it allows vertical take-off and landing and also changes from hovering flight to forward flight and back again. If the engine fails, it can come down slowly. The German version of the gyrocopter, the Tragschrauber, is built in Hildesheim. Its main building material is steel with a cabin made from fibreglass and carbon. _see_____ Photos above © A. Wegent/ Switzerland and p.106 © Annunziata Ugas

Some of today's aerial drones are based on this model, in particular very small drones, even nano-drones (generally known as UAVs – unmanned aerial vehicles), weighing only a few grams. These have been developed by the military aeronautics arm of Lockheed Martin, among others. The smallest are designed for soldiers to carry in a backpack, for use on reconnaissance missions. It is also possible to envisage parachute systems which could be released far from their landing zone for greater secrecy.

Echolocation
BATS

read   p.121

Bats, of the order of Chiroptera, essentially hunt at night. Their sight is not sufficient for getting their bearings within their airspace, even less to allow them to actively hunt. They have a sophisticated echolocation system which allows them to 'see with their ears' at night. They emit calls at ultrasonic frequencies from 20 to 120 kHz. Each bat has a unique frequency and its auditory system is specially 'tuned' to it. Each emitted burst of ultrasound* is reflected by any obstacle it meets and is bounced back to the bat's ears. This system indicates the distance to an object and reveals precise details about it, especially whether it is motionless or moving. Bats can thus locate flying prey, by means of the Doppler Effect*. In detecting frequency variations between echoes and transmitted pulses, bats can perceive the speed of a flying prey insect as well as its wing beat-rate. If the frequency of the echo is higher than that of the transmitted burst, the flying prey is coming towards the bat. Bats deduce distance from the delay between transmission and reception. Finally, bats also have the ability to deduce the size, azimuth and elevation of their prey, thanks to certain data provided by the amplitude of the echo or by the difference between the information received by each ear.

Man is barely capable of detecting sounds with frequencies approaching 20 kHz. Bat sonar systems operate at much higher frequencies from 50 to 200 kHz. These sounds are 'broadcast' in all directions and can be emitted at a rate of up to 30 bursts per second. Their echolocation system is efficient enough to enable them to avoid a wire 0.008 mm (0.00030 in) thick in total darkness.

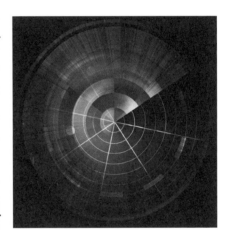

APPLICATION

SONAR is the acronym of Sound Navigation And Ranging. Contrary to a common belief, it wasn't the bat that led to the invention of sonar, but the development of sonar which allowed the bat's aerial skills to be explained. It took almost two centuries to penetrate the mystery of the bat's night 'vision'. Active sonar transmits a sound pulse and listens for its echo from obstacles that it encounters. An electro-acoustic transducer emits a signal (a 'ping') and a hydrophone acts as an acoustic-electro transducer for the received echo. Both of these may be arranged in arrays of antennas. Distance is obtained by measuring the elapsed time between transmission and reception. The speed of propagation for sound in sea water is approximately 1,500 m/s (0.93 miles/s). *see*   Photo © Argus

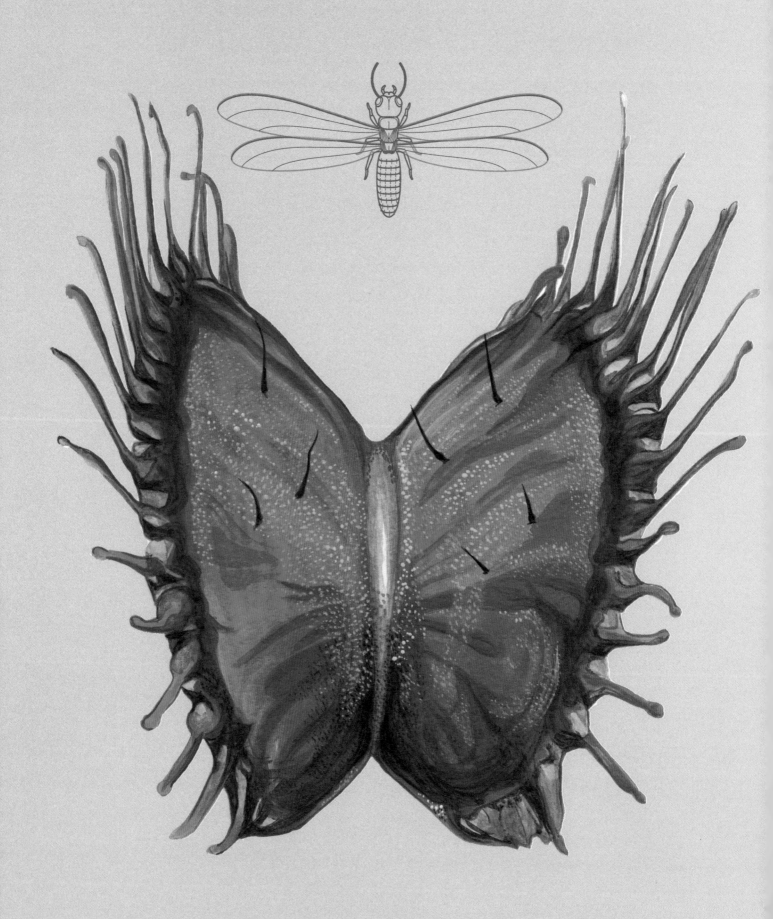

Electric current control
CARNIVOROUS PLANTS

read p.117

The Venus Flytrap (*Dionaea muscipula*) is the best known carnivorous plant and the most emblematic. In 1770 the Swedish botanist Carl von Linné named it Venus Flytrap and soon after it was fully described by the Irish naturalist John Ellis. In his 1875 publication entitled *Insectivorus plants*, Charles Darwin spoke of it as 'one of the most marvellous plants in the world' and went on to demonstrate its carnivorous abilities. Today, distribution of the Venus Flytrap is limited to the north and south Carolinas in the United States over an area of about 45,000 km² (17,000 miles²). They grow in peat bogs in acid soils that are deficient in mineral salts.

The leaves of the plant are arranged in rosettes whose diameter can reach 10 to 15 cm (4 to 6 in) in the adult plant. Each leaf blade has two parts. The upper part forms a trap, a sort of jaw consisting of two separate lobes connected by a central rib. Around the edge of each lobe there are 15 to 20 stiff hairs. In the edge of each lobe there are small glands which make and secrete a nectar rich in carbohydrates* which attract prey. On the internal surface there are three erect trigger hairs and a large number of small glands producing digestive secretions. Insects are attracted by odours given off by the trap. Three sensitive hair-like structures on the inside of each lobe that act as triggers. As soon as the trigger hairs are touched, an electrical signal is generated to close the trap. Two of the trigger hairs operate as electrical switches connected in series: two hairs must be stimulated in quick succession for the trap to close. This arrangement avoids random closures, which could be caused by raindrops for example. These biological mechanisms operate in a very short time, about 0.3 seconds.

APPLICATIONS

Some plants and animals use 'biological switches' to induce or prevent the passage of electrical signals. The natural mechanisms are similar to those controlling the flow of current in electrical circuits. *see* Photo © Nightman

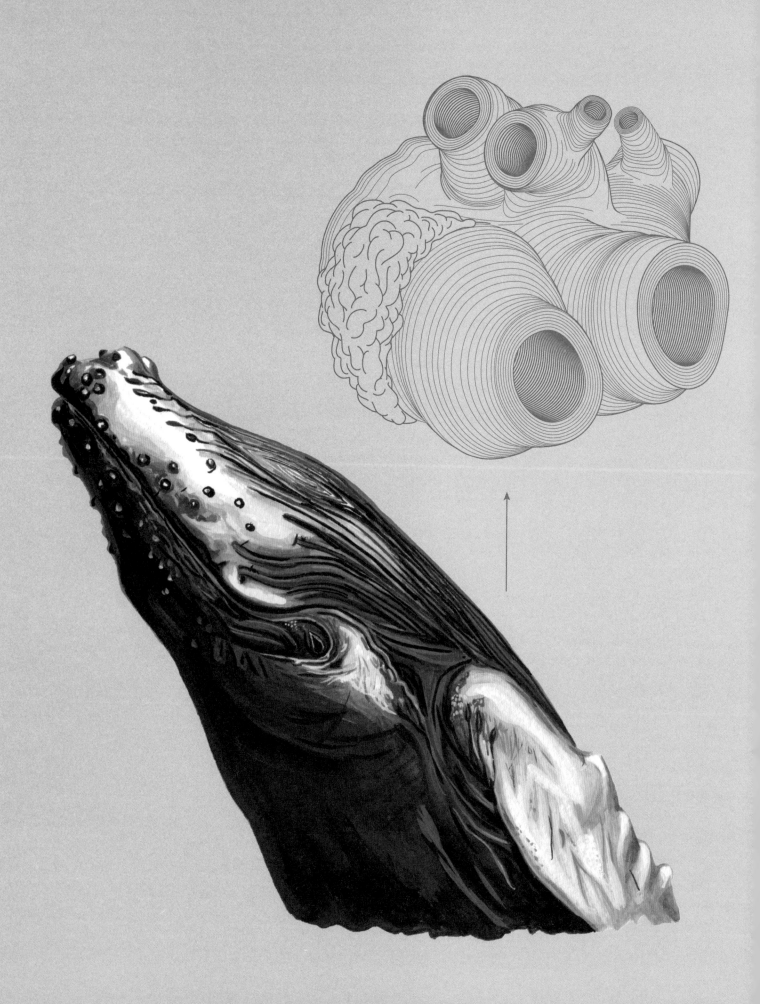

Electricity generation
HUMPBACK WHALE

read p.153

The humpback whale is a very large mammal, of the order Cetacea (whales, dolphins and porpoises), that appears in oceans and seas across the world. When the humpback whale dives, it curves its back and the dorsal fin protrudes above the water's surface – this is how the whale derived its name. The animal is quite easy to recognise by its knobbly head and jaw (which are hair follicles), its black back and its unusually long black and white pectoral fins. Individual humpback whales have uniquely-patterned tail fins.

The humpback whale can reach a length of about 15 m (49 ft) and weigh up to 36,000 kg (79,000 lb). Such an organism has a heart which, by itself, can weigh an average of 430 kg (950 lb), compared to that of the average adult human heart: 330 g (12 oz). A huge pump which is capable of propelling vast quantities of oxygenated* blood* for a lifespan variously estimated as up to 40 years. It does this at a slow heart rate (heart rate tends to fall as the size of the animal increases), in a circulatory system many times larger than that of a man.

Jorge Reynolds, one of the inventors of the pacemaker, and head of a research programme on whales in Colombia, used a submarine to study the operation of the humpback whale heart. He discovered that the contraction of the organ is controlled by nano-fibrils which transmit electrical signals, capable of reaching the myocardium (heart muscle) even though the latter is covered by a non-conducting grease layer which protects it from cold.

APPLICATIONS

These discoveries, made by way of studying humpback whales, could allow the development of a system of cardiac stimulation by means of carbon nano-wiring inspired by these animals. No longer any need for a pacemaker and its battery. The potential market is substantial: more than 350,000 people in the USA, for example, are fitted with one of these devices each year. With the solution outlined here, the cost is only a few cents, the follow-up is reduced and further surgery for battery changing is unnecessary.

Finding alternative solutions for the use of batteries in a pacemaker and other applications such as mobile phones, watches and other devices, is of increasing commercial importance. However small they are, batteries are a big drain on reserves of rare metals* such as cobalt, neodymium, rhenium, samarium, etc. There is concern for various reasons over materials for which reserves could become exhausted, and their use may involve mining, smelting and carbon emissions. Various efforts are therefore being made to develop other 'green' battery solutions.

read p.99

read ____ p.109

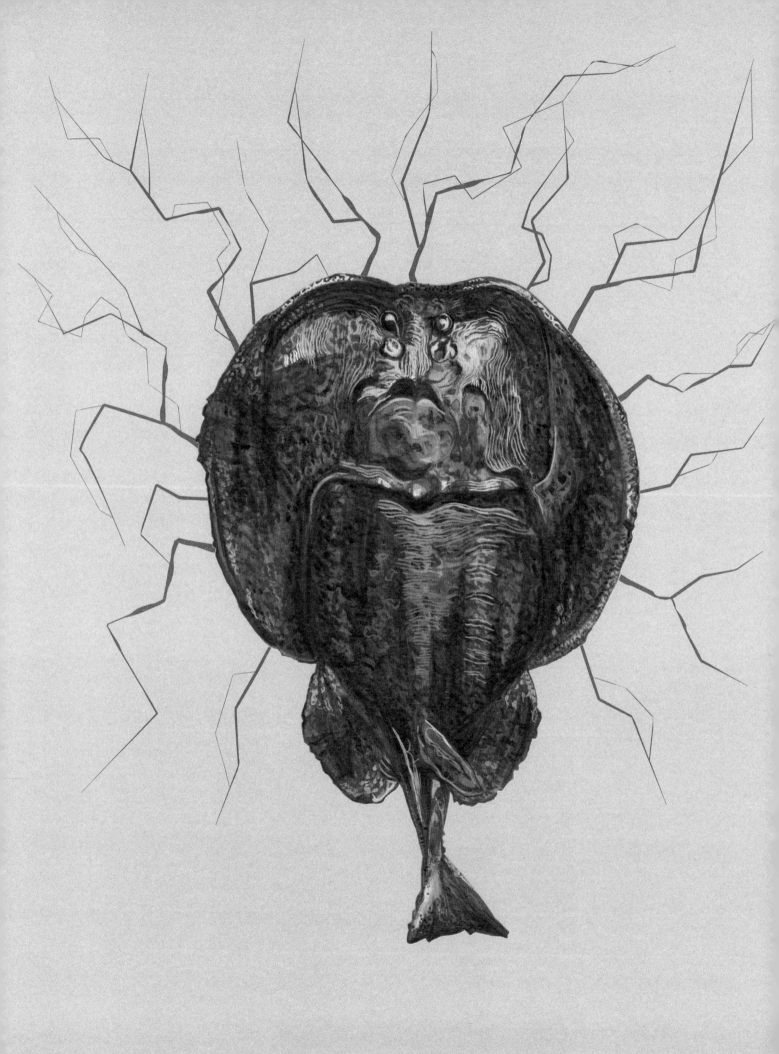

Electricity generation
TORPEDO RAYS

read   p.115

Torpedo rays are members of the family Torpedinidae. These are flat fish, also known as electric rays, the commonest species is *Torpedo nobiliana*, the Atlantic electric ray. They can weigh up to 90 kg (200 lb) and are capable of delivering electric discharges up to about 200 V with a current of more than 30 A. The ray has two electric organs located on either side of its head which consist of flat cells measuring about 5 µm (200 µin) high, with a diameter varying from 1 mm to 1 cm (0.04 to 0.4 in). The cells or, to use battery terminology, 'plates', are stacked in columns. There can be up to 360,000 plates arranged in 500 columns in each electric organ. Each cell can produce an electrical potential of the same order as that produced by any animal cell, namely a little more than 0.1 V. However, their organisation in columns, juxtaposed with other columns, constitutes a combined productive assembly producing quite a high voltage. The electric organ of the torpedo ray can be compared to a battery capable of discharging electric shocks in the form of pulses. In general, the animal uses this ability to stun and capture its prey or to protect itself against its predators. Once their electrical reserves have been exhausted, it takes several days for them to be fully recharged.

Their use of electrical power was investigated long before electricity was understood. The paralysing effect of this fish on other fish had already been noted by several of the authors of antiquity, Aristotle and Plato in particular. These fish were once used in medicine to treat certain illnesses electrically. For example, it was used to treat headaches, by application of the living fish to the top of the cranium. The discharge from an adult torpedo ray is not too dangerous for a man.

APPLICATIONS

It is likely that the study of the morphology of the electric organ in the torpedo ray was the inspiration for Alessandro Volta in his invention of the electric battery. see Photos above and p.107 © Musée des arts et métiers-Cnam, Paris / M. Favareille

Knowledge of this animal's function could allow us to optimise the production, conduction and distribution of electricity.

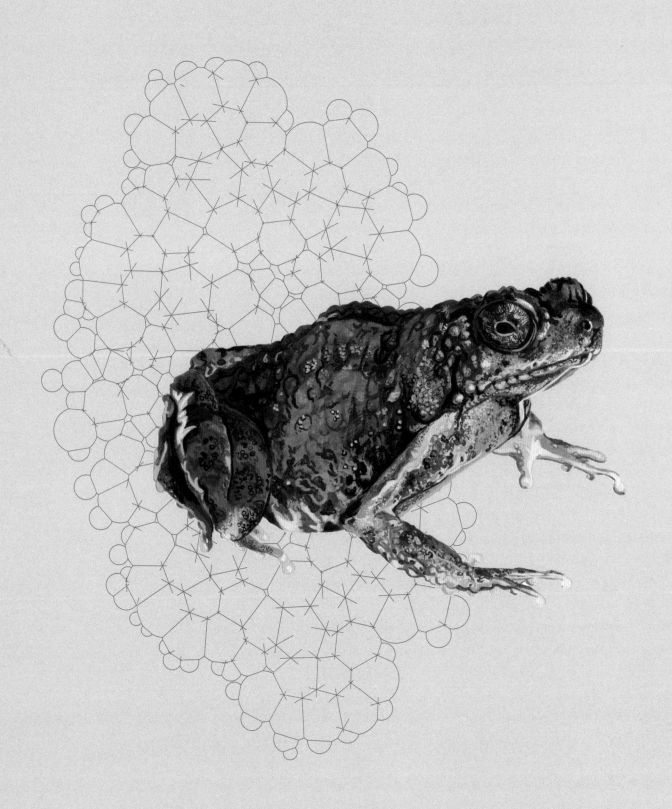

Energy generation
TÚNGARA FROG

read p.113.145.185

The semi-tropical Túngara frog, *Physalaemus pustulosus*, is a small creature of about 25 mm (1 in) long. It produces a nest from foam (or rather froth) which shelters the development of its tadpoles. The froth appears while the frogs are mating. The male carefully whips the fluid released by the female frog to create bubbles. He then places the eggs, one by one inside the created foam. This foamy nest is made next to water so that when the tadpoles hatch 2 days later, they can immediately slide into the water. In case the water level has dropped, the foam can protect the tadpoles for 5 days until rain has increased the water level.

The foam structure contains a special protein * called Ranaspumin-2. This has interesting surfactant/foaming properties, promoting the formation and association of bubbles. The material protects the eggs against dehydration, solar radiation, pathogenic attack and temperature variations. Micro-channels form along a common line on three sides of bubbles. Associations formed between enzymes* and lipid* vesicles are concentrated in these channels. The transparent, air-filled bubbles provide good access to light and CO_2. The photosynthesis* process which takes place in the froth is free of some of the constraints found in plants.

APPLICATIONS

Photosynthesis* allows the conversion of solar light energy and CO^2 into chemical energy in the form of sugar and oxygen*. Plants employ photosynthesis to obtain energy from sugar for their growth and release oxygen in the process. Inspiration provided by the Túngara frog has allowed researchers at the University of Cincinnati to develop a method for high-efficiency production of this chemical energy by artificial photosynthesis. The frog's foam nest allowed them to develop a substrate material (which is manufactured directly using the Ranaspumin-2 protein*) which contains the different enzyme* elements necessary for the process and allows light and CO_2 to play their part. The structure of the material obtained, concentrates the chemical reactions on 'fixing' carbon and producing sugar. The conversion efficiency is close to 96%. If, for example, an attempt is made to produce biofuel* by converting the carbohydrates* obtained into ethanol*, the use of this foam is of more interest than plant culture because all the sugar produced is available, whereas a plant uses a large amount of the sugar produced to feed itself. Moreover, this foam can survive in environments with a very high concentration of CO_2 (such as power station chimneys), which plants cannot do. Photosynthesis is no longer tied to plants and soil: the use of this technology therefore has no impact on arable land.

Energy generation
GREEN PLANTS

read p.111.129.145.185

All living things fabricate their own organic material from nutrients taken from their environment. Unlike animals, the special feature of plants containing chlorophyll* – green plants and green algae – is to nourish themselves solely with mineral materials. They are said to be autotrophs*, organisms which produce complex organic compounds from simple inorganic molecules*, while animals or fungi are heterotrophs*, incapable of life without the benefit of organic material. Plants containing chlorophyll are considered as primary producers. They construct their organic constituents from mineral substances: water, mineral ions and carbon dioxide.

A green plant deprived of light wilts very quickly. Light is the indispensible source of energy in the process of synthesising organic matter, known as photosynthesis*. Photosynthesis occurs only in the green parts of a plant, which is essentially in the leaves and to some extent in the stalks. The route of mineral carbon into the living world occurs in what could be described as 'synthesis factories', the chloroplasts* inside the plant cells. There are two types of reactions there: first of all the photochemical reactions* in which light energy is converted into chemical energy, then non-photochemical reactions during which carbon is 'fixed' and reduced. These reactions lead to the formation of glucides in the chloroplasts, with liberation of dioxygen*, O_2, as a waste product.

APPLICATIONS

The company SolarPrint has patented technologies of dye sensitised solar cell (DSSC) technology. These cells consist of two transparent, conducting electrodes. Light enters the cell through the working electrode, which is covered in a nanocrystalline titanium dioxide (TiO_2) layer, soaked in a dye complex which is capable of releasing electrons* upon light absorption much like chlorophyll does in plants. *see* Photo © SolarPrint

Researchers in CNRS (French National Centre for Scientific Research) have converted the chemical energy from photosynthesis into electrical energy; they developed a bio-battery which operates with the products of photosynthesis: glucose* and dioxygen. The battery's two electrodes are modified with enzymes*. This battery is inserted into a living plant, in this case a cactus. The researchers showed that this bio-battery implanted in the cactus could generate 9 μW/cm² (9 μW/0.155 in²). As the efficiency is proportional to the light intensity, more intense light accelerates the production of glucose and dioxygen (photosynthesis), there is therefore more fuel to make the bio-battery function. In the distant future, this device could possibly offer a new strategy for conversion of solar energy into electrical energy in an ecological and renewable way.

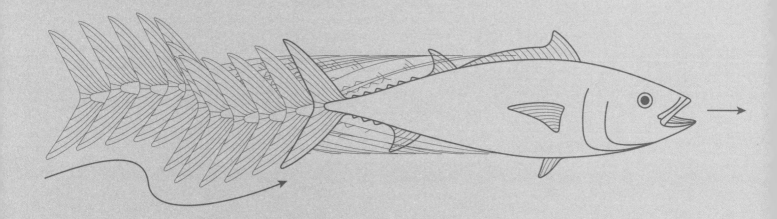

Energy generation
TUNA FISH

read p.109.197

Not all fish swim in the same way. For example, one speaks of anguilliform (eel-like) swimming, in which the body of the fish takes the form of large amplitude waves as it swims. Some marine animals such as tuna (genus *Thunnus*), mackerel or shark swim in a manner described as thunniform (tuna-like). Their lateral movements are almost exclusively determined by the orientation of their crescent-shaped caudal fin (the tail) and by the caudal peduncle (the tail's point of attachment). The remainder of the animal's muscled and streamlined body does not move. This type of thunniform swimming allows high cruising speeds to be maintained for long periods as the movements are minimised and therefore expend only a small amount of energy. The slowest speed at which tuna can swim is 8 km/h (5 miles/h) and the fastest is approximately 80 km/h (49.7 miles/h). The high swimming speed is very useful on the regular transatlantic journeys they undertake.

APPLICATIONS

The bioSTREAM™ system has been developed by the Australian company BioPower Systems for utility-scale power production from tidal currents. Its nature-inspired design (tuna fish) combines high conversion efficiency with the ability to continuously align with the current direction. It thus collects 'sea energy'. The same company has also developed bioWAVE™, based on studies of the movement of kelp algae, simulating the back and forth motion. The aim is to install submarine farms on the sea floor to generate large quantities of electrical energy. Installations that are invisible, silent and non-polluting. *see* Photo © BioPower Systems Pty Ltd, www.biopowersystems.com

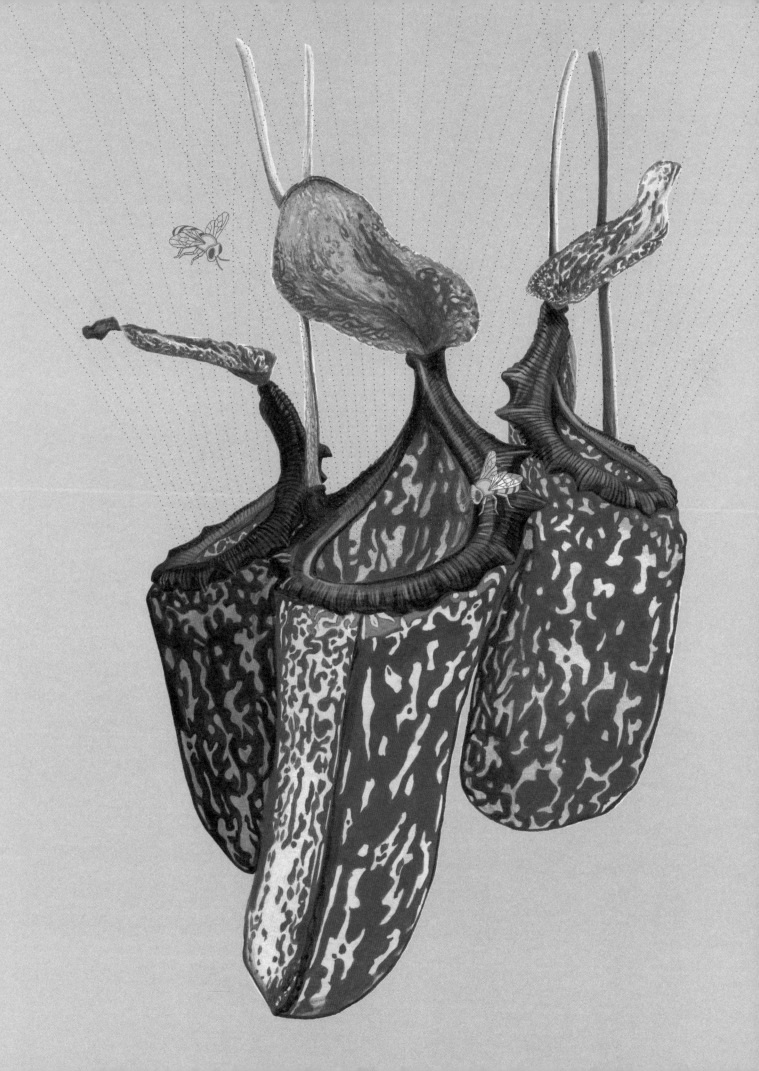

Entrapment
CARNIVOROUS PLANTS

read ____ p.93.97.103.183

_____ Carnivorous plants are adapted to life in milieus low in nutrients by feeding on small animal organisms such as insects. These plants develop different strategies involving odours which attract insects in order to trap them. Sundews of the genus *Drosera*, which grow in peat bogs, give off rotting odours which attract several species of flies. In South East Asia, there is a carnivorous plant called *Nepenthes rafflesiana*, known as a pitcher plant owing to the shape of some leaves which are modified to form deep pitfall traps. These use biochemical mimicry to lure insects into the traps, where they are digested in liquid at the bottom. Its pitchers have features in common with flowers: production of nectar, vibrant colours and ultraviolet guides which have intrigued scientists for a long time.

_____ It has been shown recently that these plants are capable of emitting floral odours to attract insects. The nature of the prey captured and ingested differs as a function of the plant's situation, either at ground level or higher up. In the higher foliage, pitchers which emit an attractive odour trap a very varied range of species, in particular flying insects, while those at ground level only capture ants. Using olfactory measurement methods, researchers have shown that, in the absence of visual stimuli, flies prefer to go towards the aromas of the higher pitchers rather than the aromas of the pitchers at ground level. Biochemical analysis of the volatile components given off by the pitcher traps shows that the aromas from the higher *Nepenthes* pitchers consist of fatty acids and above all benzene and terpine derivatives, which are generally given off by generalist pollination flowers.

APPLICATION

These recent discoveries could inspire programmes to combat insects which devastate crops and the species that are vectors for infectious diseases, for example mosquitoes. The use of perfumed traps, combined with the fluid secreted by the plant, could eventually lead to the development of biocompatible pesticides.

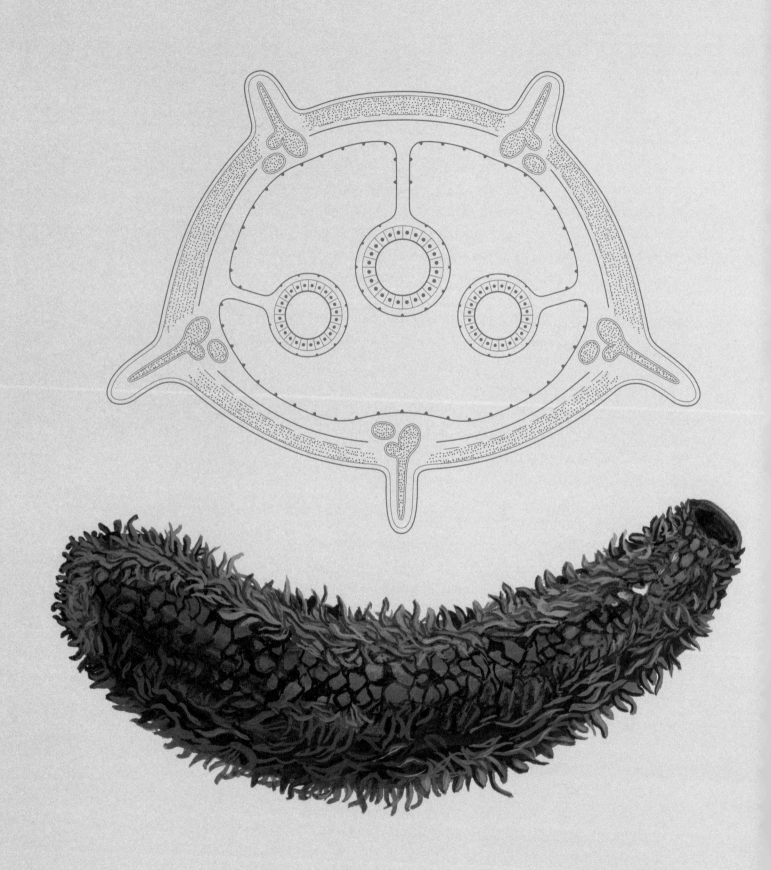

Flexibility and rigidity
SEA CUCUMBERS

_____ The sea cucumber _Actinopyga mauritiana_ is a holothurian invertebrate, oblong in shape and up to two metres (6.6 ft) in length. It is an echinoderm (Greek lit. 'spiny skin'). The mouth at one end is surrounded by so-called oral tentacles which it uses to find plankton and decaying organic material on the sandy ocean floor, or to catch food that flows by. It has a single skeleton which lies behind its mouth and serves as a point of attachment for the muscles that retract the tentacles into the body in case the sea cucumber feels threatened. Sea cucumbers can be found in all marine environments of the world, from coastal zones down to great depths.

_____ Thanks to their flexibility, these sea creatures can easily squeeze between rocks and into crevices. They have a very special feature: skin which can become rigid in the blink of an eye when they feel threatened. Their skin surface then forms a veritable armour against predators. Researchers have found that the extracellular tissue of their skin contains collagen* fibrils, which are capable of binding strongly or not with other substances surrounding them, then going from a fairly interlinked rigid state to a looser, more flexible state. Under the action of the animal's nervous system, the nature of the skin changes completely but how the observed changes take place is still not fully understood.

APPLICATION

Inspired by the skin structure of sea cucumbers, researchers in Case Western Reserve University of Cleveland have focused on a polymer material which becomes flexible in the presence of an aqueous-based solvent and becomes rigid when the solvent evaporates. The researchers foresee many applications, particularly in the medical domain where electrodes implanted in a brain could be rigid at the time of their insertion, then flexible to adapt to the texture of nerve tissues.

Flight
BATS

read _____ p.99.101.125.127

_____ Some mammals can glide for a short distance, but bats are the only mammals that can actually fly. After birth, it takes a bat 6 weeks to 4 months for its wings to develop fully to become independent. The anatomical modifications which have evolved to allow bats to fly are considerable. They have membranous wings, covered with fine, short hair. The fore limbs have metacarpals and phalanges (the main bones in mammalian hands) which are greatly elongated. The membrane of each wing is formed from a double layer of very strong skin with many blood* vessels, nerves and muscles. It extends between all four 'fingers' and from the last one to the rear limb. The 'thumb' is modified into a hooked claw.

_____ The flight of bats should be even more efficient and use less energy than birds which are comparable in size or type of flight. Wind tunnel tests with bats in Sweden and the United States have shown that, like insects, they have optimum flight efficiency when their wings beat downwards, by controlling micro-turbulence at the leading edge of the wings, turbulence* which provides up to 40% of the thrust. Unlike insects and birds, which in general have more rigid wings and are not as agile at changing direction in flight, each bat wing has more than two dozen joints covered in a thin elastic membrane which can be pulled into a shape that traps air and generates lift* in various ways. This remarkable property means that bats have extraordinary control over the three-dimensional shape of their wings during flight.

APPLICATION

Clément Ader's 'Avion III' is one of the showpieces of the Musée des arts et métiers in Paris. Ader recommended that the wings of aircraft intended for slow speeds should be modelled on bat wings and those of aircraft intended for high speeds should be modelled on those of birds. In a fruit bat, there is firstly the deployment and automatic tensioning of the equivalent of an aircraft's leading-edge flap and then the folding of the wings and hooking onto the branch of a tree. For the bat, this linked mechanism represents a safety feature. For the Ader flying machine, intended for military use, it has a double and essential function: both the tensioning and the folding of the wing to reduce the span of large wings. This has allowed the machine's wing to be rapidly extended for flight and the machine could be quickly stored again after landing. *see* _____ Photos above and p.122

© Musée des arts et métiers-Cnam, Paris / Studio Cnam

read p.121

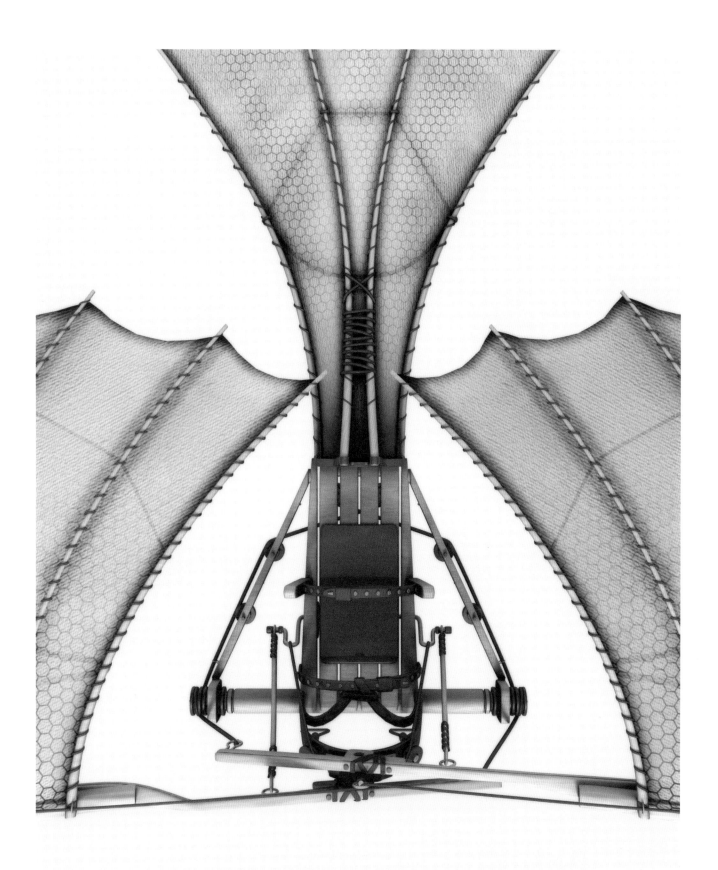

read   p.125

Flight
BIRDS

read p.73.99.121.127

The anatomy of birds reveals their perfect adaptation for the requirements of flight. Their skeleton is organised so as to be as light and as strong as possible. For these purposes, the bones are hollow and the internal structure of birds consists of various parts which articulate, distort or twist under the force of air. For example, on average the male tawny owl weighs 540 g (19 oz), its powerful musculature weighs 306 g (8 oz) and its internal organs 140 g (5 oz); the skeleton and the plumage are very light and, respectively, weigh 40 g and 53 g (1.4 and 1.9 oz, respectively).

Birds have an aerodynamic* shape which allows them to slice through the air causing few vortices*. The cross-section of a wing, in principle, is the same for all birds: the leading edges of the wings are rounded while the trailing edges are tapered. The sternum (or breastbone) is the attachment on which the pectoral muscles pull to power the wings. The feathers, also very light and flexible, give a bird its smooth shape. By preening, smoothing and readjusting its plumage, a bird oils its feathers with a secretion (sebum) from the uropygial gland on its rump. This provides waterproofing, which maintains the thermal insulation that is vital for birds. Each feather, when coated with sebum, becomes hydrophobic*. This maintenance of its surface also aids good airflow. Two flight modes can be identified for a bird: 'flapping' or 'powered flight'* which propels the bird through the air and 'planing' flight characterised by the absence of propulsion, allowing the bird to rest.

APPLICATIONS

The ornithopter is an aircraft which flies like a bird. Its wings flap, enabling it to move. Such flight has been man's dream since the time of Leonardo da Vinci. The top image is a 3D rendering by Leo Blanchette modeled after Da Vinci's sketch. The ornithopter's special feature is that the wing not only provides lift* but also thrust. After many attempts made by a team led by Professor Emeritus James DeLaurier in Toronto's Downsview Park, the dream became a reality on 8 June 2006. *see* Images top and p.123 © Leo Blanchette

Aviator George R. White built a foot-propelled flying machine and patented his version of the ornithopter. During his test flights there were many crashes. He continued to improve the ornithopter and achieved a flight of 1.3 km (0.8 mile) on St Augustine Beach in 1927. *see* Photo bottom © State Archives of Florida

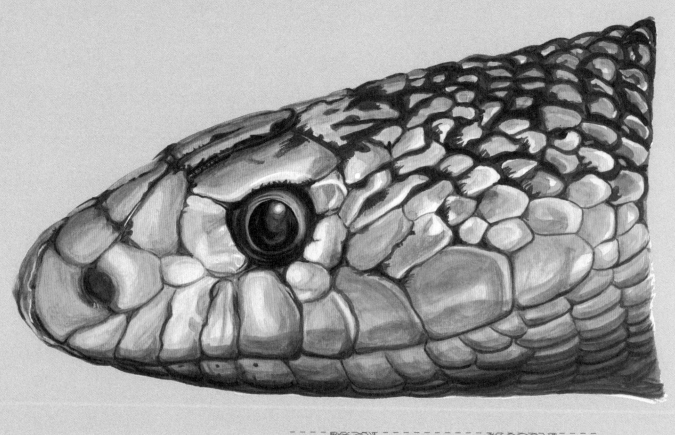
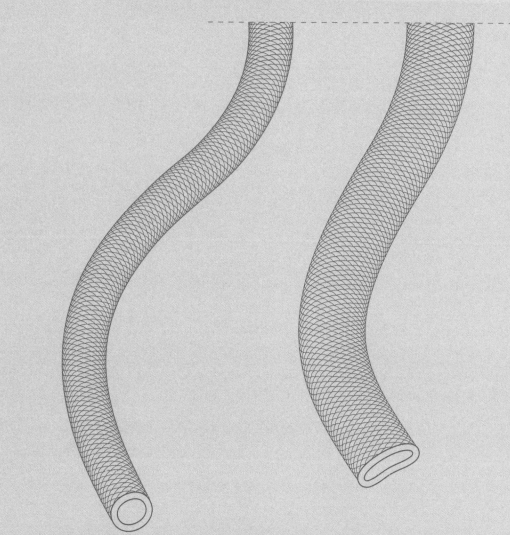

Flight
CHRYSOPELEA SNAKES

read   p.99.121.125

Chrysopelea, in the family Colubridae, are tree snakes, only mildly venomous, but they can fly. There are five species: *Chrysopelea ornata*, *Chrysopelea paradisi*, *Chrysopelea pelias*, *Chrysopelea rhodopleuron* and *Chrysopelea taprobanica*. These snakes, found in South Asia and India, are effectively capable of climbing trees in tropical forests and flying from tree to tree. They can cover up to 100 m (330 ft) in flight. They thus save a lot of energy and time and surprise some of their predators, who are not expecting them to be flying overhead.

More precisely, they are gliding* rather than flying animals. In effect they can't go higher than their point of departure, but they simply allow the air to carry them, rather like flying squirrels, which is surprising enough. This sort of leap into the air relies on the so-called parachute effect. Several teams of researchers are investigating this ability to fly without the use of wings or any other limb whatsoever. Jake Socha's research group from the Virginia Polytechnic institute succeeded in following the snakes closely and filming repeatedly. They now know that one of these snakes, which measures about 1 m (just over 3 ft) in length, is capable of flattening itself in flight, with its head and body each taking up a particular angle in the air, the animal becoming a wing capable of gliding flight. Once launched into the air from a tree trunk, the snake continuously sways laterally to increase the air pressure under its arched body for optimum flight. It would seem that there is a correlation between the size and the ability of the animal to glide, small snakes being more skilful at slicing through the air.

APPLICATION

This very special type of flight is unique in the animal kingdom and in the world of aeronautics. A close study of the snakes could therefore open up new fields for the development of flying vehicles. The American army is very interested in this phenomenon and is subsidising certain research.

Flow regulation
PLANTS

read ____ p.113.145.157.167

In the living world, every species develops control systems for its metabolic* pathways to ensure its survival and its adaptation to differing variations of the milieu in which it lives. The biological mechanisms, which govern this type of functional regulation at the molecular, cellular and tissue levels of the whole organism, involve delicate processes for adjustment of the flows of energy and organic material.

For example, nature has endowed plants with systems enabling them to regulate the production of molecules* at speeds which are sometimes 1000 times greater than those recorded under normal conditions. These control mechanisms are essential to avoid breakdown of the store of molecules present in the cell or again to cope with congestion which would slow down the plant's growth and inevitably lead to cell death. These regulation mechanisms come into play in plants when energy sources such as light suddenly increase after the passing of a cloud or when the surrounding temperature quickly falls a few degrees when the wind blows, thus reducing the rate of cell activity by half.

APPLICATIONS

Researchers at the CNRS (French National Centre for Scientific Research), CEA (French atomic energy authority) and INRA (French national institute for agricultural research) constructed a mathematical model for the pathways along which amino acids* are synthesised in the plant *Arabidopsis thaliana*. This model mimics a metabolic system with many pathways and systems employing different kinds of controls: synergy, feedback, inhibition, activation, double control.

Control problems encountered in biological systems are undeniably close to those inherent in the control of electrical networks or control of industrial manufacturing lines supplied by a parts stockpile which varies in size. This type of mathematical model opens up the possibility for designing biological systems to regulate the flow of material and energy and thus contribute to better control of resources.

In the early history of electronics (1920s), it was discovered that if part of the voltage from the output of an amplifier (made from glass 'valves' or 'tubes' rather than transistors) was fed back to oppose the input, a valuable facility for steady control was obtained: 'negative feedback'. When this idea was introduced to research in biology it had a significant influence on our understanding of biological control systems.

Food conservation
KING PENGUIN

read p.83.193

It's easy to remember the magnificent images in the film *The March of the Penguins*, King Penguins going off to find food and their return, at all costs, to feed their young chick that stayed on land with the other parent. In this species, the male and female take turns with incubation but it's generally the male which takes care of this for the last weeks, the female coming back at hatching time to feed the chick. Penguins mostly feed on *myctophids*, commonly known as lanternfish owing to their use of bioluminescence. The largest biomass of these fish is found at the polar front, 400 to 500 km (250 to 300 miles) from land. In some years, the polar front moves further south and the duration of the King Penguin food journeys can increase by ten or more days.

Researchers at the Centre for Ecology and Energetics Physiology in Strasbourg discovered some years ago that the male King Penguin which returns with food in its stomach (when it returns to the colony to provide the final incubation period, which lasts 2 to 3 weeks), is capable of conserving the food in its stomach without digesting it, while it fasts and as a consequence lives on its body's reserves. The researchers sought to identify the mechanisms likely to account for this conservation of food in the stomach. They thus discovered antimicrobial substances in the penguin stomach contents, which could be involved in the food conservation mechanism. One of these substances was isolated, spheniscin*. This is active against a large number of micro-organisms (bacteria*, fungi), some of which are pathogenic in man (in particular, it completely inhibits the growth of a species of fungus frequently involved in human and animal pathology).

APPLICATIONS

By imitating this method of conservation in the penguin stomach, an attempt could be made to make a distinct improvement of agro-food preservation techniques. A patent has already been registered by the researchers.

Applications in the biomedical field are also envisaged.

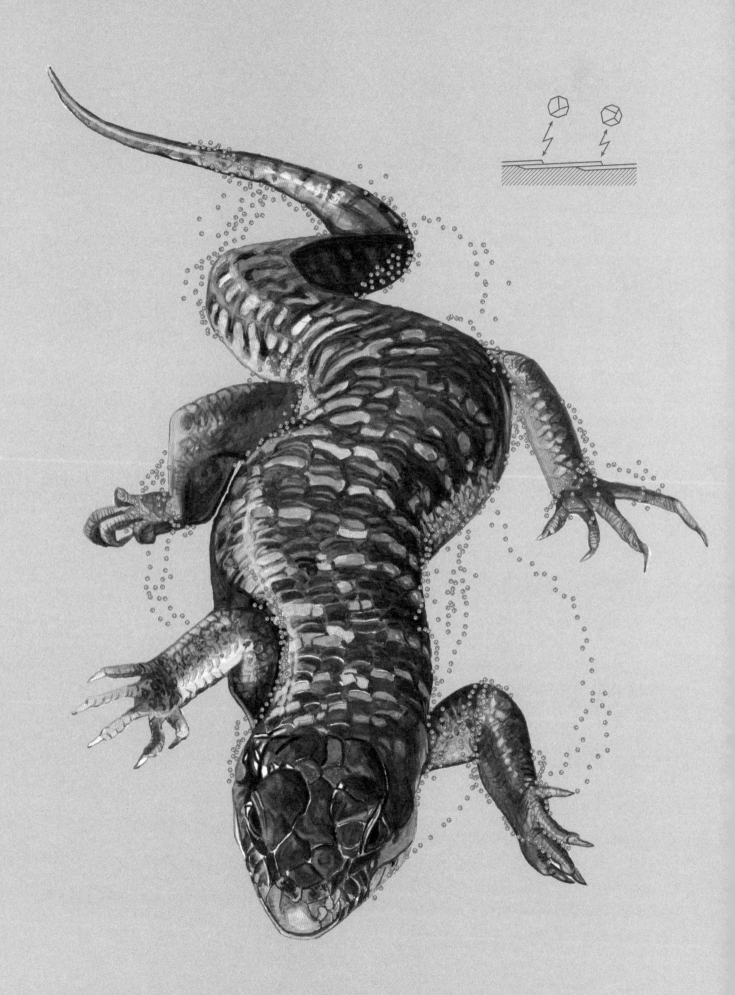

Friction reduction
'SANDSWIMMER' LIZARD

read ——— p.203.237

——— The sands of North Africa and the Arabian Peninsula are the habitat of a lizard, *Scincus scincus*, a skink with very short legs, commonly known as the sandswimmer because it literally 'swims' through sand. A sandswimmer can reach approximately 20 cm (8 in) in length. The reason for its 'swimming' behaviour is that the sand offers the lizard both shelter from the hot desert sun as well as protection from predators. From its underground shelter it can detect vibrations coming from insects moving on the sand's surface. The lizard can even establish the insect's location to quickly emerge and catch its prey. When it swims it folds its limbs against its body and propels itself forward, moving surprisingly fast.

——— The Technical University of Berlin has taken a close look at this interesting reptile, which seems capable of movement through sand because it experiences very low friction (and minor damage caused by abrasion). The keratin* skin of the animal proves to be chemically strengthened by various molecule* and is covered by nano-spikes. The nano-spikes are so small – 400 nm (16 µin) apart – that a single grain of sand will touch 20,000 spikes. The contact area is thus hugely reduced and the level of friction becomes very much lower than it would be otherwise. There is also a theory that micro-ridges on the skin of the lizard have a negative electric charge which may also assist the lizard's movement in some way.

APPLICATION

Friction reduction is obsessively studied in many industries, with a view to optimisation of mechanical and electrical systems for example. Today there are various solutions to achieve low friction: ball-bearings and many lubricants, but also silicon carbide and nano-crystalline diamond, the latter two being counter-intuitive. Observations made on the sandswimmer skink could allow major advances to be made in reducing friction, in particular the development of a film made from cheap materials (sugar and keratin*) at an ambient temperature.

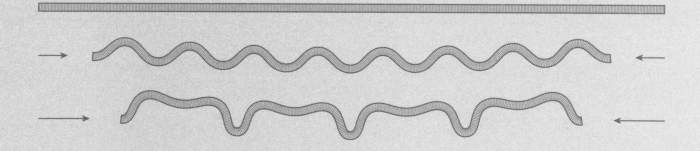

Generation of regular shapes
FOLDS

read p.137

In October 2010, the *Nature Physics* journal published studies on the formation of folded structures carried out by the Franco-Belgian Statistical Laboratory (CNRS/ENS Paris/Université Paris Diderot/UPMC) and the Laboratory of Interfaces and Complex Fluids at the University of Mons in Belgium.

If a thin layer of solid material is compressed lengthways, it bends systematically over the whole length, a phenomenon known as buckling. If this rigid sheet is glued to a soft, thick substrate, compression then forms small, perfectly regular undulations on the surface. The distance between them is called their period. This can be observed by compressing the skin on the back of the hand between thumb and index finger. If the compression is continued, a new phenomenon then arises. The amplitude of some undulations increases, while for others it decreases. One in two folds concentrates all the deformation energy. If the compressive forces are increased still more, a quadrupling of the initial period will be obtained.

The researchers also showed that the fundamental mechanisms which govern the appearance of period doubling in folded structures are similar to those involved in the frequency of oscillation in variable-length oscillating mechanical systems such as pendulums. This means that there is some similarity between equations describing oscillations in space and those relating to time.

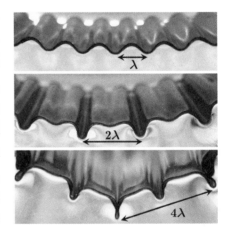

APPLICATIONS

An illustration of shape generation: 01 A thin film is bound to a soft elastomeric substrate. 02 A moderate horizontal compression of the sample yields a sinusoidal folded surface. 03 Further compression leads to altered shallow and deep folds. *see* Image © Fabian Brau

This work opens up perspectives in the field of technology, in particular for the development of new methods of microfabrication likely to be used for modelling material by creating regular micrometric structures.

Research conducted in this domain is gradually allowing description of the innermost mechanisms of morphogenesis* brought about by mechanical instabilities. The latter phenomena are common in nature, for example in the folding of geological layers or in the morphogenesis of living tissue consisting of two layers of different cells (skin, intestine wall, or brain). A better understanding can lead to the ability to predict the occurrence of these structures.

Generation of regular shapes
FRACTALS

read p.135.191.197

In 1975, Benoît Mandelbrot (1924–2010), the father of fractal mathematics, defined the terms 'fractal' and 'fractal object' (from the Latin adjective *fractus* meaning 'broken' or 'irregular'). He discovered a common feature in certain geometric shapes, the distribution of interference on signal transmission lines, coast lengths, terrestrial relief, stock exchange values, river flood levels, filtration, branching structures such as: trees, soft corals, rivers, crystallisation in the form of dendrites (tree-like crystal formations), snowflakes, nerve cells, branching in lungs and vascular systems, and the distribution of galaxies. A classic example of fractals is illustrated by the Von Koch curve (Von Koch snowflake) obtained by simple geometric construction. This curve is obtained by applying a transformation to each side of an equilateral triangle: each side is divided into three parts and the central third part becomes the base of another equilateral triangle. The first iteration produces an image close to that of the Star of David and as more and more successive iterations are made, the shape starts to resemble a snowflake.

Whatever magnification is used, the same details will still be revealed. Fractal objects are too irregular to be described effectively in terms of traditional geometry, but fractal mathematics allows them to be described and their dimensions defined.

Fractal shapes can be linked to cause and effect relationships and are then known as 'deterministic fractals', or to random effects, when they are known as 'stochastic fractals'. They appear very often in the study of chaotic systems.

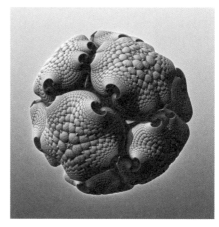

APPLICATIONS

Computing, graphic arts, literature, cinema and music are all affected by recent advances in this branch of mathematics. Tom Beddard carries out experiments in the visualisation of mathematical and generative graphics, creating fractal art.

see Images above and p.138 © Tom Beddard

Fractals have also allowed significant advances in the understanding of development in living things: the structure of plants, leaves and branches, bud formation and the development of bacteria*. In geology: the structure of rocks, relief, coasts and watercourses, and avalanche phenomena. In palaeontology: laws concerning the appearance and extinction of species; in animal and human physiology, the structure of organs (lungs, vascular system, neurons*, cardiac activity and electroencephalography). In meteorology: clouds, vortices*, ice flows and turbulence*. In vulcanology: eruptions and earth tremors. In astronomy: the structure of the universe, galaxies and exoplanets (planets outside our solar system). There are also applications concerning economics (stock exchange rate fluctuations) and electronics (wideband antennas in mobile phones).

read p.137

read p.141

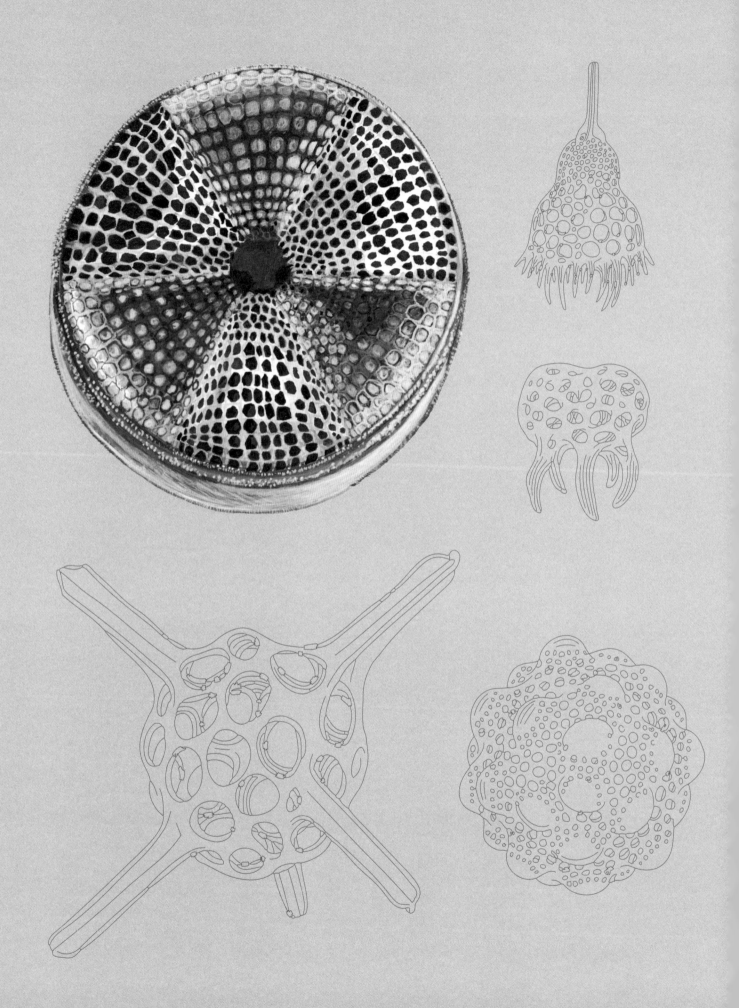

Glass production
DIATOMS

read p.223

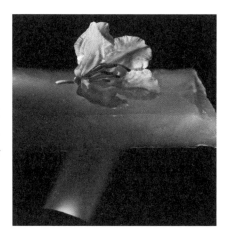

Diatoms are microscopic algae which are part of the marine plankton (drifting organisms, Greek *plank-tos* 'wandering'). Their special feature is the creation of an exoskeleton, known as a frustule*, formed from amorphous silica* – glass – without any contribution from heat. These unicellular organisms take in minute amounts of silica dissolved in sea water and make protective cell walls of astounding geometric and architectural complexity.

The frustules created by diatoms during mitosis* (non-sexual cellular division for reproduction) consist of assembled balls of silicon dioxide (SiO_2 – silica), obtained from silicic acid, $Si(OH)_4$ present in sea water. By successive elimination of water molecules* (polycondensation*, a form of chemical condensation) and with the aid of appropriate proteins* and enzymes*, oxygen* is brought into play as a bridge between silicon atoms to form silica, all of this taking place at temperatures less than 20 °C and in less than 2 hours. When one remembers that glass is made/worked much more slowly at around 1,000 °C, the considerable advantages of finding the key to understanding this method of glass fabrication can be seen.

Furthermore, frustules are porous structures. The silica grain arrangements include gaps of just a few nanometres or micrometres, allowing exchanges to take place with the external environment. Diatomite, an ocean-floor rock which consists essentially of diatoms, is exploited as a porous material for its filtering power. The study of such porous solids now allows consideration of synthesis of materials with high gas absorption power for storage of large quantities of CO_2 for example.

APPLICATIONS

Research on diatoms has allowed the development of so-called technical sol-gel materials: a 'soft chemistry'* method for fabrication of vitreous materials such as glass without the high temperature fusion stage that is normally necessary. Glass is then synthesised by a process which approaches that of a known polymerisation method for fabrication of the familiar plastics materials. Sol-gel comes from 'sol' for 'solid dispersed in a liquid phase' and 'gel' for 'liquids dispersed in a solid phase'. Aerogel is a porous solid material with an extremely low density*, also referred to as 'solid smoke', manufactured through a sol-gel process*. *see* Photo top and p.139 © Pascal Goetgheluck

Among other things, these fabrication techniques allow the creation of thin protective layers of glass on the surface of materials, like on these bottles, and development of hybrid organo-mineral hybrids. Applications are already numerous and give hope for wide development in the desirable context of 'green' chemistry. *see* Photo bottom © Pascal Goetgheluck

Heat resistance
CAMELS

read   p.85.163.165.177.193.205.227.231. 233

        The desert is characterised by very low atmospheric humidity, hot cloudless days at temperatures of 40 °C to 50 °C (104 °F to 122 °F) and cool nights. There is no dew and there are almost no water sources. These extreme conditions pose real problems for people. Exposed to 50 °C, a person sweats and loses about one litre (0.26 US gallon) of water per hour. Sweating is essential in the desert as it allows the 'steam' to escape. However, if the water loss exceeds 11 litres (2.9 US gallon), on average 12% of body weight, the person is in danger of imminent death: without enough water, blood* thickens and organs can no longer be supplied with blood.

     Camels are not confronted with these difficulties. When a camel loses a quarter of its weight under the effect of sweating, only 1/10th of the water in its blood is lost. A camel can thus be exposed to the sun for 8 days without drinking, lose 100 kg (220 lb) in body weight, but not die. The dromedary and camel are the only mammals with blood cells that are oval rather than round. These blood cells are capable of responding to osmotic problems by a 240% increase in volume without rupturing, while in other species this limit is only 150%. They can thus drink a large quantity of water in one go without running the risk of their red blood cells bursting. If they are dehydrated, camels are capable of allowing their body temperature to rise to 41 °C (106 °F) during daytime. They therefore do not lose water in maintaining their thermoregulation. Internal heating in the camel is quite slow as the fat-content in its hump(s) is a poor heat conductor. A camel only starts to sweat when its internal temperature reaches 40 °C (104 °F).

APPLICATION

Application proposed by asknature.org: Thanks to research on the camel's abilities, numerous developments are envisaged in the domain of liquid storage, liquid flow management in machines subjected to temperature variations, as well as in the medical domain to facilitate blood* flow in patients.

Heliotropism
COMMON SUNFLOWER

read p.111.113.129.185

The common sunflower, *Helianthus annuus*, is an annual plant in the Asteraceae family (Greek *aster* 'star'), named for the common flower shape in this family. The French *tournesol*, Italian *girasole* and Spanish *girasol*, all meaning 'sunflower', actually say rather more than that as they literally mean 'turn with the sun'. This plant is in effect heliotropic (Greek *helios* 'sun' and *tropos* 'turn') before it flowers, that is to say that it 'follows' the sun as the Earth turns throughout the day.

Several plants exhibit heliotropism*, for example the alpine buttercup of glaciers, *Ranunculus adoneus.* Receiving a maximum of sunlight helps them, among other things, to heat up and attract warmth-seeking insects who in turn pollinate the flowers.

Once the sunflower blossoms it is no longer heliotropic, but as it still *grows* in the direction of the sun, this is often mistaken as heliotropism. The phenomenon of directional growth is known as phototropism and is due to the presence of a hormone known as auxin*, which causes cellular elongation. Auxin has a tendency to migrate to the unlit side, therefore the cells are larger on the shady side and the unbalanced stem bends towards the sun, giving the impression that it is following the latter.

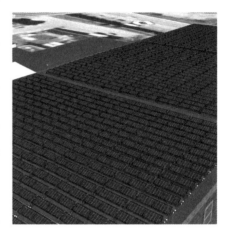

APPLICATION

Solar panels are generally immobile devices, oriented as well as possible to capture solar energy throughout daylight. However, it is obvious that if the panels cannot 'follow' the sun, their efficiency is not maximised. Systems which are servo-controlled* are capable of following the sun (and are almost 40% more efficient as a result) but following the sun in this way involves using some energy and spending more money. A group of researchers at MIT has developed a system which reacts to the 'movement' of the sun with no additional energy supply and no maintenance being necessary. The solution is to mount solar panels in an arc constructed from two different metals, aluminium and steel. The behaviour of these two metals changes as a function of temperature, between zones exposed to sunlight or not exposed, inducing panel movement so that the panels are constantly oriented towards the sun.

see Photo © SunPoint Technologies, Inc.

Humidity assessment
HERCULES BEETLE

read p.189.239

Dynastes hercules is a rhinoceros beetle from the rain forests of Central America, South America and the Caribbean zone. It is considered to be the largest rhinoceros beetle in the world. The male elytra*, or front wings (modified to cover the rear wings at rest), can change colour from black to yellow/green, then back again to black within a few minutes. This is a phenomenon rare in insects. In a dry atmosphere, the elytra appear green/khaki. If the humidity increases, the elytra then start to darken until they are black. The colour perceived as green originates in a porous layer $3\,\mu m$ $(120\,\mu in)$ below the external surface, or cuticle, of the insect. This layer has a three-dimensional structure of photonic crystals. In a dry situation, nanoscopic holes are filled with air, which takes up water according to the ambient humidity. This results in changes in the refractive index, which causes variations in the visible colour as a function of the water content of the atmosphere.

The beetle is still quite mysterious. Some suggest that the phenomenon is involved in the insect's protection: night time is humid, and darkness is then a good safety precaution. Others think that there is a relationship between the absorption phenomenon and the heat of the night.

APPLICATION

Researchers at the University of Namur in Belgium used the latest imaging techniques to study the beetle's elytra: a scanning electron* microscope was used to analyse the structure and spectrophotometry* used to determine the interaction of light with the structure. In effect, light interferes with the structure to produce green colour, but when water penetrates through the porous layers, it halts the interference phenomenon, resulting in black colouration. A study published in the _New Journal of Physics_ provides details of work carried out on the structure of the special protective skin of this insect, which could facilitate the design of 'intelligent' materials. Such materials could serve as humidity sensors and could, for example, be used in food processing factories to monitor humidity levels. A humidity sensor inspired by the beetle is currently under development at the University of Sogang in South Korea. At a 25% humidity level, the sensor shows blue/green, while at 98% it becomes red.

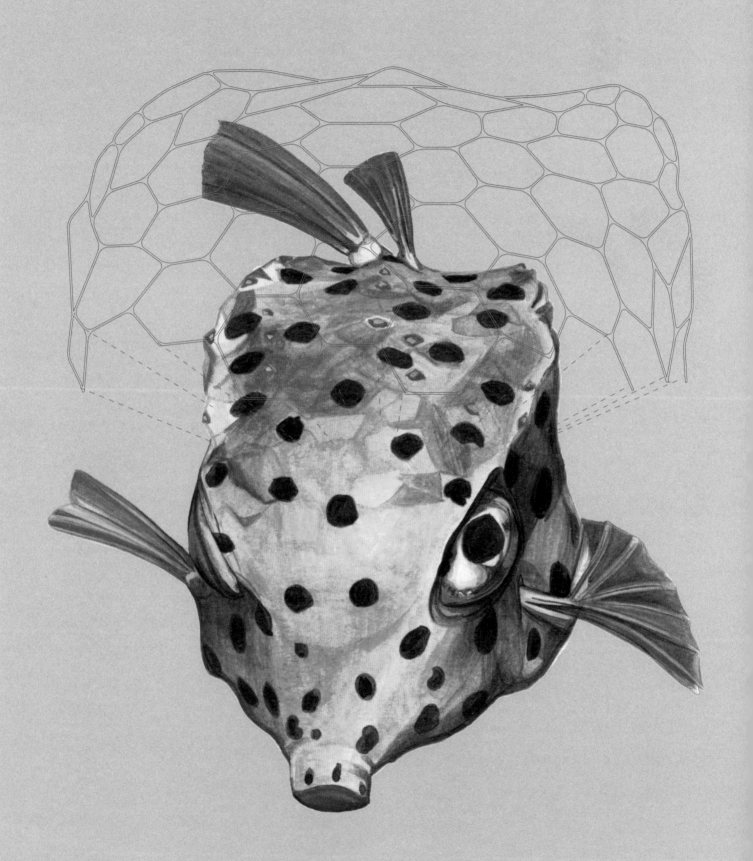

Hydrodynamics
BOXFISH

read   p.73.153.155

_____ Boxfish, one of the 25 species belonging to the Ostraciidae family, swim in tropical waters around coral reefs. They reach a maximum length of 45 cm and feed mostly on algae, sponges and molluscs. It is clear where the boxfish derived its name. The young ones have a slightly rounded shape but it becomes more box-shaped as they mature.

_____ The quasi-parallelepiped shape is formed by a rigid structure. This unusual geometry doesn't allow the body of the animal much flexibility and it moves in water by means of a complicated combination of movements of its five fins. However, it moves slowly, making optimum use of its stable hydrodynamics*, even in turbulent water. Useful qualities when it must manoeuvre where it normally lives in the confined spaces among corals. It can also reverse and expends the least possible energy in its movements.

_____ The skin of boxfish is also of interest for the way it is formed: it must be ready to resist impacts and is in fact a sort of armour, formed by hexagonal, interlinked bony plates following the example of a honeycomb. This gives rigidity, protection and stability, the latter thanks to small vortices* which are generated along its body when it moves.

_____ Boxfish appear to defy all the laws: they seem to be the exact opposite of a hydrodynamic shape while in fact it is optimised for its environment.

APPLICATION

In 2005, Daimler automotive engineers produced a Mercedes-Benz bionic* car, based on a boxfish shape, as a concept vehicle. Among other things, the wind resistance of the vehicle is improved by 65%. _____*see*   Photos above and p.150 © Daimler A.G.

read   p.149

read p.153

Hydrodynamics
HUMPBACK WHALE

read p.73.105.149.155

———— Humpback whales (*Megaptera novaeangliae*), despite their size, up to 15 m (49 ft) long and consequent weight, up to 36,000 kg (79,000 lb), are rather agile in water and able to manoeuvre at low speed. They have a hunting technique of swimming in a circle, creating a 'bubble net' which traps their prey. They are also known for their acrobatic manoeuvres which often includes breaching and slapping the water, showing their long black and white tail fins.

——— Their pectoral fins, which are proportionally long compared to other animals in the order of Cetacea (whales, dolphins and porpoises), have an uneven leading (front) edge and are revealed to be more hydrodynamic* than the smooth-edged blades on water or wind turbines for example.

——— The protuberances on the fins, called tubercules, form water swirls which provide better 'lift'* and avoid risks of slip in turns. This slip corresponds to the moment when a wing ceases to have a lift and/or directional role. After carrying out studies in a wind tunnel, Laurens Howle of Duke University found that this resistance to slip is 40% greater thanks to the tubercules.

APPLICATION

Canadian company WhalePower has taken a lesson from these humpback whales and applied the principle of the tubercules to blades in wind turbines, computer cooling fans, ceiling fans, and other products. The results are convincing: the devices generate less noise, are more stable and, in the case of the wind turbines, capture more energy from the wind. see ——— Photos above © Whale Power and p.151 © WhalePower / Joseph Subirana

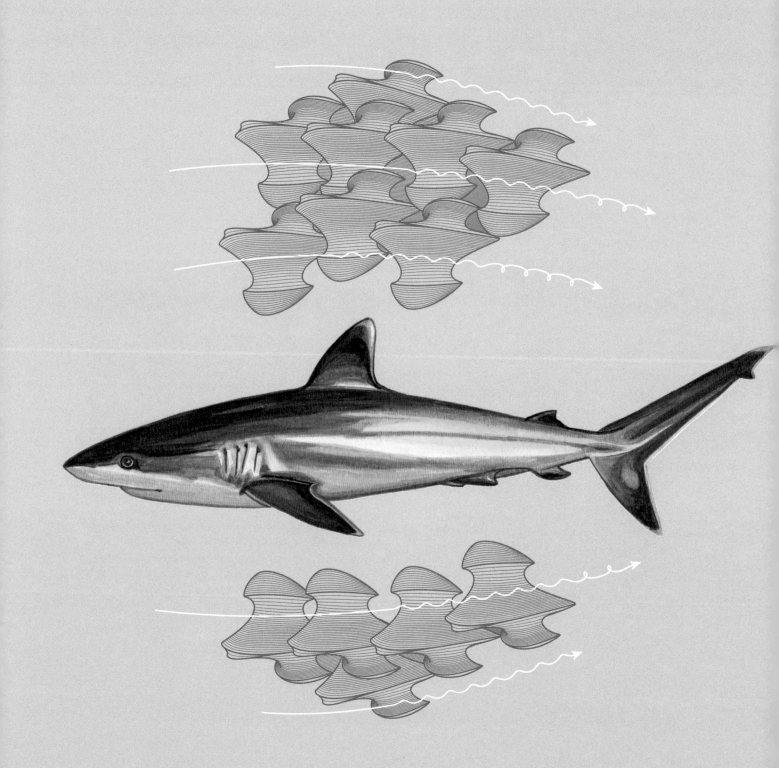

Hydrodynamics
SHARKS

read p.73.75.149.153

To the eye*, sharkskin seems to be perfectly smooth and thus in keeping with the slender shape of the animal. To the touch, it is immediately obvious that it is in fact very rough, abrasive tissue. Sharkskin is covered with dermal denticles, rather like small teeth or tiny fins, which have micro-grooves on their surface, called riblets, all parallel to the swim direction. This is known as the 'riblet effect'*. Sharkskin from some species of shark was in fact used for scrubbing decks on wooden sailing ships.

When a smooth body is moving fast through water, the water approaching the body surface is disturbed and slows down. The speed differences between the water 'layers' (close and further away) cause disturbance, vortices* and currents, absorbing energy and slowing the moving body. The unusual structure of sharkskin modifies the behaviour of the water around the animal. First of all, the grooves channel the direction of the flow. Then, the water at the surface is accelerated since it has to squeeze between the denticles and grooves where passages are narrow and, as in a river, where the passage narrows the flow must accelerate to maintain a constant flow rate. The lower the difference in speed between the water close to the skin surface and the water further away, the more any possible disturbances are reduced: movement is easier and requires less energy. Finally, by the same principle, the water flow at the surface is divided by its passage through this complex structure and the eddies created are smaller than they might otherwise be and therefore less restricting.

APPLICATIONS

In 2004, Speedo developed a textile inspired by sharkskin, designed to improve swimmers' performance by reducing drag by 4–8%. Michael Phelps wore the Fastskin® FSII material in his numerous victories in the Athens Olympic Games in 2004.
see Photos above and p.160 © Pascal Goetgheluck

The riblet effect* could be used in the design of ground and aerial vehicles to reduce fuel consumption, improve their performance and also perhaps to reduce friction in major pipelines.

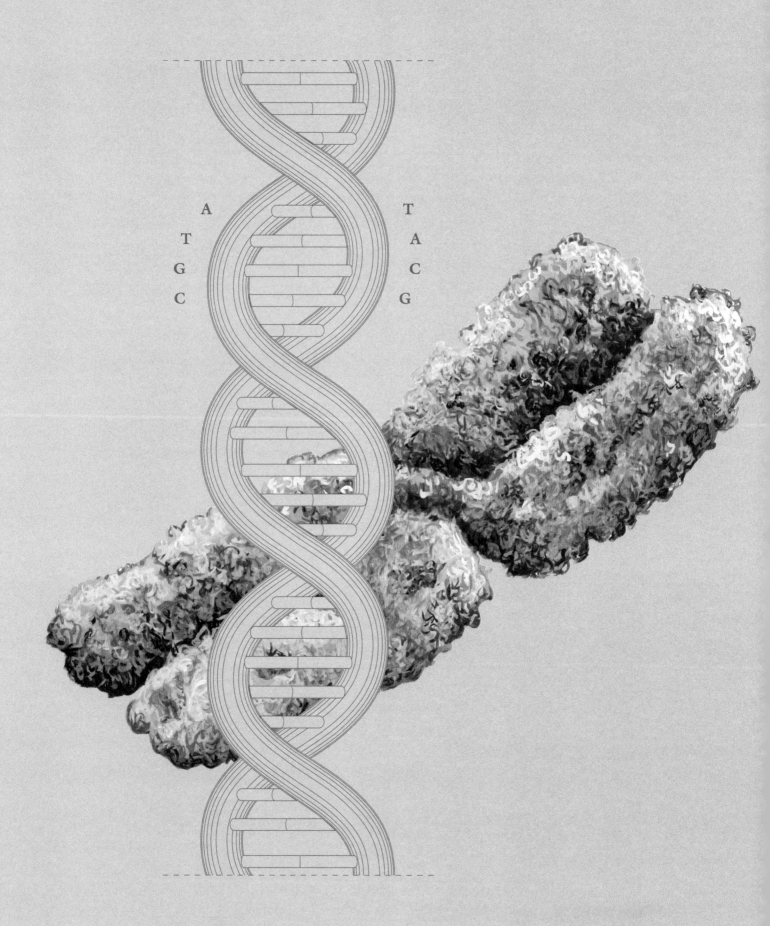

Information storage
DNA

read   p.129.159

The characteristics of a cell are determined by the genetic information stored in its chromosomes*. DNA* is the essential constituent of chromosomes. The latter are always present in the cell nucleus* and their number is a characteristic of a given species; in man the number of chromosomes is 46, in 23 pairs. Each chromosome contains a DNA molecule* representing a large number of genes. This DNA molecule is formed from two strands twisted into a double helix, built from four types of sub-units called nucleotides*, referred to by the letters A, T, C and G: the initials of their main constituents (A – adenine, T – tyrosine, C – cytosine, G – guanine). Each of the two strands is a chain formed from a succession of nucleotides which are interlinked so that A in one chain is always opposite to T and C is always opposite to G. With this universal structure (the same for all cells, individuals and species), only the number and order of nucleotides explains the variability of the genetic message. It can be said that the biological identity of each individual or living species is universally 'written' in a language using a four-letter alphabet: A, T, C and G. One gene, a fragment of DNA (sequence of a few thousands of nucleotides), contains the information necessary for accomplishing a particular cell activity.

The information storage capacity in the long DNA molecule is considerable: the 46 human chromosomes consist of about 6.5 billion pairs of nucleotides. If the content of human DNA were to be printed in the form of an encyclopaedia, it would amount to 500 volumes of 800 pages each.

APPLICATIONS

For some years, scientists have been trying to develop a synthesised version of DNA in order to make use of its very high storage capacity. Japanese researchers recently announced the creation of the first DNA molecule consisting almost exclusively of artificial components. A calculating system using DNA would rely on encoding mechanisms that are fundamentally different from those of a conventional computer: in our normal machines, it is the manipulation of electrical charges carried by electrons* within the electronic switching devices (transistors) which makes the information encoded in binary form materialise. In DNA-based computers, the information would be translated into chemical units of DNA. These DNA-based computers are promising because they do not have the limitations of silicon-based chips: there is no shortage of supply as DNA exists in all living things, there are no toxic side-products and size is minute (a computer the size of a drop of water will be more powerful than the most powerful super computers of today).

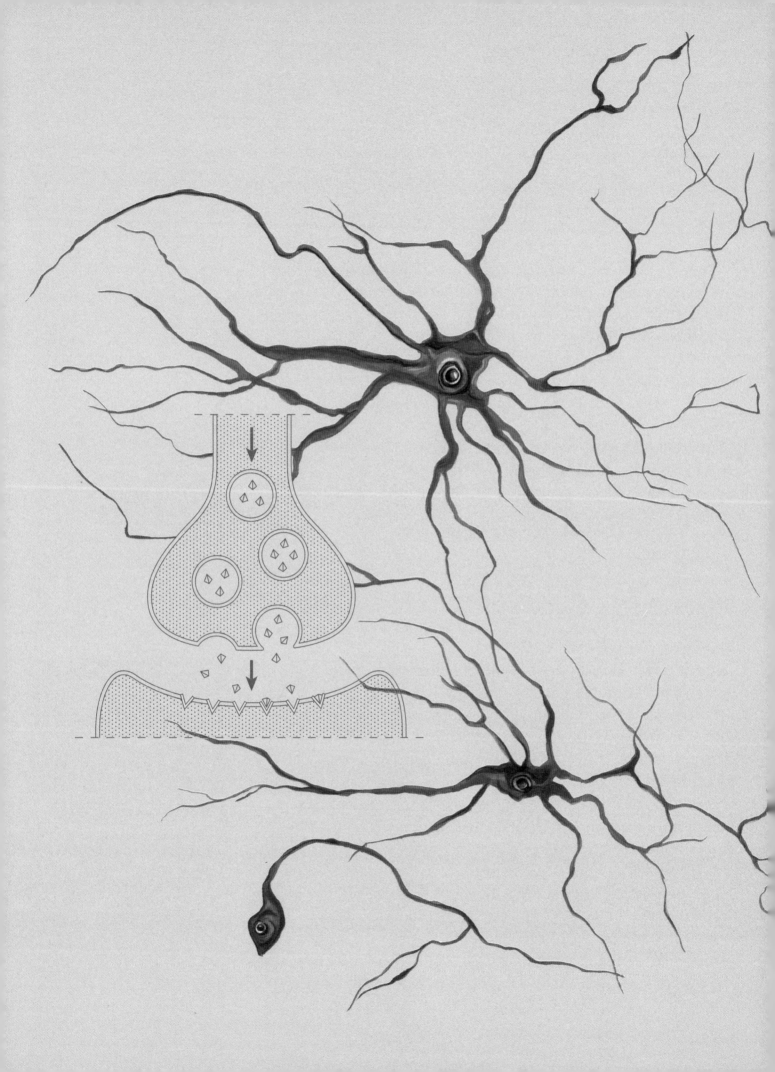

Information transmission
NEURONS

read p.157

———— It is now known that transmission of information along nerves is a chemical process. When a neuron* (nerve cell) is activated, an action potential* generated in its cell body is carried along the axon* to the nerve termination. The action potential is a propagated electrical wave which gradually depolarises the neuron membrane. In the nervous system the neurons, which are contiguous, and the nerve terminations 'contact' their target neurons in a zone called the synapse*. Here, the pre- and post-synaptic membranes are about 60 nm (approx. 2 µin) away. This zone is called the synaptic cleft. The presynaptic element (nerve termination of the neuron) has vesicles of different shapes and sizes containing molecules* called neurotransmitters*. When the action potential arrives at the termination, the vesicles migrate rapidly towards the membrane of the presynaptic element. Some merge into the membrane and liberate their content into the synaptic cleft. The liberated molecules attach themselves onto the receptor molecules fixed in the membrane of the target neuron (postsynaptic element). This attachment triggers the opening of 'channel' proteins*, also present in the postsynaptic membrane, inducing the exchange of ions between the extracellular milieu (synaptic cleft) and the interior of the postsynaptic element of the target neuron. The flows of ions across the postsynaptic membrane create an electrical potential difference which will be propagated along the neuron dendrites (extensions), to the cell body. If the depolarisation threshold is reached in the initial segment (cell body axon emergence zone), it will be possible for an action potential to be generated in the target neuron.

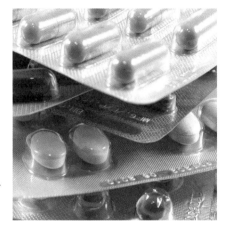

APPLICATIONS

In 1902, neuro-anatomist Santiago Ramon y Cajal suggested that nerve cells were not in continuity but contiguous, thus establishing the synapse* concept. The first demonstration of chemical transmission of a nerve message was obtained by Otto Loewi with the discovery of the first neurotransmitter, acetylcholine*, in the parasympathetic nervous system. This substance was to be identified subsequently as the neurotransmitter in the neuromuscular junction. Work by Henry Hallett Dale would later confirm the role of neurotransmitters throughout the nervous system. Today, more than 20 neurotransmitters have been identified in the brain and the molecular structure of a great number of their specific receptors has been decoded. Progress in this field has allowed chemists to construct neurotransmitter agonist or antagonist molecules capable of binding to or blocking receptors, valuable therapeutic tools in the treatment of certain diseases of the nervous system. *see* ———— Photo © Evgeny Rannev

read p.155

read p.163

Insulation
POLAR BEAR

read p.143.165.177.227.231.233

The polar bear (*Ursus maritimus*), also known as the white bear, is a semi-aquatic carnivorous marine mammal encountered on ice floes in the arctic regions around the North Pole. It lives its life in continuously cold conditions, which it can withstand by having a thick layer of fat and an insulating fur coat. As the name 'white bear' indicates, it is consider to be white, an obvious camouflage advantage in its icy environment. However, studies have shown that on the one hand its skin is black, allowing it to absorb as much energy as possible from sunlight to warm itself, while on the other hand its coat in fact has hairs that are colourless, translucent and hollow. The whiteness effect occurs by reflection of light on the internal surface of the hollow hairs. A long-held hypothesis was that these hairs acted as optical fibres, conducting the light down to the skin of the animal to keep it warm. It has now been proved that this idea is incorrect.

Astonishingly, polar bears are almost invisible at infrared wavelengths, the wavelengths at which bodies emit heat in general. It seems in fact that their very special hairs have low emissivity* close to that of snow and this property is involved in their thermal insulation, avoiding heat loss.

Global warming* is having a major impact on polar bears, which are now considered to be in danger of extinction. The bear's thermal insulation is so well developed that it has to swim to cool down at temperatures above 10 °C.

APPLICATIONS

It may not look like it, but the Singapore Arts Centre is inspired by the bear. The rounded surface, dreamed up by Atelier One in collaboration with DP Architects and Michael Wilford & Partner, is covered with aluminium diamond shapes or lozenges, which play the same role as the hairs of the bear. Their orientation is controlled by sensors. As a function of climatic conditions, the lozenges open in bad weather to allow in light and heat for the building, while in fine weather they reclose to reduce the solar gain. When closed, the lozenges do however still allow light to pass indirectly, reflected by their aluminium surface. *see* Photos above and p.161 © Peter Marlow MAGNUM / Courtesy of Atelier One

Once discovered, the secret of the polar bear's exceptional thermal insulating abilities leads to devising numerous applications for coping with extreme conditions or else camouflaged clothing to avoid detection by infrared emissions.

Insulation
REINDEER

_____ The insulation properties of a fur coat are a function of the amount of air trapped between the hairs and the resistance of the coat to movement of air between the hairs by convection. The length, diameter and density* of the hairs determine the thermal efficiency of the fur.

____ The reindeer has the highest density of hairs per unit area in the whole family of Cervidae. Its fur has two types of hair: woolly hairs and guard hairs. The woolly hairs are fine, flexible, short and wavy. Their surface (the cuticle) consists of upturned scales which allow the strands of hair to link to each other. This felting effect provides excellent thermal insulation. The density of the reindeer's woolly hairs is about 2,000 hairs per cm² (13,000 per in²) and their diameter is 0.025 mm (0.001 in). The guard hairs are thick, long and stiff with a smooth cuticle. The density of the guard hairs is about 60 hairs per cm² (400 per in²) and their diameter is 0.25 mm (0.01 in). A 65 kg (143 lb) reindeer can have fur that is at least 32 mm (1.25 in) thick in certain areas.

____ Associated with each hair there is a sebaceous gland and a smooth erector muscle, which makes the hair stand up in cold weather (the familiar 'goose pimples' effect) and also triggers the secretion of sebum. The sebum lubricates and waterproofs the surface of the hair, which allows the coat to remain dry. Reindeer are not affected by rain or snow. Reindeer in fact have two coats: a summer coat and a winter coat. In summer, the fur is more scattered and contains fewer woolly hairs, allowing good heat dissipation. The skin is thin and the sweat and sebaceous glands are well developed. In winter, the number of hairs increases.

APPLICATIONS

Applications proposed by asknature.org: The study of animal fur allows progress in the development of insulating materials to be predicted, for protection of piping and insulation of buildings as well as to allow the manufacture of high-performance clothing.

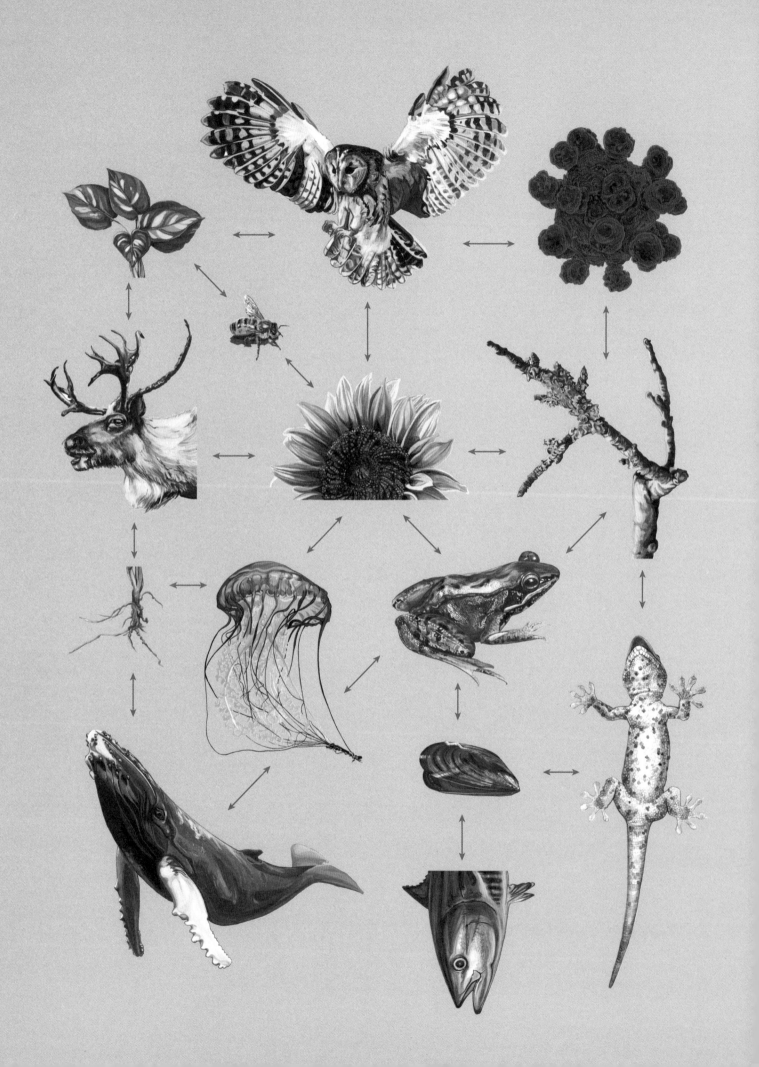

Interconnectivity
ECOSYSTEMS

read p.129.225

A British botanist called Arthur George Tansley introduced the notion of an ecosystem* in 1935 as the basic unit in nature. This is a group of interconnected living things and their environment, relying on a network of exchanges of energy and material which ensure the upkeep and development of their communal life. Ecosystems exist in many sizes, the Earth itself is an ecosystem, as is a forest or a lake. The various systems are also interconnected.

An ecosystem consists of two components that influence each other: the physical biotope* and the living community. The abiotic biotope consists of components such as temperature, light, wind and water. The biotic part consists of all living things; producers (plants), consumers (animals) and reducers (bacteria* and fungi).

Ecosystems combine numerous animal and plant species in more or less complex ways and tend naturally towards a state in which stability is assured. We speak of dynamic stability in that an ecosystem is in a constant state of flux, arbitrating all parameters and trying to maintain a balance between all parties involved. Each entity of an ecosystem takes its share of responsibilities and plays its part. It is therefore important to ensure the preservation of all participants in the relevant ecosystem.

APPLICATION

French scientist Antoine Lavoisier said about nature, 'Nothing is lost, nothing is created, everything is transformed'. Taking inspiration from this lesson, industrial ecology* suggests that industrial systems are considered as special ecosystems, as they also manage flows of material, energy and information. The Danish industrial city of Kalundborg is a model for this. Several companies that are established there have built a system for efficient exchanges: the power station sells part of its steam production to the pharmaceutical factory and oil refinery. It also sells ash to the cement works and hot water to the city for heating. The refinery itself returns treated water to the power station for use in its cooling circuits. The power station also heats water for a fish farm which produces trout and turbot as well as supplying by-products such as fertilisers to local farms. These farms also use waste materials from the pharmaceutical factory, and so on. This 'eco-industrial' park is now used as a model in different countries. *see* ____ Photo © Kalundborg Symbiosis

Light production
BACTERIA, FIREFLIES, ALGAE, ETC.

_____ In the deep ocean environment 95% of marine life collected from below a depth of 4,000 m (13,000 ft) are natural light emitters. However, the majority of bioluminescent species are found in the world of bacteria*. Also, certain algae and common fungi produce light.

____ Bioluminescence is the result of a chemical reaction in which chemical energy is converted into light energy. The light produced is a cold light. In the majority of cases, the chemical compound at the origin of luminescence is luciferin. Its oxidation by a specific enzyme* called luciferase, produces the light. The emitted light decreases in relation to the oxidation of luciferin by luciferase. In the majority of cases the emitted light is in the blue and green parts of the light spectrum, but certain species emit red and infrared light*.

____ When the bioluminescent reaction occurs inside an organism it is called intracellular bioluminescence. In this case, uric acid crystals are involved to reflect the light outwards. Extracellular bioluminescence results from the synthesis of luciferin and luciferase and their storage in glandular cells in the skin. Excretion of these two molecules* causes the formation of luminous clouds.

____ Symbiotic bioluminescence is the commonest form in the animal kingdom, found mainly in marine animals. These animals have vesicles containing luminescent bacteria on their bodies.

____ Bioluminescence plays a major role in various aspects of behaviour: illumination of the visual field, camouflage, attraction of prey, attraction of a sexual partner and communication.

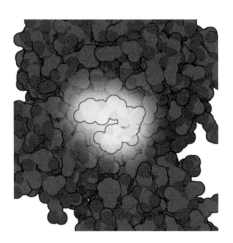

APPLICATIONS

Within the anti-cancer field, tests directly inspired by bioluminescence in the glow-worm are now used to select the right treatment. _In vitro_*, tumours are targeted thanks to luciferase. They emit light and if an anti-cancer molecule* is efficient, it is visible as the light disappears when the tumours dies.
see _____ Image © June 2006 Molecule of the Month by David Goodsell – doi: 10.2210/rcsb_pdb/mom_2006_6

In the United States and in Canada bioluminescence has been used in a meat safety health protection context, to develop ultrafast tests for salmonella, staphylococci* and listeria organisms. In the field of ecology*, methods inspired by bioluminescence have led to the development of particularly sensitive tests to detect low levels of pollutants such as mercury or aluminium in water samples.

Consider the possibility for safety clothing which could light up automatically when the wearer falls into water.

Lightweight and resistance
BEES

read p.79.175.177.211.223

The hives of wild bees are always highly organised and very clean. The internal structure of hives has been carefully studied. No space or material is wasted. The cells that the worker bees construct from wax, to store honey and pollen or house the larvae, are in fact juxtaposed prisms. In one respect, they display a well-known hexagonal shape, in another respect the cells comprise an assembly of three identical interlocked lozenge shapes or rhombi. This rhomboid shape was actually identified rather belatedly in the 18th century. The angles of the interlocked rhombi were calculated precisely by Maraldi, astronomer at the Paris Observatory in 1712. He obtained 109.28° and 70.32°. These values correspond exactly to those from mathematical calculations made by the German geometer Koenig and then the Scottish mathematician Maclaurin in 1743, in response to the following question: 'of all the hexagonal cells basically composed of three equal rhombi, determine which is constructed with the least material'.

Each cell is in fact assembled, offset with three other cells thanks to the rhombi. There are different types of cells with different shapes and functions. The bees take part in a mass effort of cell fabrication and they start by constructing a wax shelf in the hive. The wax is a natural thermoplastic material which is worked as a function of the temperature generated by the bees. This shelf will be the base for the honeycomb. The wax from the inner surfaces is taken and extended towards the exterior. Two teams of bees work simultaneously on either side of the foundation shelf thus constructed.

APPLICATIONS

So-called honeycomb materials take inspiration from the cellular structure built by bees to offer light materials which are resistant to compression. Many honeycomb products are available on the market today, made out of aluminium, paper, cardboard or plastic. Shown here is a thermoplastic* elastomer* product developed by the American company Supracor. Lightweight and resistant, honeycombs are used in various fields, from aerospace to medicine and architecture. *see* Photo above © matériO

Studio Libertiny's project Made by Bees is not an example of biomimicry* but of bio-utilisation*. A vase-shaped hive, constructed by the designer, was colonised by 40,000 bees who built the hexagonal-shaped combs around it, creating the vase. *see* Photo p.172 © Studio Libertiny

read ___ p.171

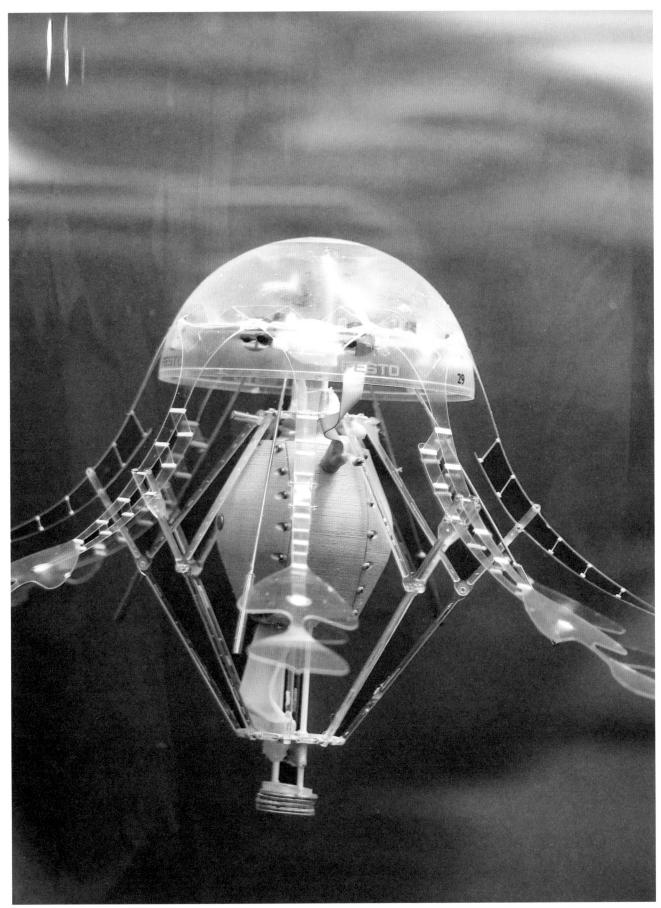

read   p.179

Lightweight and resistance
TREES

read p.171.177.211.219.223

Trees are extremely high-performance living organisms, especially in relation to their mechanical strength. The fibres in wood are oriented in the direction which gives the greatest resistance to shear forces. A tree also distributes its material strategically. At the trunk/branch junctions for example, it compensates for increased stresses by adding material.

Wood is in fact a very sophisticated natural organic composite material*. It is essentially composed of cellulose* and lignin*. Cellulose forms the wood fibres and is found in all species of vegetation. The role of lignin is to provide adhesion between the cellulose fibres, thus making them rigid. Like cellulose, lignin is a natural polymer, one of many with some similarity to synthetic 'plastics' materials, and is thermo-softening. This is why wood can be heated to form it into a curved chair back, for example.

A tree is literally a bundle of fibres which essentially run along the axis of the trunk and branches. This main orientation also determines the grain of the wood and explains why the material behaves differently as a function of the direction considered: wood is anisotropic*. A vascular system transports sap throughout the tree, from the roots to the leaves. This capillary structure is a good example of optimisation of quantity distribution/resistance.

APPLICATIONS

Study of the internal structure of trees is useful in the design of extruded parts. The polymer parts shown above are made out of wood powder and thermoplastic*. The extruded shapes are optimised to have the highest possible strength with the lowest possible amount of material. This WPC (wood polymer composite) is manufactured by the Germany company NATURinFORM. *see* Photo © matériO

Observation of the internal structure of wood, as well as careful observation of bones, for example, has allowed the development of high-performance composite materials*, allying strength and lightness. This brings energy economy in the automotive domain, for example where fibrous materials are used in a vehicle to increase safety and strength and to reduce weight.

Lightweight, strength and insulation
TOUCANS

read p.143.163.165.171.175.211.213.227.231.233

The Toco Toucan (*Ramphastos toco*) of the Ramphastidae family is the biggest of the toucans. It lives in the canopy of the tropical forests of South America. Their diet mostly consists of fruit but they also eat insects and small lizards.

These very colourful birds are distinguished by a huge, vascularised yellow beak which helps the animal to reach insects deep inside tree trunks. The main function of the beak, however, is that it provides thermal regulation for the animal. The abundant supply of blood* flowing in it acts as a liquid coolant: the blood vessels contract with cold and avoid the loss of body heat, whereas they dilate and diffuse excess heat to the environment when the temperature increases. This temperature control system is well-known to scientists. The African elephant has the same via its large ears. The toucan's beak is however even more efficient.

The toucan beak has yet another structural mechanism in addition to this thermal regulation ability: studies now show that despite its size and astonishing strength, the beak represents only 5% of the total body mass of the bird. It is very hard and very light, meeting the bird's requirements for foraging, defence or attack while still allowing it to fly. The strong external part of the beak consists of successive layers of hexagonal keratin* scales, about 50 µm (2,000 µin) in diameter and 1 µm thick (40 µin) 'glued' together, while the inner part of the beak consists of a ventilated bony foam structure separated by membranes with a composition similar to keratin.

APPLICATIONS

The fabrication of composite materials* inspired by the toucan beak should thus make it possible to obtain lightweight and very strong products, with a good capacity to absorb energy and to insulate. Uses may be imagined in the automobile field, for materials with crash resistance, or in the aerospace field.

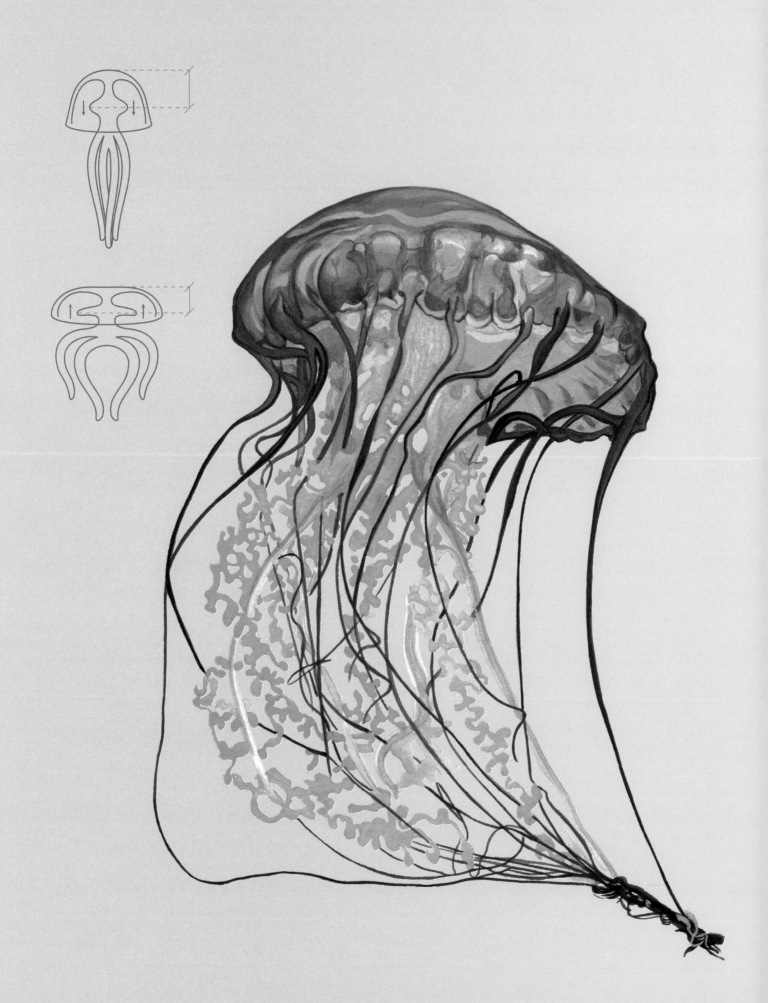

Neutral buoyancy
JELLYFISH

_____ Jellyfish are very ancient aquatic animals which appeared on Earth before the dinosaurs, about 600 million years ago. There are several hundred species of jellyfish, of different shapes, colours and sizes. In arctic seas there are jellyfish that measure more than 2 m (6.5 ft) in diameter, with tentacles 40 m (130 ft) in length. As these animals are not actually fish, their name is a bit misleading. So they are also referred to as 'jellies' or 'sea jellies'.

_____ Jellyfish move elegantly in the sea (some rare species live in freshwater), floating at the whim of marine currents, but able to move themselves in slow pulses as well. They take the shape of an umbrella, their 'head', with an edge from which tentacles hang, and the manubrium, which is a tube hanging down in the centre, ending in a mouth.

_____ Jellyfish float without effort as their density* is close to that of the surrounding water. In effect, they consist of more than 95% water. This allows them to be free of the influence of weight. Their slow, pulsing movement is produced by contraction and expansion of muscles in the umbrella at a rate controlled by the heart. At each contraction, water is ejected to the rear and the animal is pushed forward.

APPLICATION

Can the movement of jellyfish in water provide inspiration for an aerial propulsion system? This is the question raised by the Festo company, specialists in robotics and automated devices. Aviation history has many examples of analogy between the aquatic medium and the aerial medium. AquaJelly, developed by Festo to gain further insight into jellyfish, is an artificial autonomous jellyfish in water, a self-controlling system which emulates swarming behaviour. AquaJelly consists of a translucent hemisphere and eight tentacles for propulsion. The centre of the AquaJelly is a watertight laser-sintered body. It houses a central electric motor, two lithium-ion polymer batteries, a recharging control unit and servo motors for the swash plate. Festo also created AirJelly, whose environment is the air.

Noise reduction
OWLS

read _____ p.73

_____ Owls belong to the order of Strigiformes. They are nocturnal predators with 80% of their diet consisting of mice. They have several tools that help them to find and catch their prey efficiently. Large forward-facing eyes* provide them with excellent far-sighted vision. As the eyes are fixed in their sockets, they have to turn their entire head in order to see anything that is not in front of them. Owls have the ability to rotate their heads 270º. They cannot see well at close range however, which is the reason why they cannot build their own nests and thus take over the nests made by other birds. Another hunting tool is their good sense of hearing, which helps them to locate prey.

_____ Furthermore, owls are astonishingly silent in flight. For this reason they are able to catch their prey, even though the latter is timid and very vigilant. The most important feature: feathers which are much softer than those of diurnal birds, with very fine barbules – small hooks at the end of the feather filaments – which reduce air friction. These barbules, on some of the primary feathers in the wings of these birds, are arranged in 'comb' or 'sawtooth' form. The serrations thus formed generate tiny eddies, which tend to break up the large eddies which are generally the origin of noise.

APPLICATIONS

For railways, today's challenge is no longer just to get travellers to their destination faster, which is feasible, but rather to achieve mastery over some of the inherent consequences of fast movement, such as noise. Below 200 km/h (124 miles/h), the noise generated by a train comes from the wheels running on steel rails. Beyond this speed it is in fact the noise generated by the movement of the vehicle through the air – aerodynamic noise* – which is the source of nuisance. The pantograph, the device which electric trains use to collect current from an overhead catenary cable, is the source of a major part of this aerodynamic noise, created as the air hits it. Study of the owl's silent flight has inspired modification of the pantograph design on the Shinkansen, the Japanese high-speed train, whose frontal shape is already inspired by the kingfisher beak. By studying the serrations on owl feathers and creating similar forms on the pantograph, engineers have succeeded in considerably reducing the noise of trains running through urban areas, where the noise regulations in force are the most stringent. *see* _____   Photo © Yuzi Kanazawa

The principle of creation of a multitude of eddies is known as 'vortex* generation' and is also applied to aircraft and the boots or helmets of professional skateboarders.

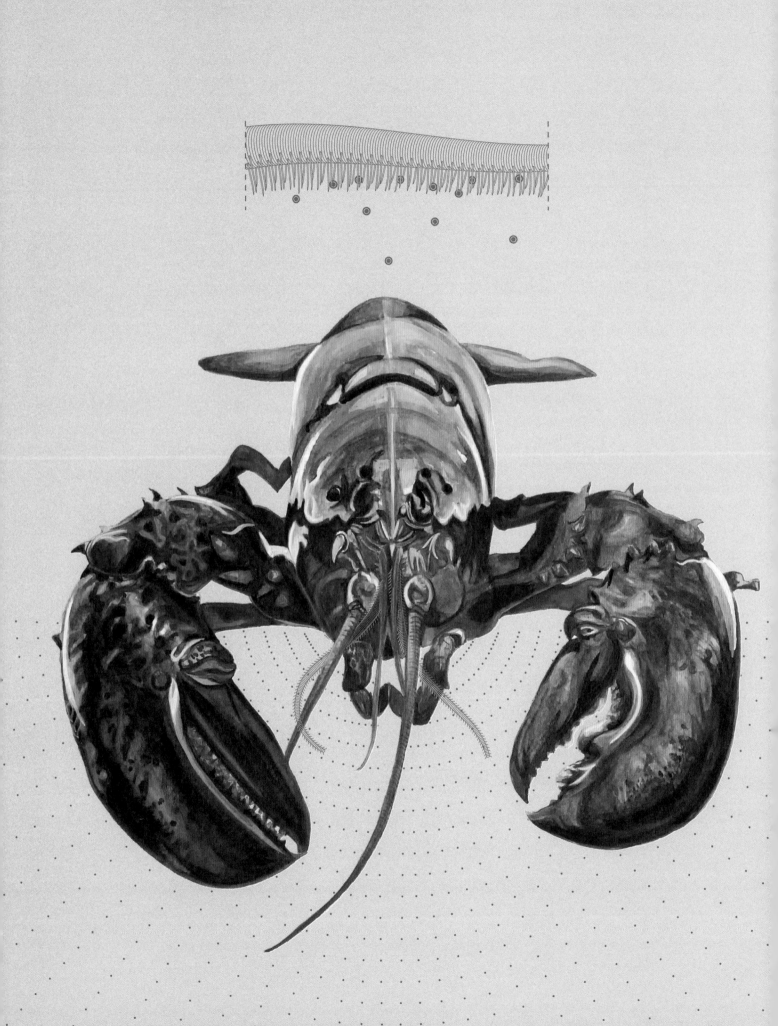

Odour detection
LOBSTERS

read   p.117

Crustaceans such as crabs, crawfish and lobsters use their sense of smell both to find their food and to escape from predators. Different studies on lobsters have allowed the physiological mechanisms relating to their sense of smell to be discovered.

Work carried out in the United States particular at Stanford and Berkeley Universities, has demonstrated that these crustaceans possess a very sensitive olfactory organ. Lobsters have three pairs of antennae: one large pair and two small ones. These antennae are in fact sense organs, which serve both as touch organs, allowing the animal to find its way around, and as organs for processing chemical signals present in the water as odours. Lobsters smell by pointing their antennae towards the source of odours. Chemically-sensitive cilia (hair-like structures), arranged like brushes on the small antennae (known as antennules), come into contact with odour molecules* moving in the marine environment. These generate electrical signals which are carried by nerves to the nerve centre. In order to smell, a lobster waves its antennules in the water, increasing contact between odour molecules and cilia. The speed at which it moves its antennae forwards and backwards is optimised for maximum water movement between the cilia. In going forward again, it moves more slowly so that water trapped in the cilia remains almost motionless, enabling odours to be captured and differentiated.

APPLICATIONS

Studies conducted by a team led by Dr Mimi A.R. Koehl at the University of California, Berkeley on the physiological mechanisms involved in the lobster's olfactory organ, led to the construction of a robot they called Rasta Lobsta. This was designed to precisely imitate the beating of the cilia on the antennules. By using different odours, the team of researchers was able to show that the sensitive cilia were capable of detecting very tiny differences in the concentration of odour molecules: the cilia possess a high-resolution discrimination system. Even if the mechanisms for transmission of the messages are yet to be determined in detail, innovative potential applications for the use of such robots can be imagined. The design of artificial olfactory antennae will possibly allow exploration of dangerous zones in a safer manner rather than using deep-sea divers. This type of robotic application may be of great interest to navies for coastal mine detection operations.

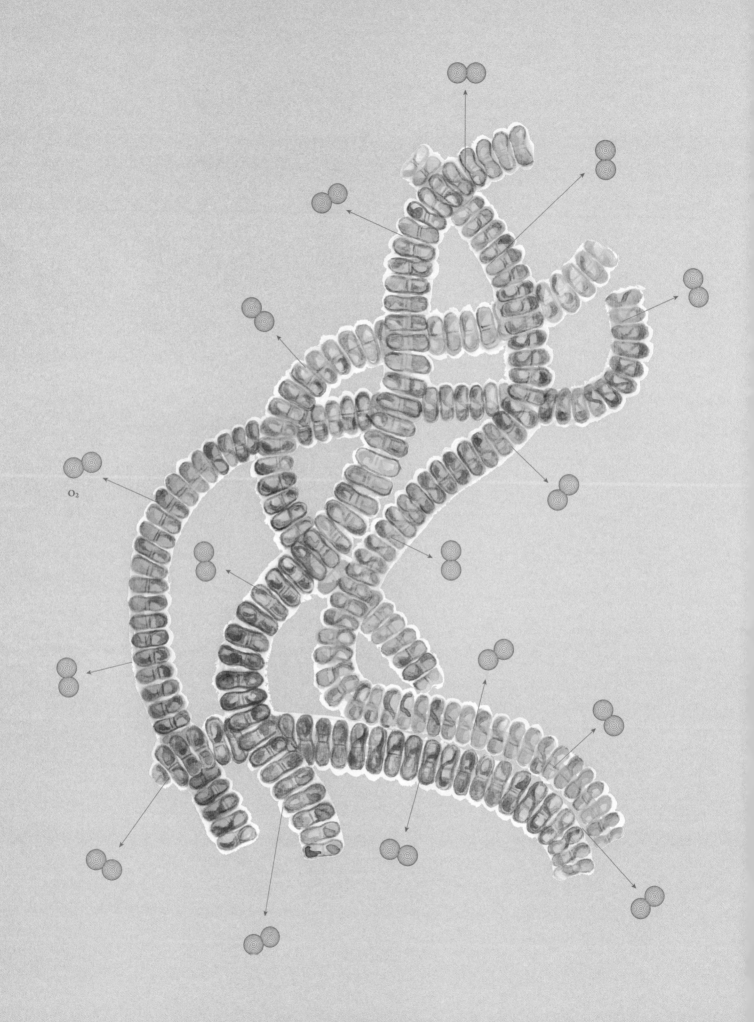

O₂

Oxygen production
SPIRULINA

read p.111.113.145

Spirulina is an edible cyanobacterium of the genus *Arthrospira* often referred to as a blue-green alga. *Spirulina* is the Latin word for 'little spiral', referring to the algae's spiral structure. It is found in alkaline or soda lakes around the world where it is difficult for other organisms to survive. Lake Nakuru in Kenya is one of its natural habitats. Here the spirulina provide a source of food for the Lesser Flamingos that populate the lake and actually owe their pinkish colour to the spirulina.

Known for centuries, it is also used as food by men and is now cultivated on a large scale. Spirulina contains vitamins, minerals, trace elements, enzymes*, fatty acids and essential proteins*. Available in powder or liquid form, its pharmaceutical virtues are also valued in the cosmetics domain.

This living unicellular organism has the ability to generate oxygen* by photosynthesis*. Over the course of a day, the surface of a sunlit bowl containing spirulina shows small bubbles of oxygen which are produced by photosynthesis, taking in carbon dioxide* in the process.

APPLICATIONS

A genuine domestic lung, the 'O' device devised by designer Mathieu Lehanneur, generates pure oxygen* in occupied buildings. In large towns, the oxygen level is 90% lower than the level necessary for our body under optimum conditions. Using an oxymetric probe, the O device continuously monitors the oxygen level in the air and when it detects too low a level, it uses light to activate the micro-organisms the device contains: *Spirulina platensis* – the living organism with the highest oxygen production yield. It produces oxygen, which diffuses into its environment. As soon as the oxygen level returns to the optimum level, the light (and agitation) stop and the spirulina falls back to the bottom of the tank. This project remains more an example of bio-utilisation* of a living organism than a genuine biomimetic* application. *see* Photos above and p.186 © Véronique Huygues / Mathieu Lehanneur

NASA is currently conducting in-depth studies into this subject with a view to long-duration journeys by its astronauts.

read p.185

read p.189

Production of colour effects
MORPHO
BUTTERFLIES

read p.87.147

A butterfly wing consists of complex multi-layered ribbed structures, covered with scales. Butterflies belong to the order Lepidoptera (Greek *lepidos* 'scale' and *pteris* 'wing'). The colours and patterns perceived on the wings are a function of the shape, size and arrangement of the scales. Some, the pigment scales, contain pigments which produce colour directly, others produce colour as a function of their structure and the way light plays on this structure to produce the perceived optical effects. In the latter case the scales are known as structural scales. The pigment and structural scales both have a network of parallel striations and counter-striations on their upper surface. These cause light diffraction and their upper membrane consists of several layers of chitin (the scale material) and air. A butterfly wing therefore consists of several strata of different types of scales (bottom scales and covering scales), the scales themselves being complex and multi-layered. The scales overlap like tiles on a roof, sometimes with the types mixed together. For some butterflies, such as the Morphos of the family Morphidae for example, the iridescent* colour effect is explained by the presence of structural bottom scales which produce the colour and create light interference patterns which are visible through the transparent covering scales. Each structural scale behaves as a photonic crystal (optical nano-structure). The bottom scales, rectangular and non-convex, are of the order of a certain maximum of microns (μm) in size, acting as a selective mirror and dispersing the light. The resultant optical effects of these combinations of scales are quite astonishing.

APPLICATION

Morphotex, developed by the Japanese company Teijin Fibers, is a fibre which allows an amazing burst of colour to be obtained without the use of any pigment. This fibre, inspired by the wing structure of the South American Morpho butterfly, captures light and reveals colour. The fibre consists of 61 closely-packed, superimposed layers: each thickness (70–100 nm) having a different refractive index of polyester and nylon. By controlling the thickness of the layers, colour variations can be produced (red, green, blue, yellow) as a function of the angle and intensity of incident light. Morphotex is a material needing no dye or pigment, no water or energy and no metallic surface treatment to create a surprising colour effect.

Random pattern creation
LEAVES

read p.137

The autumn season sees the leaves of trees such as plane, oak or chestnut change colour and then fall to the ground. A carpet of dead leaves always makes a composition in various colours, the leaves of all different shades, from green to brown through reddish, or even purple for example. The random patterns which result from the fallen dead leaves are always aesthetically pleasing to the eye. A good example of nature's capacity to make disparate elements work together, in a sort of organised chaos. This can also be found elsewhere, for example the pebbles of a riverbed, all different sizes, shapes and colours.

The study of randomness goes way back in ancient history, being intimately linked to chance and fate, but mathematicians only started to formalise such a concept in the 16th century. Long considered as an obstacle, randomness is now one of the rulers of computing science. Algorithmic randomness proves itself to be even more efficient than deterministic methodologies in some cases. Physics is also very fond of the concept, especially for quantum mechanics *, and biology too, to some extent, admitting that not all the characteristics of a living organism are determined by its genes and environment, but that randomness does have a say in destinies. Randomness is all the more interesting as a concept because, aside from the mathematical probabilistic theory attached to it, it also plays on the verge of religious beliefs and superstition. It calls upon our ability to let go of some of the control, which humans seem to seek desperately for reassurance, and in the context of creativity, randomness appears to be an opportunity for surprises and against all odds, real efficiency.

APPLICATION

Inspired by the random patterns offered by dead leaves, the InterfaceFLOR company, a major manufacturer of carpet tiles, had the idea of offering a range called i2™ Modular Carpet in which tiles are laid in a random manner. This results in substantial savings in material and labour as it is no longer necessary to put a tile in a particular place. Whatever their arrangement, the result will be aesthetically pleasing. The average for offcuts is only 1.5%, while during a normal installation of rolled carpet there is sometimes 14% wastage. Laying is easy because there are no joins to check and no direction of laying and no separate tile replacement because the care needed to have the same colour batch throughout is not necessary. *see* Photos above and p.194 © InterfaceFLOR

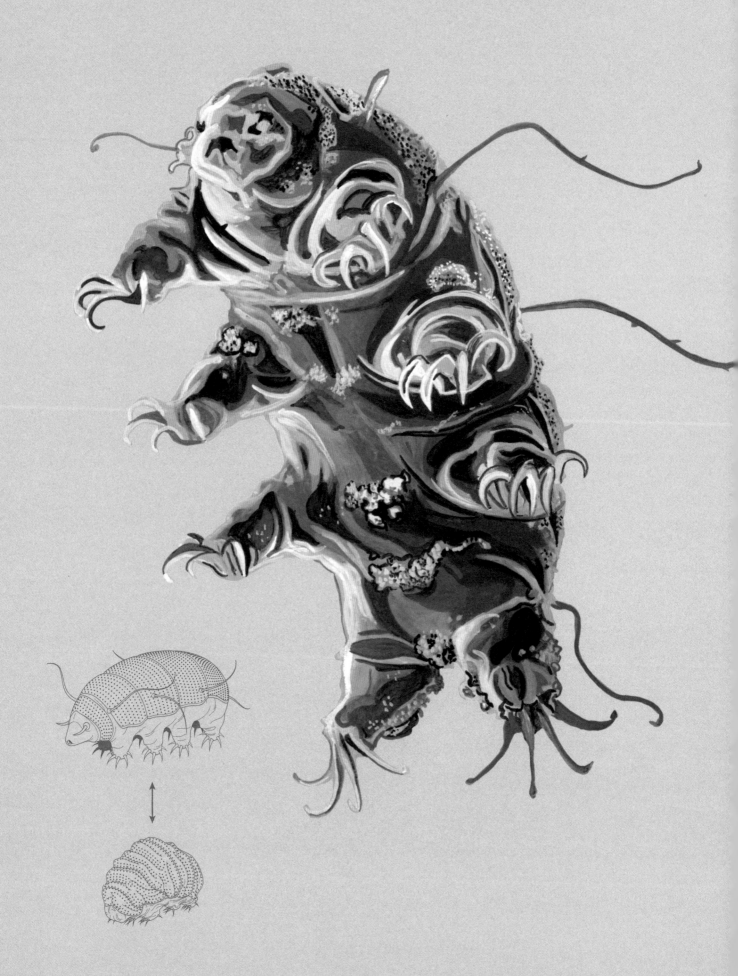

Resistance to extreme conditions
TARDIGRADES

read p.83.131.143

Tardigrades or 'water bears' are tiny multicellular animals with a maximum length of 1.5 mm (0.06 in). Excluding the head, there are four segments with a pair of legs on each. Each leg ends in a claw. Tardigrades live mainly in forests and tundra where the mosses and lichens which form the basis of their diet are found. They are able to live in extreme conditions at an altitude of 6,000 m (almost 20,000 ft), in the depths of the oceans at 4,000 m (13,000 ft), or in polar and equatorial regions, in ice, snow, wet sand, saline* sediments or freshwater.

Their normal lifespan is a few months but they have characteristics which allow them to survive for a very long time and resist extreme conditions. They are resistant to X-rays, toxic products which are lethal for the majority of species, exposure to vacuum, exposure to high pressure and high temperatures (150 °C = 300 °F) for several minutes, or exposure to extreme cold close to absolute zero (approx. -273 °C or -459 °F) for several days. They are also especially resistant to desiccation. Their resistance to extreme cold has been studied, revealing a mechanism called cryptobiosis* (i.e. a state of 'hidden life'). Tardigrades enter an ametabolic state in which their metabolism* is reduced to 0.01% of normal. They can then return to normal life after as many as 8 years in a cryptobiotic state. This state is accompanied by a 99% water loss, retraction of the legs and replacement of the water in the organism by synthesis of a special sugar which acts as an antifreeze and prevents cell damage. To complete its protection, a dehydrated tardigrade encases itself in a layer of wax. When environmental conditions return to normal, the water bear becomes active again in a few minutes.

APPLICATIONS

Understanding of the cellular and molecular mechanisms of the cryptobiosis* phenomenon, in particular those relating to the metabolism of sugars with antifreeze properties, opens up prospects in the food processing industry and medicine. The unravelling of these mechanisms should in time bring improvements in the freezing of food and also possibilities in plastic surgery and improvements in the transport and preservation of organs for transplantation.

read _____ p.191

read p.197

Resistance to strong currents
GIANT BULL KELP

read ___ p.115.137.219

_____ The long brown alga *Nereocystis luetkeana*, known as giant bull kelp, forms submarine forests that are mostly found along the west coast of North America and along the New Zealand coast. Fish, sea urchins, snails, crabs and otters use these forests as shelters. The alga is an annual species, consisting of a root-like structure that anchors the plant to the seabed, and a flexible long stem from which long strap-like blades grow, creating a golden canopy (the upper part of a forest) near the water's surface.

_____ The alga is capable of resisting the power of the ocean as it hits the shore, able to grow and hold its place in very strong currents. It resists storms without damage by curling into spirals which offer the least possible resistance to the force of the sea. This geometric form, a logarithmic spiral, has proven its effectiveness in nature. It has been the subject of several studies, for example by René Descartes and later by the mathematician Jacob Bernoulli who gave it the name *Spira mirabilis*, the 'miraculous spiral'. In mathematical terms, the logarithmic spiral – also designated as equiangular spiral – is related to the golden ratio and Fibonacci numbers. From any point in the curve of the spiral, the angle formed by the radial vector and the tangent is constant. Like fractals, these spirals are self-similar no matter at what scale you look at them.

APPLICATIONS

The spiral fans from the PAX Scientific Technology company are inspired by, among other things, the behaviour and capabilities of giant algae to resist powerful marine currents. The fans offered by the company are quieter and consume up to 75% less energy than the conventional devices. This technology, developed over many years of research and observation of nature by Jayden Harman, the founder of Pax Scientific Technology, can be applied in various domains: computer fans, vehicle fans, mixers, pumps and other fluid handling devices, etc. *see* _____ Photos above and p.195 © PAX Scientific

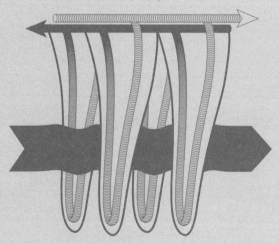

Respiration underwater
FISH

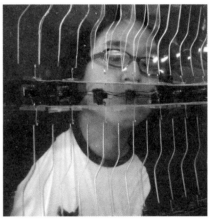

_____ All living species absorb oxygen* and dispose of carbon dioxide*. Respiratory exchanges can take place in air, in its gaseous state, or in water. In water, dissolved gases including oxygen are present but in much smaller quantities than in air. A pulmonary membrane must filter about 25 litres (1,525 in³) of air to extract 1 litre (61 in³) of oxygen (the yield is moderate, air being 21% oxygen), but gills have to pass 300 to 500 litres (80 to 132 US gallon) of water to obtain the same quantity. However, water on the other hand is 800 times more dense than air and 60 times more viscous. Gill systems can therefore make a maximum amount of water pass in one direction with a minimum amount of muscular effort.

_____ Gills, whether internal or external organs, are literally tissues with a good blood* supply which are turned inside out to form a respiratory exchange sur-face. They function in a way comparable to lungs, by means of their form they constitute a very extensive exchange surface within a re-stricted volume. Their membrane serves as a filter, allowing oxygen to pass one way, to the inside of the organism, and carbon dioxide to pass out of the organism. Water enters by the mouth and exits via the gills, a sufficient flow of water being created by the movement of the animal and by pumping movements of the mouth and/or gills. For species with external gills, only the movement of the body allows passage of water through the gills. On its way, the blood has captured some of the dioxygen*, O_2, dissolved in the water and has disposed of carbon dioxide already dissolved in the blood, by osmotic diffusion.

APPLICATIONS

Like-A-Fish Technologies has developed a device employing a method that extracts dissolved air from the water. A one-kilo battery should be able to provide enough power to extract air for a one-hour dive. However, because of its bulkiness, it may be more suited for submarines and underwater habitats than for individual divers. This technology is planned to be used at Expo 2012 in South Korea under the theme, 'The Living Ocean and Coast'. A sub-aqua prototype is in the making. _see_ _____ Photo top Courtesy of Like-A-Fish Technologies

The Living Glass by David Benjamin and Soo-In Yang is a window that uses a shape memory alloy to open and close its surface like gills. The designers embedded Flexinol wires in cast silicone; the wires contract due to an electrical stimulus, causing the gills cut into the surface to open and close. With minor changes the system could be tuned for environmental control, detecting carbon dioxide* in a room and 'breathe' when levels are high. _see_ _____ Photos bottom and p.200 © The Living

read p.199

read p.203

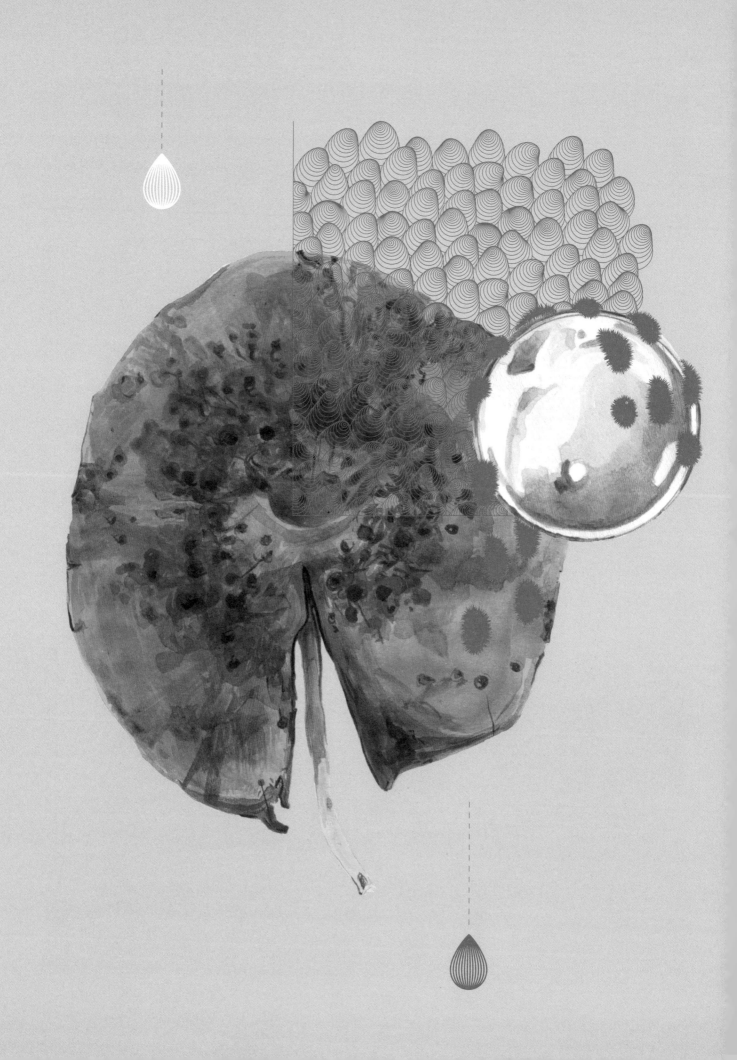

Self-cleaning
LOTUS LEAVES

read p.91.133.237

Lotus leaves are symbols of purity and are sacred in the Buddhist religion. They have a notable peculiarity: they always appear clean. This phenomenon of cleanliness is related to their surface structure, which makes them super-hydrophobic (very water-repellent): water droplets hardly stick at all to the leaves and roll off, simultaneously taking with them any dust on their surface. The latter is covered by a wax micro-structure, the elements of which are from 1 to 10 μm (millionths of a metre) in size. This surface demonstrates something known as the 'fakir' effect. Wax is by nature hydrophobic and water on the leaves is unable to enter the intervals between the very fine, rough structure of the wax. The water therefore rests mainly on air, just as it does in a cloud. With no possibility of hanging on, it streams away, taking dust particles in its way.

These properties of super-hydrophobia* and self-cleaning ability are found on the leaves of other plants such as cabbage, reed and nasturtium. Some insects have wings which react to water in the same way. The key feature is the fact that the contact between the surface involved and the water is reduced as much as possible, to only a few percent of the available surfaces.

APPLICATIONS

The textile coating product Mincor® PES, developed by BASF, reproduces the self-cleaning ability of lotus leaves. It can be applied to textiles composed of synthetic fibres and covers them with a nanoporous layer. *see* Photo top © Pascal Goetgheluck

Designed by Rusan Arhitektura, the Lumenart office building, also called 'House of Light', is situated in Pula, Croatia. Intense whiteness dominates the exterior that features Sto's LotuSan® paint coating. Over time, external façades of buildings become more and more clogged with dirt. LotuSan® external paint coating has an extremely water-repellent surface, based on the lotus effect. Its micro-structure is modelled on that of the lotus leaf in order to reduce the surface contact area with water and dirt to a minimum. Treated façades thus remain dry and clean. *see* Photos bottom and p.201 © A. Kaunat

Glass panels can have lotus effect surface treatment to facilitate maintenance.

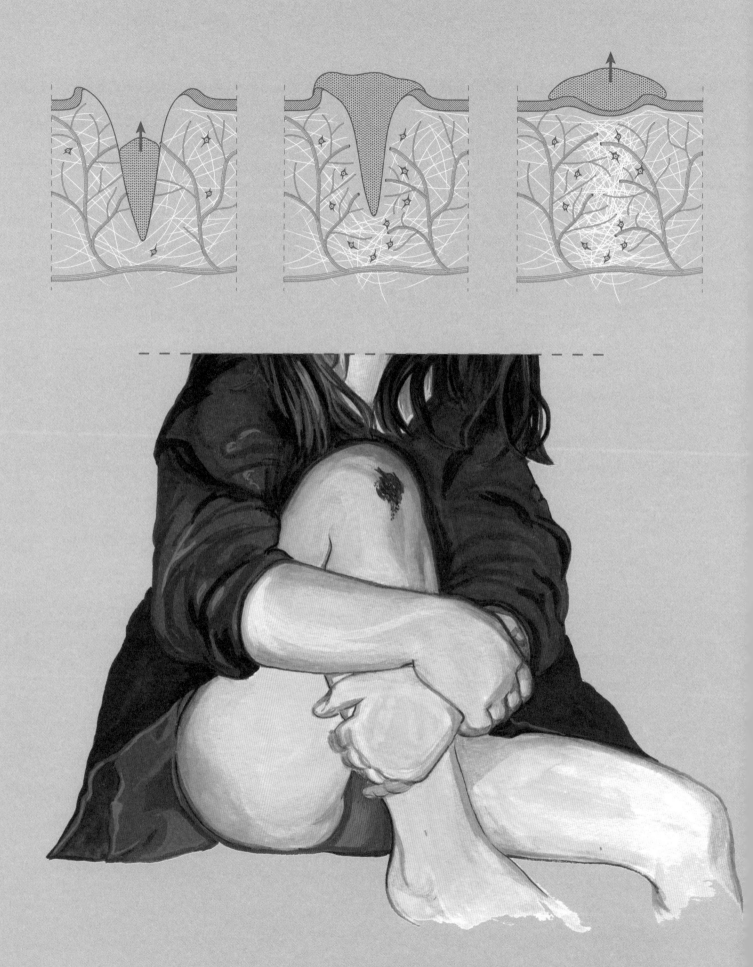

Self-healing
SKIN

read p.85.143.207

All human and animal tissues are capable of self-repair and regeneration. Human skin consists of three layers of cells constituting successively, from the exterior to the interior, the epidermis*, the dermis* and the hypodermis*. In the event of tissue damage, several reactions are triggered to repair the wound. If the lesion is superficial and reaches only the epidermis, healthy cells located at the interface between the epidermis and the dermis will divide and migrate to the wound to fill it in. If the lesion is deeper and reaches the dermis for example, several stages are necessary. At first, the body seeks to avoid potential infection and special cells ensure that the zone is cleaned by the absorption of bacteria*, damaged tissues and possible foreign bodies under the newly-formed blood* clot. Next, the blood flow in the zone is renewed and the blood clot becomes a scab under the action of fibrin*, a fibrous protein* which appears at the moment of blood coagulation. New tissue is fabricated under this scab to progressively fill in the hole left by the wound. Finally, the wound will finish by retracting and the tissue created will be transformed into scar tissue, with the generation of a new area of epithelium (the most superficial layer of the skin).

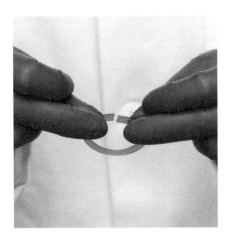

APPLICATIONS

Arkema developed the Reverlink™ range of 'semi-crystalline polymer'* resins and elastomers* with remarkable properties of selfhealing. They've been produced by means of supramolecular chemistry* and use renewable raw materials. They are in effect obtained from fatty acid oligomers in vegetable oils, which comprise a minimum 60% of their composition. A feature of supramolecular materials is that they make so-called 'reversible' (non-permanent) inter-molecular links, unlike the polymers arising from traditional chemistry, which rely on so-called 'irreversible' (permanent) links. This characteristic of reversibility gives rise to a whole family of high-performance materials which are distinguished by their complete-break properties in comparison with traditional materials, among other things the self-healing ability: a crack or break occurring in these materials can be repaired by simple contact between the opposing surfaces of the break under light pressure, recovering most of the initial strength. *see* Photos above and p.208 © Arkema

Nissan developed a polymer-based coating called Scratch Guard Coat. Depending on the depth of the scratches and the ambient temperature, it's capable of recreating a perfectly smooth surface in a few days.

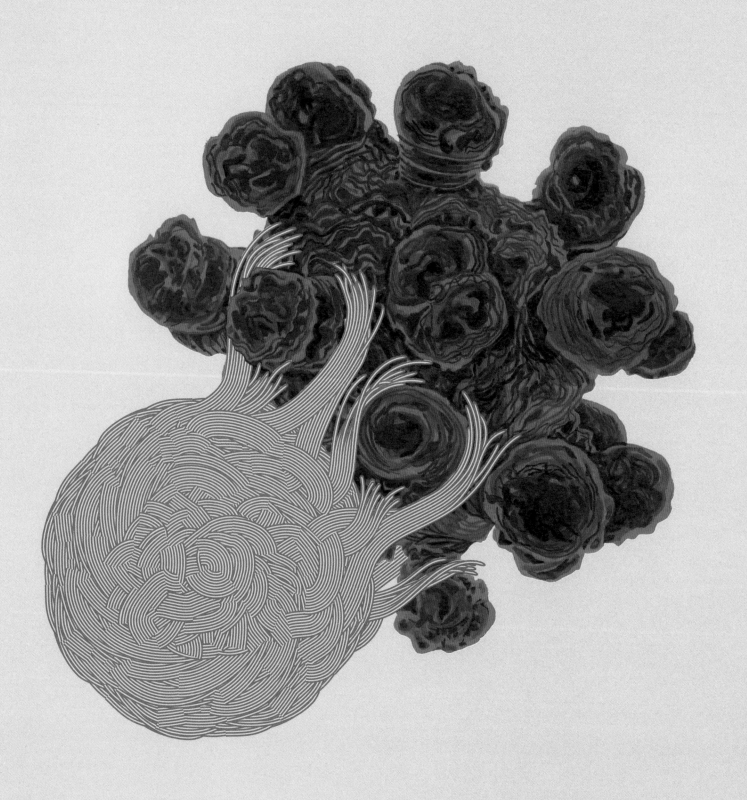

Self-protection against attack
IMMUNE SYSTEM

read p.75.85.205

In living organisms, an immune system is a set of coordinated processes capable of discriminating 'self' from 'non-self' for recognition and defence purposes. Pathogenic elements such as viruses, bacteria*, parasites or certain foreign molecules* are recognised as 'non-self' and are destroyed. Identifying pathogens can be difficult as they've proven themselves to be very adaptive, changing quickly to avoid the action of the immune system and consequently succeeding in infecting their host.

In mammals, two types of defence mechanisms are brought into play: non-specific defence mechanisms (natural or innate defence) such as protective skin and mucous membranes, phagocytic cells and even tears; specific defence mechanisms such as action carried out by lymphocytes and the production of targeted antibodies. The latter specific mechanisms constitute the immune response.

When an organism encounters a pathogen, it immediately starts to produce antibodies which are going to recognise the invader and destroy it. When the first viral or bacterial infection has been stamped out, the organism conserves some antibodies. These will be ready to intervene in case of a new infection, without it being necessary to detect all the infected cells. This ability of memorising an efficient response to pathogens in order to combat them if they re-appear, is called 'acquired immunity'. The principle of vaccines is based on this very specific memory.

APPLICATIONS

The immune defence processes described for living organisms are entirely applicable in the computing domain, especially for the development of software for defence against viruses which infect computers. With the development of networked computer systems and the World Wide Web, when a computer is infected by a virus, connected computers are immediately contaminated in their turn. Inspired by nature, a large number of computer companies attempt to develop 'immune defence' systems to protect their networks against viruses. Using appropriate software, IBM has undertaken research in this field by creating a laboratory capable of detecting the presence of one million plus currently identified viruses to isolate them in a secure manner.

Computer viruses are 'intelligent' programs capable of self replication, designed to infiltrate computers and to partially or totally damage them, just as in living organisms. Virus identification programs search all the code in the computer's memory to find signs of viruses previously identified and stored in the memory. Computer viruses have recognisable signatures. When these are found, the protection program indicates that the computer has been infected. Protection is however not a built-in feature as new viruses can appear within a few hours. Researchers in the field now attempt to develop new defence strategies even closer to those of natural immunity defences.

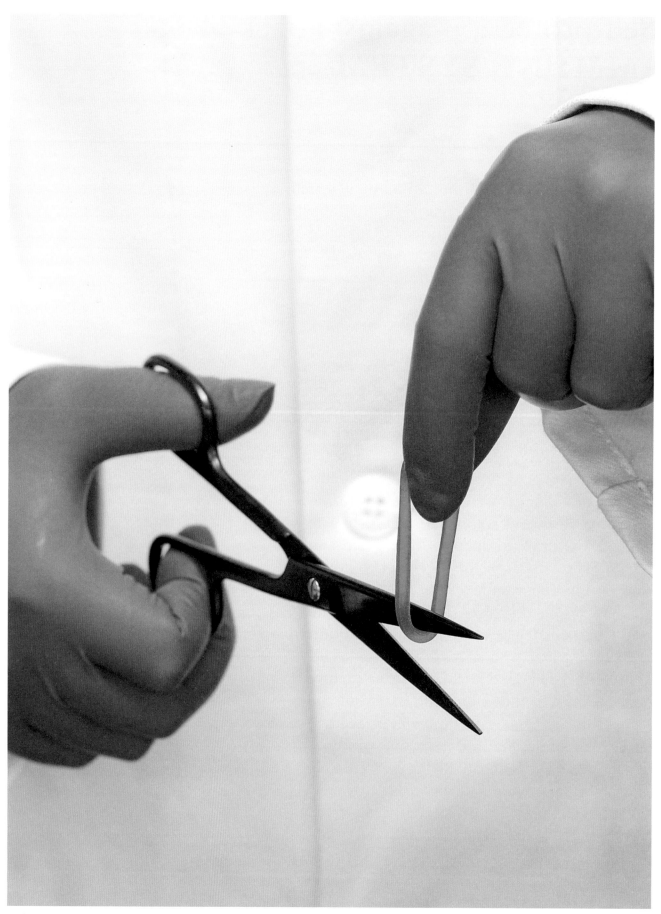

read p.205

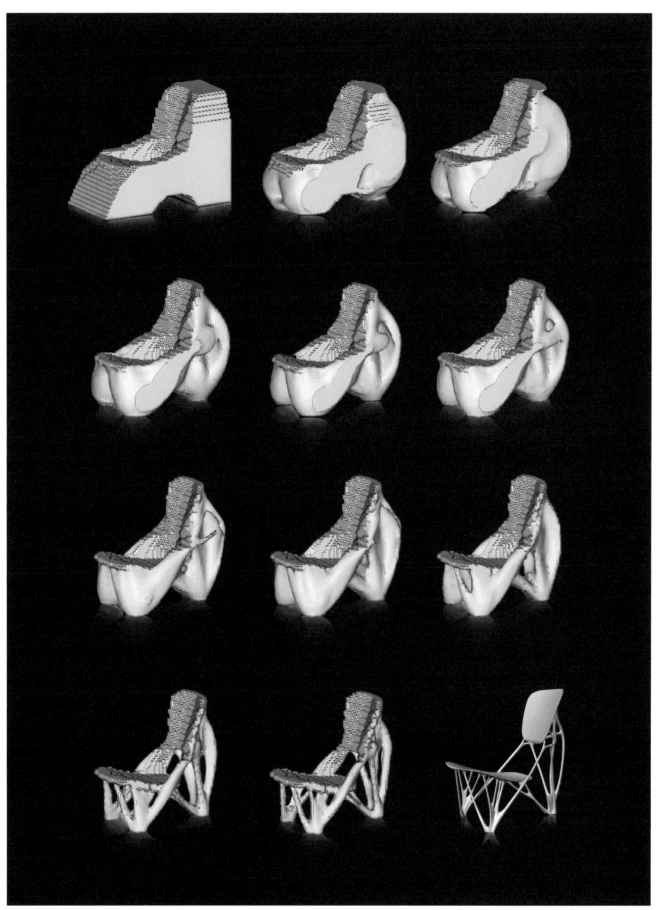

read p.211

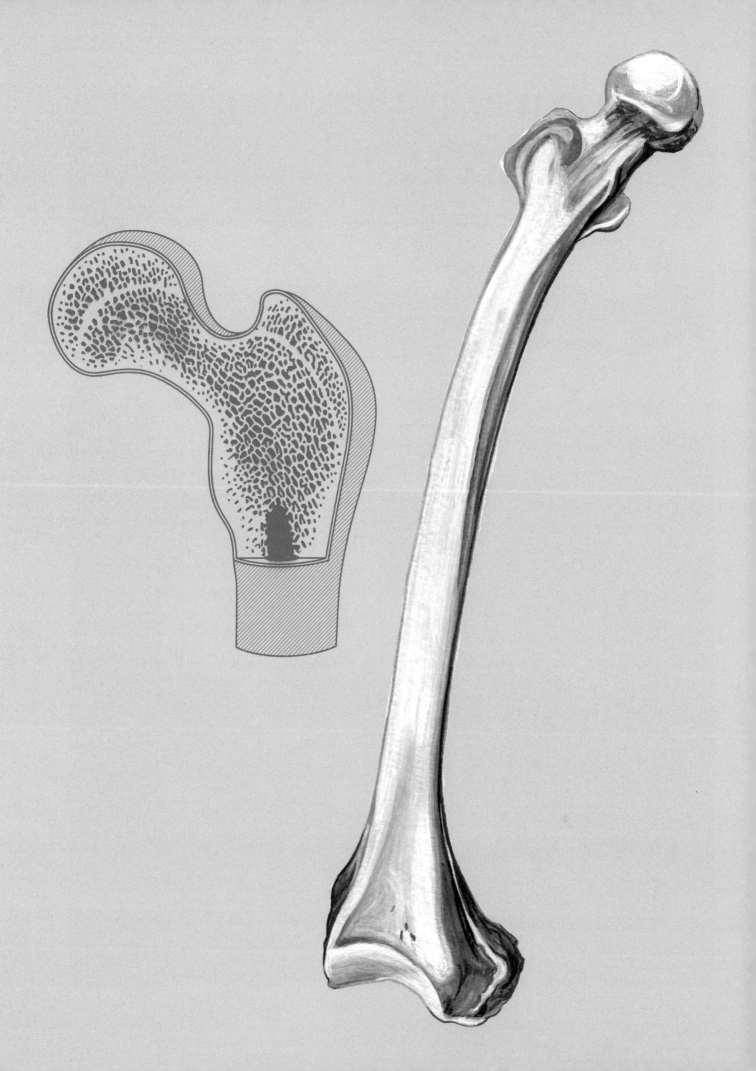

Strength
BONES

read p.91.171.175.177.213.215.223

It's possible to imagine the skeleton in the human body as the equivalent of the reinforced concrete frame in a building. With each step, the femur (thigh) bone bears a weight equivalent to three times the weight of the whole body and when a pole vaulter lands after his jump, each square centimetre ($0.15\,in^2$) of his pelvis is subjected to a pressure of 1,400 kg (3,000 lb). Engineers estimate that the strength of bone is six times greater than that of steel. And yet the bare skeleton is only 4 to 5 kg (9 to 1 lb) of the weight in the human body. While an architect can call on a range of materials – steel, aluminium, concrete – the skeleton makes do with bone, but this has a high degree of organisation which manifests itself by the existence of hierarchical structures fitted together (also found in the carapace of a crab), capable of adapting to various external stresses. The femoral bone is particularly representative of this economy of material on the one hand and of structural organisation on the other, which allows resistance to major stresses of up to 300 kg/cm² ($4,267\,lbf/in^2$). The efficiency lies in the fact that, just as trees add wood to the parts which are subjected to major tensions, nature reduces superfluous bone mass and does so in a progressive manner.

A lot of effort is currently going into understanding mechanotransduction*, that is to say how macroscopic mechanical stress exerted on bone regulates the activity of bone cells. The stakes in the materials domain are considerable. The key being the idea of one day having materials capable of developing as a function of external stresses.

APPLICATIONS

Generating constructions using the exact same principle as bone growth – first developed by Claus Mattheck, not only to optimise an existing shape, but to actually sculpt from a block with the underlying codes of Mother Nature – designer Joris Laarman came up with a series called Bone furniture. This series contains the first aluminium chair, a rubber chaise, a marble/resin armchair, a marble/resin rocker, a tungsten/aluminium table and a bronze bookshelf. These were all studies in shape, strength and different materials. Together with Vitra, the Joris Laarman Lab is now working on a low-cost and efficient industrial interpretation of the concept. *see* Photo above and image p.209 © Friedman Benda Gallery, New York

The Soft Kill Option (SKO), adapted to the requirements of the Opel company, has allowed developers to construct components as if they were bone. All superfluous material is eliminated by tiny amounts in order to obtain the best strength/weight ratio, the holy grail of the automobile industry. To date, several Opel models are fitted with a bionic engine mounting which, while meeting very high physical constraints, is 75% of the weight and twice as strong as its predecessors.

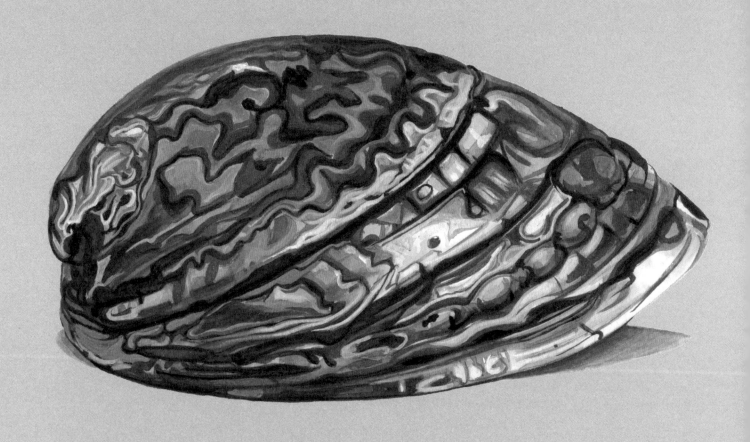
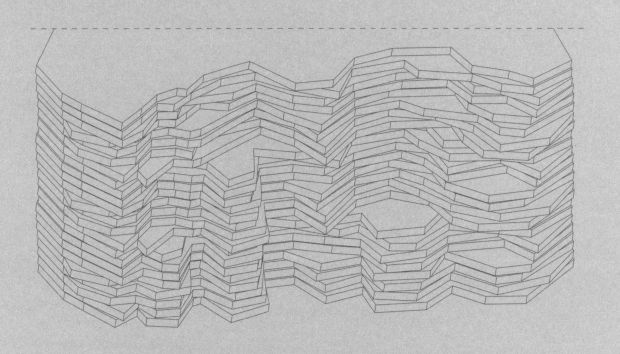

Strength
NACRE

_____ The marine environment is a dangerous one for soft-bodied organisms like bivalve molluscs (mussels, oysters, etc.), gasteropods (snails, limpets, etc.) or a cephalopod (nautilus). Evolution has therefore provided them with an advanced system of nano-structured armour: a shell. Its internal surface, nacre*, is a sandwich material consisting of layers of aragonite* crystals and layers of organic material (conchiolin*). Its strength is much greater than that of its single mineral material constituent. Pupa Gilbert, a physics professor at the University of Wisconsin-Madison, states that it would be 3,000 times stronger than aragonite. Physicists have now proved that the tiny fraction of organic material plays a major part.

_____ To delve into the secrets of the structure of nacre, researchers submitted it to analysis using synchrotron radiation*. Using more common methods, nacre appears to be rather like a brick wall, consisting of entirely mineral crystalline masses welded together by the organic fraction. However, polarised synchrotron radiation reveals crystals in different orientations. A larger-scale structure then appears, formed from columns in which crystals are arranged so that the direction in each is different from that of its neighbours. It seems that the secret of nacre's strength lies in these multiple, crossed orientations. They avoid the appearance of cleavage planes which can form preferred pathways for propagation of a fracture. Furthermore, nacre has the capacity for reconstituting damage or holes. Commonly known as mother-of-pearl, it is the material used by an oyster to deal with the intrusion of a foreign body by forming a pearl, which in itself suggests great potential.

APPLICATIONS

Following the example of the Mayas, who were already using nacre for replacement teeth, small prostheses cut from this biomaterial are now being made. It will be possible for them to be used in reparative surgery for bone substitution and regeneration.

As nanotechnology methods advance, the creation of artificial nacre and other high-performance armour plating is becoming more and more realistic says Christine Ortiz, Department of Materials Science and Engineering, MIT (source: _Journal of Materials Research_, September 2005).

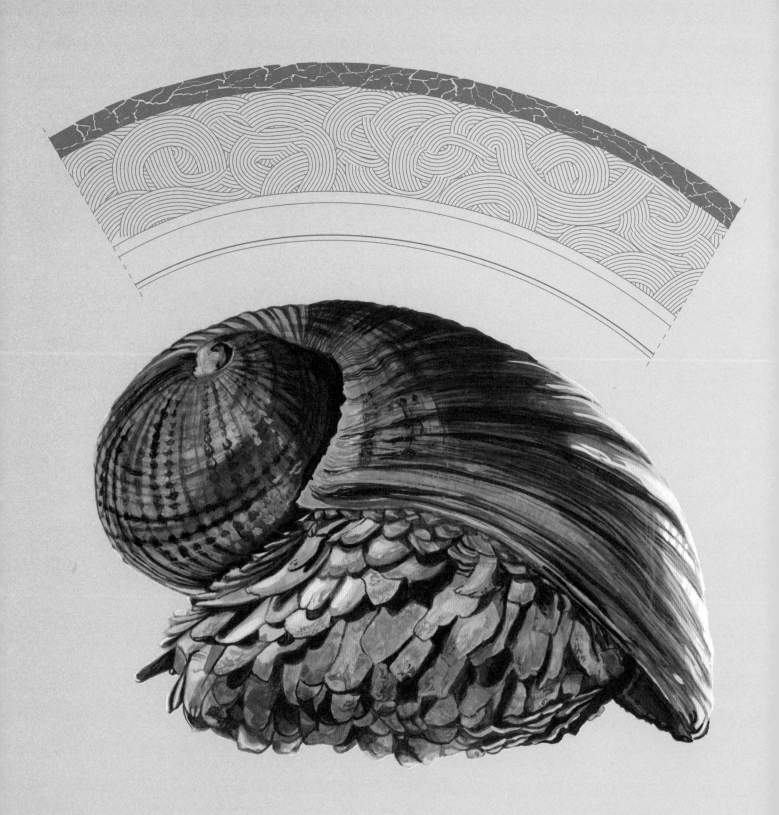

Strength
SNAILS

read p.177.211.213

The gastropod (snail) *Crysomallon squamiferum*, commonly known as the scaly-foot gastropod, lives in the Indian Ocean at a depth of more than 2,400 m (7,900 ft) close to hydrothermal vents known as 'black smokers', rather like small undersea volcanoes. This marine mollusc is distinguished from its relatives by a foot covered in scales and a shell capable of resisting its very acidic environment, where any normal mollusc shell, consisting of calcium carbonate*, would be rapidly dissolved. It's shell is not only insensitive to acids but is also capable of resisting attacks from crabs which also live around hydrothermal vents. Christine Ortiz, a scientist from the Massachusetts Institute of Technology explains that the shell of this snail in fact consists of three different layers which dissipate energy when, for example, squeezed by a crab. The external surface of the shell consists of iron sulphide* granules mixed with a material secreted by the animal. This layer cracks when absorbing and dissipating energy exerted by a claw, but the micro-cracks and deformation thus created, prevent further breakage. The intermediate layer which is the thickest, consists of a softer material and also absorbs energy, and the innermost layer of the shell is calcium carbonate for strength, protected from the acidic environment by the two layers above it.

In addition to this very specific and unique type of shell structure, the animal's 'foot' is also protected by scales of the same iron-based nature (iron sulphides), basically transforming the snail into an armoured gastropod.

APPLICATIONS

The shell of *Crysomallon squamiferum* is of interest on many levels for the development of composite materials*. In aeronautical engineering in particular, it has been the practice to assemble layers of materials with complementary properties, but these always have to be composites with stable and homogenous structures. This particular shell, as well as the exoskeletons of sea urchins or certain beetles, could perhaps allow high-performance protective materials to be developed for military use, for example.

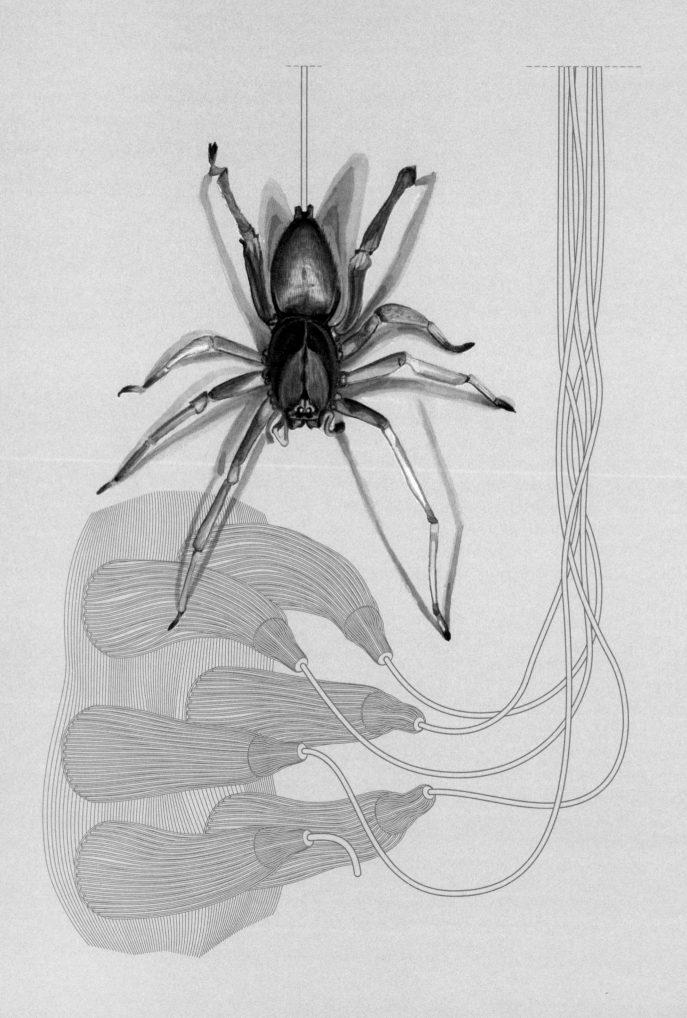

Strength
SPIDERS

read p.223

Spiders, of the order Araneae, are predatory animals with eight legs. They produce silk threads which allow them to move, protect themselves, catch and store prey, demarcate their territory, etc. They have, on average, six small protuberances called spinnerets, on their abdomen. From these they can express different types of liquid silk produced by silk glands. The silks are different as a function of the final use they are intended for. The silks are very light, about $1.3\,g/cm^3$ ($0.047\,lb/in^3$), very strong, elastic and resistant to abrasion. Silk spider threads, with a diameter between 25 and 70 microns (0.000984 to $0.002755\,in$), are often compared with steel. They are actually tougher than the latter. They are also more elastic than latex, for example.

The silk consists of a protein* core filament, fibroin*, covered with a type of adhesive based on another family of proteins: sericins*. Fibroin is in fact a copolymer*, consisting of different types of aminated acids (principally glycine and alanine), constructed in hydrophilic* and hydrophobic blocks.

Silk comes out of the animal in the form of a gel and is drawn into a very fine thread. This particular polymeric material has the astonishing property of never being water-soluble once the thread has dried. Spider silk also seems to have a 'shape memory' phenomenon in that it always returns to its initial configuration.

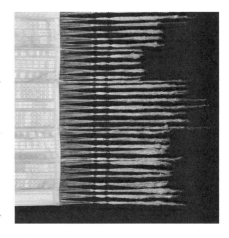

APPLICATIONS

Simon Peers and Nicholas Godley followed the path that Frenchman Francois Xavier Bon took in 1709. From 2004 to 2009 they examined spider silk in the highlands of Madagascar in the same light as the silk of the Chinese silk worm. Peers and Godley reinvented the various processes for obtaining spider silk and began to collect and 'silk' golden orb spiders (*Nephila Madagascariensis*). The result of this intensive and exhaustive work is a woven textile using silk thread from over one million spiders. *see* Photo © Simon Peers and Nicholas Godley

A great deal of research is being done today in trying to collect or synthesise spider silk. There could be many applications in the biomedical domain (spider silk has already been used as a suturing material), in the manufacture of bullet-proof vests, for fishing nets or in the sporting domain. Farming spiders is complex, as they are carnivorous and cannibalistic. One of the major routes explored by Nexia Biotechnologies of Canada is the recovery of fibroin from the milk of transgenic goats. In effect, there are great similarities between the silk-producing glands of spiders and the mammary glands of goats. The gene which codes for spider silk is inserted into the gene pool of the goat and the desired protein appears in its milk.

Strength
TREES

read p.175.197.223

Nature often uses a helical shape. It occurs in the construction of the nautilus shell and in the organisation of certain algae to optimise their hydrodynamic* strength. For example: the insect trachea and some parts of diatom skeletons have increased mechanical strength owing to the spiral organisation of the material.

This spiral effect is also found in trees which experience bad weather conditions (wind and snow). Tree fibres are capable of deviating between 30° and 50° off the vertical, thus creating a trunk and branches with a helical structure. This particular growth ensures a consistent distribution of nutriments between the tree's roots and branches allowing it to have increased resistance to drought or a varying water supply. In general, the branches are supplied vertically because the roots below them are capable of drawing in water. If roots are cut on one side of a tree, any branches in direct connection with them are going to die. When tree fibres and transport tissues are organised in a spiral, they more or less cover the whole of the tree, thus assuring the survival of the whole tree. In addition, the spiral structure gives the wood material extra strength: the branches are more able to bend under the action of the wind or a weight of snow rather than breaking.

APPLICATIONS

Today, there are many spiral structures in everyday objects, for example the reinforcing on gas pipes.

The Portuguese mineral water brand Vitalis, a member of the Unicer group, has asked Logoplaste Innovation Lab to develop a water bottle made from PET (polyethylene terephthalate), which is lighter than traditional bottles of the same material and yet is just as strong. Inspired by the spiral growth of the fibres of *Pinus albicaulis* (the whitebark pine), the shape of the bottle allows a saving of 250 tonne (275 US short ton) of material per year: less material, a strong spiral structure and a heightened image for the brand. *see* Photos above and p. 220 © Logoplaste

read p.219

read p.223

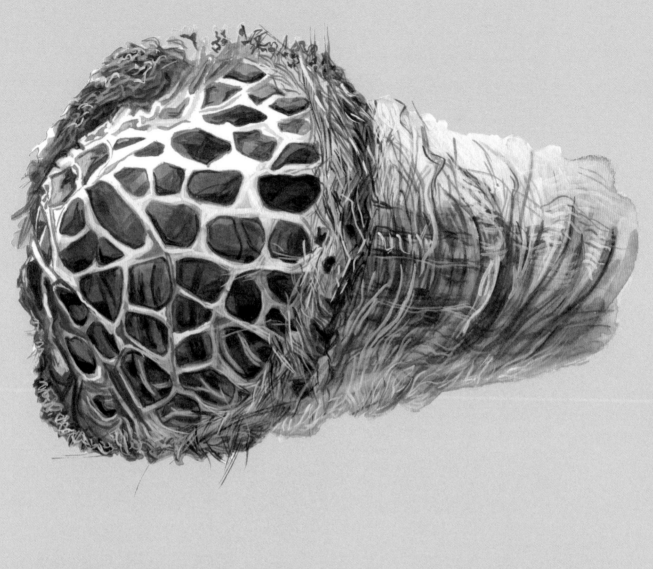

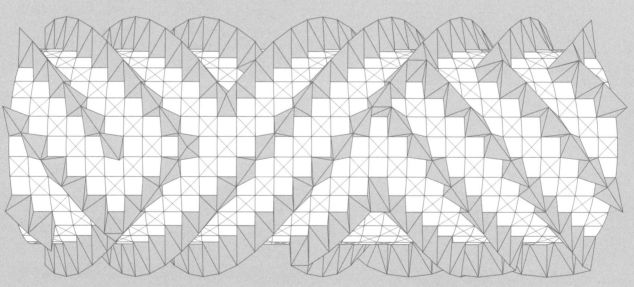

Strength
VENUS FLOWER BASKET

read p.91.141.171.175.211.217.219

Sponges are simple multicellular marine animals. There are more than 30,000 species, of which a small number live in freshwater. The majority of them have no defined shape, some form crusts on the surface of rocks or crustacean shells, others take the shape of urns, cups or shrubs. However, all sponges have one characteristic in common: a lacy surface through which water can penetrate, bringing in food and oxygen*. This water is then expelled via a single orifice called an osculum*. Sponges are sedentary, just able to contract.

Euplectella aspergillum, the Venus Flower Basket, class Hexactinellides, is called a 'glass sponge' or shrimp sponge, the former name from its appearance, the second from its commensal* relationship with a pair of shrimp which live within its complex structure. The sponge generally lives in deep water, beyond 200 m (660 ft) and is characterised by a curved tubular silica* skeleton, which can be up to 1 m (just over 3 ft) in length, resembling lacework. The skeleton actually consists of siliceous spicules, glass particles in this case, and is extremely crack resistant and stiff. These spicules, called hexactines, have six points oriented on three axes. Like diatoms and radiolaria*, this *Euplectella* sponge makes glass by a cold process. The complexity, regularity and strength of their skeleton is astounding. The spicules have a structure similar to that of optical fibres: a core which is a few micrometres in diameter enclosed in a sheath of about 50 µm (2,000 µin) with a lower refractive index. This sheath is itself covered by a tough lamellar structure.

APPLICATION

The head office building of Swiss Re in London, a tall landmark, popularly known as 'The Gherkin', designed by Sir Norman Foster and a team of engineers, is based on a cylindrical architecture similar to that of glass sponges. Opening windows in the steel exoskeleton allow natural light and fresh air to penetrate the structure, just like food penetrates the structure of the sponge. Because of its cylindrical shape, wind can easily wrap around the building instead of blasting downwards onto the street. Also, vents at the bottom level suck in wind and swirl it upwards just like a sponge does with water. Besides resistance to wind and breaking, the complex framework also assures a better ventilation management, cutting air conditioning costs.

see Photos above and p.221 © Nigel Young / Foster + Partners

Symbiosis
LICHENS, CLOWNFISH, SEA ANEMONES, ETC.

read p.167

———— As unassuming plants, often unnoticed by most people, lichens colonise a very wide variety of surfaces: tree trunks, bare rocks, concrete, mosses or even other lichens. They are capable of growing in places where no other vegetation exists. They are in fact composite plants, an alga living with a fungus. When scraped off, the whitish or greyish lichens are revealed to be green inside and small cup-shaped organs which are 1–2 mm (0.04–0.08 in) in diameter can be seen. When seen under the microscope, these elements are essentially the same as the reproductive organs of fungi in the genus *Peziza*. This association offers a very specialised kind of life solution. There are many conditions in which an alga or fungus, taken separately, could not survive, but their close relationship allows them to survive together in a wide variety of conditions. An alga, using photosynthesis* among other things, makes metabolites such as carbohydrates* which the fungus needs to live. In exchange, the fungus offers protection for the alga against wind and excessive sunlight. It also provides the alga with water, carbon dioxide*, mineral elements and organic molecules* such as acids which protect the lichen from bacteria* and molds.

———— Clownfish and sea anemones also share certain interests. The tentacles of sea anemones carry cells which can sting, paralyse and kill fish. Clownfish are immunised against the stings and even seek refuge amongst the tentacles to escape their predators. In turn, they defend the anemone against attacks from butterfly fish, which feed on sea anemones. The anemone also benefits from some of the food eaten by the clownfish.

APPLICATIONS

Beyond the direct use of these organisms, it is their symbiotic relationship which inspires thoughts as to the type of partnership we can encounter in nature. There is no doubt that this type of exchange of 'services', guaranteeing the survival of each species, is to be taken up in different domains such as agriculture, management or industry.

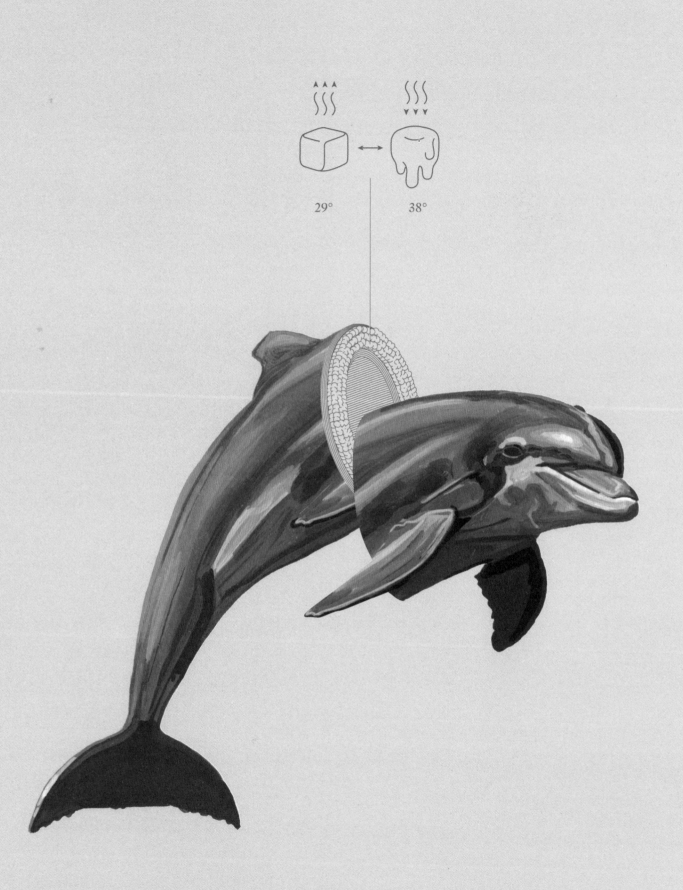

Temperature regulation
BOTTLE-NOSED DOLPHIN

read p.143.163.165.177.231.233

Tursiops truncatus, the bottle-nosed dolphin, well-known from water parks and in television programmes, is a popular, intelligent cetacean mammal. It can reach 4 m (13 ft) in length and weigh up to 650 kg (1,400 lb). The dolphin likes to swim in the warm temperate waters across the world with its team mates. Dolphins mainly live in pods (also called schools) of up to a dozen individuals for mating, hunting and protecting each other.

To search for their prey, like fish, shrimp or squid, they use an echolocation system, just like bats. Each animal has a large lump on its head called the melon, which is situated just in front of its blowhole. This is in fact a fatty mass which transmits and receives ultrasound, a sort of ultrasound* radar. This aspect of the animal is under study and already a source of inspiration.

Dolphins also have an excellent ability to regulate their temperature with the aid of, among other things, the fatty layer which covers their body. This fatty covering consists of fatty acids identified as phase-change materials with a melting point between 29 °C and 38 °C (84 °F and 100 °F). This quite specific fat composition is matched with a highly developed vascular system. The vascular adaptations control heat loss by acting on the blood circulation. The combination operates very efficiently and, coupled with the properties of the phase-change fatty acids, gives a very effective thermal regulation system.

APPLICATIONS

Phase-change materials (PCM*) are already in use in the textile domain, offering garments capable of providing their owner with constant thermal comfort. The special textiles, manufactured by Schoeller, contain millions of microcapsules filled with PCM and create a personal comfort climate. *see* Photo p.228 © matériO

There are also wall coverings (paints or panels) which include phase-change materials and are capable of providing effective thermal regulation in a room. Micronal® PCM, manufactured by BASF AG, is a phase-changing polymer. It consists of micro-encapsulated wax globules which function as latent heat accumulators to increase the thermal mass of lightweight construction materials. It can be, for instance, employed in building materials to maintain the indoor temperature at a constant 23 °C. *see* Photo above © matériO

The study of fatty acids and the system of the combined PCM/vascular network complex opens further interesting pathways in the textile and construction domains.

read p.227

read ——— p.231

Temperature regulation
PINE CONES

read p.143.163.165.177.227.233

Pine cones are in fact the reproductive organs of conifers and show that pines are gymnosperms*. There are female pine cones and male pine cones. These cones consist of scales which overlap and are distributed around a central axis. The scales carry the reproductive organs of the plant.

On looking into the way pine cones function, it can be noted that they are capable of opening when dry and closing once they become wet. The scales are two-layer elements which react to variations in atmospheric humidity. Once exposed to dampness, the cellular tissues in the external scale layer have a tendency to expand lengthways, causing the scales to close, the internal scales following the movement passively. When the environment becomes drier, the opposite occurs and the same tissues shrink, opening the scales. These cellular dimensional variations are controlled, among other things, by this reaction and the arrangement of the cellulose * microfibrils in the pine cone.

The behaviour of a pine cone scale is in fact a natural version of a bi-metal strip, the two parts of which are bonded together, each taking the other with it in their movement, as a function of temperature.

APPLICATIONS

The shoe lining material c_change™ textile, developed by Swiss company Schoeller contains a membrane inspired by observation of pine-cone scales. At high temperatures or during intense activity, the membrane structure opens when the body perspiration increases. Excess heat can then escape to the exterior. After a reduction in body perspiration during a cold or inactive period, the structure recloses to retain body heat within the garment. *see* Photos above and p.229 © Schoeller Textil AG

Temperature regulation
TERMITES

read   p.143.163.165.177.227.231

Termites are highly-organised insects. They are 'eusocial', which is the highest level of social organisation identified. Bees and ants, for example, are also considered eusocial. This social model is studied in depth and inspires humans in terms of organisation of systems and even societies. The model is characterised by a strong hierarchy in which the queen ensures the reproduction of the species, while sterile insect workers protect her and deal with everyday tasks, providing a suitable environment for the swarm to live in.

Some termites of the genus *Macrotermes* specialise in building structures complete with air conditioning. *Macrotermes bellicosus* is a mound-building termite found in tropical Africa, where it is capable of constructing mounds up to 6 m (20 ft) tall and 3 m (10 ft) in diameter, using earth mixed with saliva. Termite mounds are almost as hard as concrete and have walls up to 30 cm (12 in) thick. The interior of these 'buildings' is a labyrinth of cavities and corridors variously reserved for raising young, storing food and for moving around. One of the unusual features of these termites is that they cultivate species of fungi as their primary food source. To enable them to do this, a mound must have a constant temperature between 29 °C and 32 °C (84 °F to 90 °F), whatever the external temperature, which may vary over a range of 40 °C (104 °F) in a day. The design of the mound, with its ventilation, heating and cooling systems, has been studied extensively. The insects are able to regulate the temperature by opening or closing air passages.

APPLICATION

Since 1996, the Eastgate Centre building in Harare, Zimbabwe, has been open. This building has passive air conditioning which requires no input of energy, a short and long-term economic efficiency from an inspired design by architect Mick Pearce, in collaboration with Arup. *see*   Photo © David Brazier

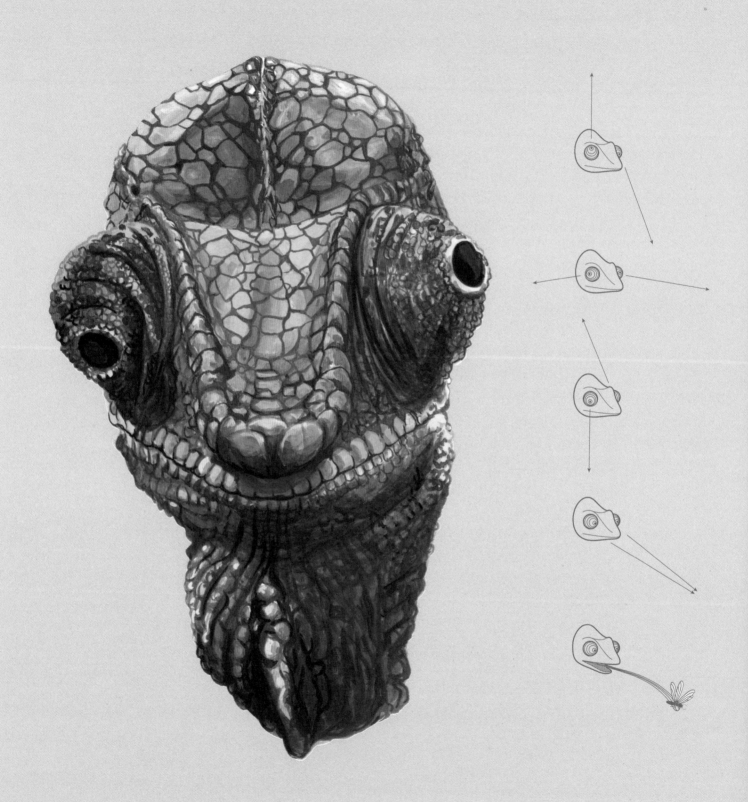

360° Vision
CHAMELEON

read p.79.89

Chameleons are highly-specialised lizards of the Chamaeleonidae family. There are more than 150 different species of chameleons, known mainly for their ability to change colour depending on their surrounding environment, thanks to the presence of chromatophores* in their skin, just like in cuttlefish. They don't possess any ears, but they have very characteristic and rather astonishing vision: their huge eyes* bulge and swivel independently, giving chameleons 360° vision.

They capture their prey – which include insects such as grasshoppers, but for the biggest chameleons it even includes small birds or other lizards – by shooting out their tongue very quickly and precisely, sometimes up to a distance of more than three times their own length, which can be up to 70 cm (27 in). Their unusual eyes allow them to monitor their entire surroundings without moving, which has the double advantage of not scaring their prey, and also not drawing their predator's attention. Once one eye has located the prey, the view points of both eyes converge on it, thus providing binocular vision to enable them to judge the distance to the prey. This analysis of the eyes' accommodation, that is to say analysis of the deformation of the lens which allows focusing, shows the chameleon where to act. The lens is stretched by the muscles of the iris in the eye and the chameleon's brain assesses the extent of the stretching as a measure of the distance to be covered.

APPLICATION

The operation of the chameleon's eyes is of interest in various fields, from aeronautics to the military. This high-performance vision, adapted for surveillance systems, could considerably improve the performance of security cameras.

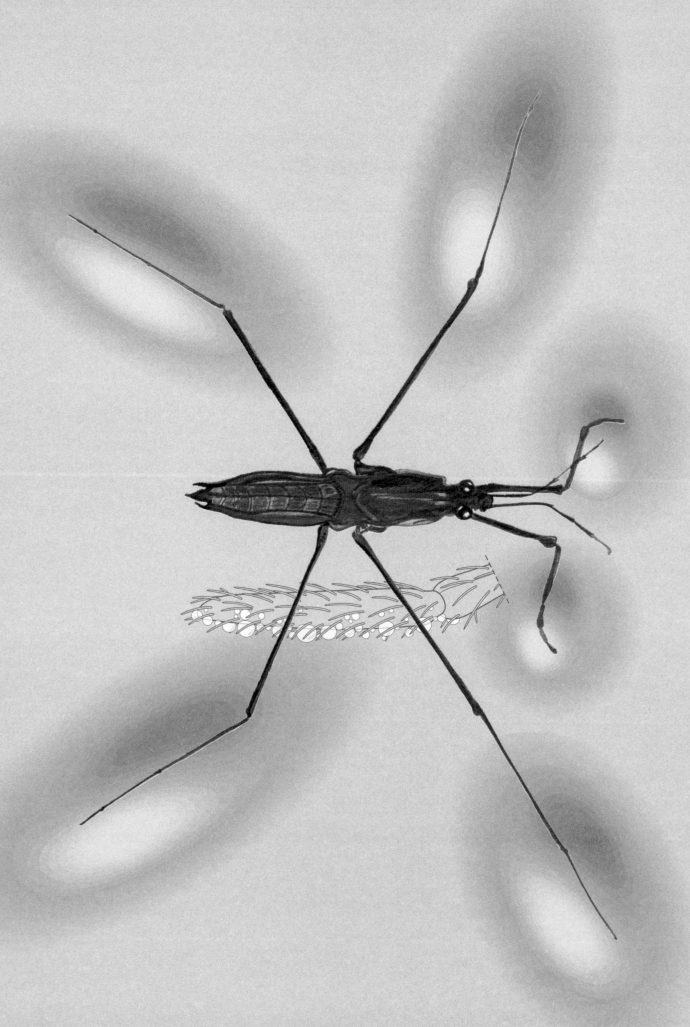

Walking on water
GERRIDAE

_____ Insects of the Gerridae family of the order Hemiptera have the astonishing ability to walk on water. They are often called 'pond skaters' or 'water striders' and live on the surface of calm waters. At rest, the weight of these insects, characteristically 0.01 g (0.00035 ounce) is held up by the surface tension* of the water. The skater's six feet, covered in hair and hydrophobic* wax, rest on the water surface, creating depressions up to 4 mm (0.16 inch) deep without breaking the elastic film produced by surface tension. The insect can support up to 15 times its own weight and still stay on the surface.

_____ Researchers at the Institute of Chemistry in Beijing have shown that, although the hydrophobic wax secreted on the feet is certainly involved in the ability of the animal to move on water, having hairy feet is the primary explanation of the phenomenon. Each foot has thousands of micro-hairs, with a diameter of the order of nanometres to a few microns (µm), 50 µm (2,000 µin) in length and set at an angle of 20° in relation to the surface of the foot. Each of these hairs has micro-grooves and air is trapped between the hairs and the grooves, forming cushions which increase the animal's ability to float.

_____ A simple hydrophobic surface would allow the Gerridae to stay on the water surface but the particular configuration of the feet allows them to move very quickly as well.

_____ The Gerridae are also indicators of water cleanliness. In effect, if the surface tension is reduced by the addition of detergents for example, the insects are no longer capable of resting on the water surface. Their presence is therefore a good indicator.

APPLICATIONS

Micro-robotics engineers could possibly develop robots capable of walking on water like pond skaters. One might imagine man himself being capable of evolving in the same way.

Studies on the skater's feet remain promising in terms of understanding the phenomena of super-hydrophobia*, which may have applications in the field of impermeable textiles, among other things.

Water collection
NAMIB DESERT BEETLE

read ___ p.147

Beetles of the genus *Stenocara* live in the African Namib Desert, one of the driest places in the world, not receiving more than a few millimetres of rain per year. These beetles are able to capture minute traces of moisture from the air by an ingenious method. Researchers Andrew Parker and Chris Laurence looked into this intriguing subject in 2001 and discovered how the insect captures this vital fluid in such a hostile environment. The beetles have rough elytra* (wing covers), a surface on which hydrophobic* (water-repellent) hollows coated with wax, alternate with hydrophilic* (water-attracting) ridges. In the early hours of the morning a beetle positions itself on the crest of a sand dune, bending its head down, its body creating a 45° angle to the ground. Fog is one of the only sources of humidity in these deserted areas. Fast-moving at almost gale speed, it comes from the Atlantic Ocean and blows over the desert, just a few times per month and normal condensation of any moisture seems impossible. However, the beetle's hydrophilic ridges retain traces of moisture. Minute droplets of water, just a few microns (μm) in diameter, form on the ridges. The droplets expand until, at a certain point, they cannot be held on the hydrophilic ridges, so they run down into the hydrophobic hollows, from which they are channelled directly to the mouth of the insect. The beetle – adequately hydrated – is then ready to face its hot and dry day.

APPLICATIONS

By combining raised hydrophilic* areas with lower, super-hydrophobic* areas, as demonstrated by the Namib beetles, it is possible to make materials able to capture minute traces of moisture from the air and convey them along a channel. Designed by Kitae Pak of Seoul National University of Technology in South Korea, the Dew bank was inspired by the Namibian beetles collecting moisture. Its steel body helps to assimilate the morning dew and to channel it into a bottle immediately.

see ___ Photo © provided by the Industrial Designers Society of America

A team of researchers of Oxford University and the UK defence technology firm QinetiQ are collaborating to develop a device to collect drinking water and agriculture water in dry regions of the world.

One can also imagine that this model could be put to other uses, to collect substances other than water, for example toxic elements.

TIMELINE

PRECAMBRIAN

13.700.000.000

Big Bang, expansion of the universe, birth of the Earth

PALEOZOIC ERA (PRIMARY ERA)

4.550.000.000 — First traces of Life

3.400.000.000 — First cells

2.000.000.000 — Continental surface areas increase

1.800.000.000 — Oxygen appears in the atmosphere

1.400.000.000 — First eukaryote (complex organism) cells

540.000.000 — Invertebrates

510.000.000 — Spread of shell and skeleton

Nature takes the exact amount of time it needs

Marine Jacques-Leflaive

PREHISTORY

MESOZOIC ERA (SECONDARY ERA) **CENOZOIC ERA (TERTIARY ERA)**

STONE AGE

QUATERNARY PERIOD

PLEISTOCENE

400.000.000	220.000.000	150.000.000	135.000.000	65.000.000	60.000.000	7.000.000	3.800.000	3.500.000	1.800.000	500.000
Development of life on the continents	Dinosaurs, crocodiles appear	Development of flowering plants	Birds, mammals	Disappearance of dinosaurs	Ammonites disappear	Hominidae, *Sahelenthropus tchadensis* 'Toumaï'	Stone tools	*Australopithecus afarensis* 'Lucie'	*Homo erectus*	Organisation of habitat

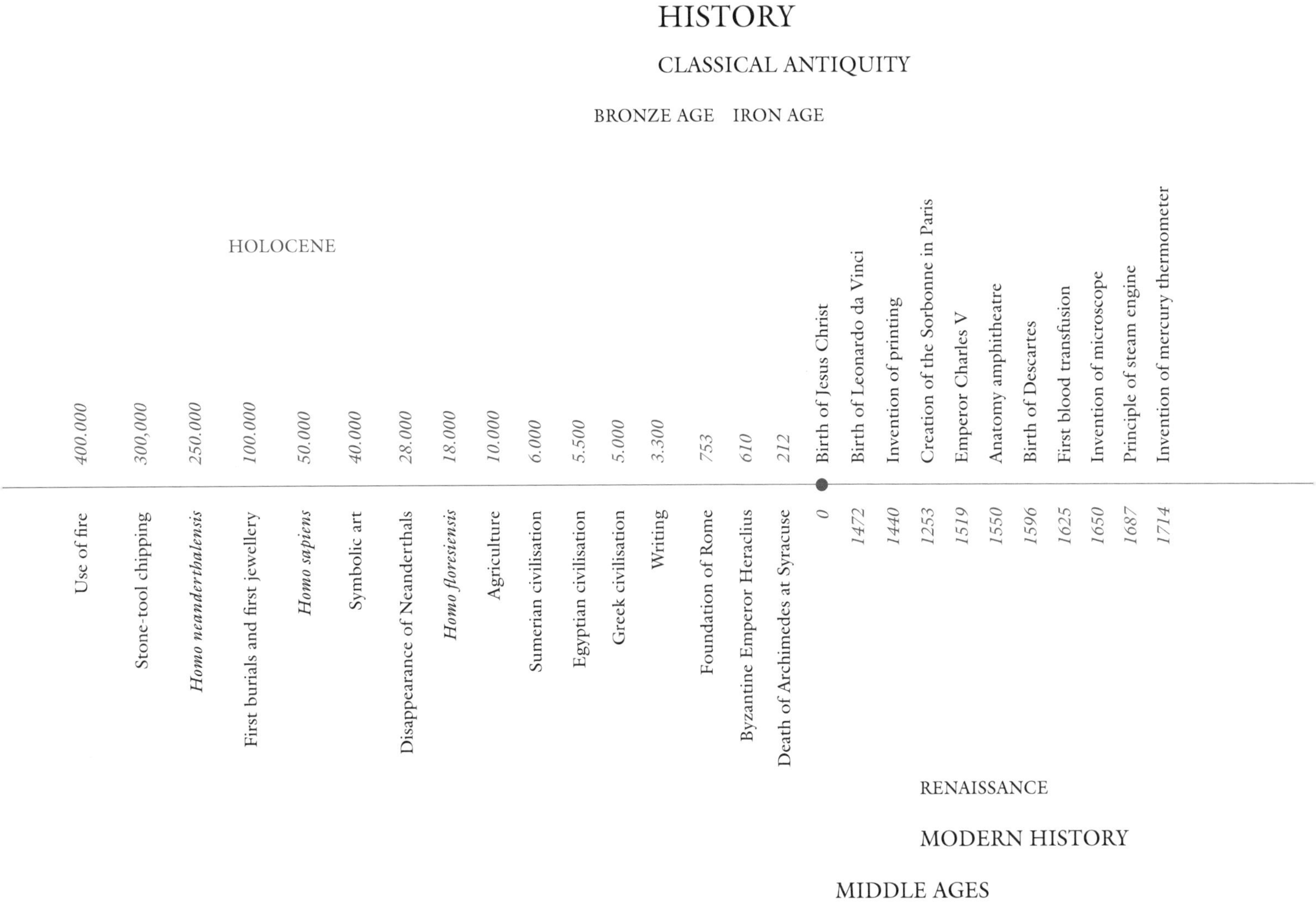

HISTORY

CLASSICAL ANTIQUITY

BRONZE AGE   IRON AGE

HOLOCENE

Year	Event
400.000	Use of fire
300,000	Stone-tool chipping
250.000	*Homo neanderthalensis*
100.000	First burials and first jewellery
50.000	*Homo sapiens*
40.000	Symbolic art
28.000	Disappearance of Neanderthals
18.000	*Homo floresiensis*
10.000	Agriculture
6.000	Sumerian civilisation
5.500	Egyptian civilisation
5.000	Greek civilisation
3.300	Writing
753	Foundation of Rome
610	Byzantine Emperor Heraclius
212	Death of Archimedes at Syracuse
0	Birth of Jesus Christ
1472	Birth of Leonardo da Vinci
1440	Invention of printing
1253	Creation of the Sorbonne in Paris
1519	Emperor Charles V
1550	Anatomy amphitheatre
1596	Birth of Descartes
1625	First blood transfusion
1650	Invention of microscope
1687	Principle of steam engine
1714	Invention of mercury thermometer

RENAISSANCE

MODERN HISTORY

MIDDLE AGES

1745	Leyden jar
1751	Diderot and Alembert encyclopaedia
1752	Franklin's lightning conductor
1756	Vaucanson's automata
1758	Volta's battery
1778	Lavoisier identifies oxygen
1789	French Revolution
1820	Invention of galvanometer
1831	Invention of current generator (Faraday disc) by M. Faraday
1831	Darwin embarks on the Beagle
1848	Abolition of slavery
1856	Birth of Sigmund Freud
1875	Invention of telephone by A.G. Bell
1879	The invention of 2-stroke engine by K. Benz
1885	Vaccination against rabies by L. Pasteur
1889	Eiffel Tower
1890	First flight by C. Ader
1900	Flight of the Zeppelin LZ1, invented by Count Ferdinand von Zeppelin
1901	Transatlantic radio message
	Compact and modern vacuum cleaner invented by Hubert Booth
1902	Air conditioner invented by Willie Carrier
1903	Double-edged disposable safety razor produced by Gillette Safety Razor Company
	Controlled, powered and manned flight by the Wright brothers
1904	Vacuum diode (known as the 'Fleming valve') invented by John A. Fleming
1905	Albert Einstein's special theory of relativity published
1906	Kellogg's® Corn Flakes on the market
	Sonar type listening device invented by Lewis Nixon
1907	Synthetic plastic, Bakelite®, invented by Leo Baekeland
	Colour photography process launched by Auguste and Louis Lumière
	Piloted helicopter flight by Paul Cornu
1908	Gyrocompass invented by Elmer A. Sperry
	First Ford automobile sold
	Process for making artificial nitrates developed by Fritz Haber
1909	Flight across the English Channel by Louis Blériot
1910	Neon light demonstrated by George Claude

INDUSTRIAL REVOLUTION

AGE OF ENLIGHTENMENT

CONTEMPORARY HISTORY

Start of the Mexican Revolution

Instant coffee marketed by the G. Washington Coffee Company

Light bulbs with ductile tungsten on the market, invented by William Coolidge

Motorised tank idea submitted to the British War office by Lancelot de Mole

Sinking of the Titanic

Small-format camera developed by Leica

Start of the First World War

Pyrex® glass ovenware developed

Modern zipper patented by Gideon Sündback

Start of the Russian Revolution

Alternating current welding invented by Claude Joseph Holslag

Band-Aid® invented by Earle Dickson

Insulin discovered by Sir Frederick Grant Banting

First 3D movie released

Patent filed for Television Systems by Vladimir Kosma Zworykin

Vitamin D synthesised by Harry Steenbock

Western disposable paper tissues introduced by the Kimberly-Clark Corporation

Quick-freezing method for food developed by Clarence Birdseye

PEZ Candy invented by Eduard Haas III

Quartz clock developed by Warren Marrison

Atlantic Ocean crossed by Charles Lindberg

Penicillin discovered by Sir Alexander Fleming

Bubble gum invented by Walter E. Diemer

Scotch Tape patented by 3M engineer Richard G. Drew

Neoprene developed by Wallace Carothers and DuPont Labs

Differential analyser – one of the first computer devices – built by Vannevar Bush at MIT

Electron microscope invented by Max Knott and Ernst Ruska

Stratospheric balloon flight by Auguste Piccard

Cyclotron built by Ernest Lawrence

Radio telescope built by Karl Jansky

Frequency modulation (FM radio) patented by Edwin Howard Armstrong

Artificial radioactivity discovered by Irène and Frédéric Joliot-Curie

Nylon invented by Wallace Carothers and DuPont Labs

Radar patented by Robert Watson-Watt

Voice recognition machine developed by Bell Labs

Colt revolver patented by Samuel Colt

Start of the Spanish Civil War

Xerography invented by Chester F. Carlson

Ballpoint pen patented by Ladislo Biro

1911
1912

1913
1914
1915
1917

1919
1920
1922

1923
1924

1927

1928

1930

1931

1932
1933
1934
1935

1936

1937
1938

1939	Tetrafluoroethylene polymers (Teflon) invented by Roy J. Plunkett
	LSD synthesised by Albert Hofmann of Sandoz Laboratories
1940	Start of the Second World War
	Colour television technology demonstrated by Peter Goldmark
1941	Launch of Elna # 1, the first compact, portable, electric sewing machine with a free arm
	Z3, the first programmable, fully automatic computing machine, designed by Konrad Zuse
	First artificial nuclear reactor, Chicago Pile-1, constructed by a team led by Enrico Fermi
1942	Electronic digital computer built by John Atanasoff and Clifford Berry
	Turboprop engine in production, designed by Max Mueller
	Kidney dialysis machine invented by Willem Kolff
1944	Synthetic cortisone invented by Percy Lavon Julian
1945	Atomic bombing of Hiroshima and Nagasaki
	Start of the Indochina War
1946	Microwave oven invented by Percy Spencer
	First mobile telephone call
1947	Transistor invented by John Bardeen, Walter Brattain and William Shockley
	Tupperware seal patented by Earl Silas Tupper
1948	Velcro® invented by George de Mestral
	Polaroid instant camera on the market, invented by Edwin Herbert Land
1950	First credit card charge by Frank McNamara, Ralph Schneider and Matty Simmons
	Start of the Korean War
1951	First electricity-generating nuclear power plant
1952	Successful detonation of the hydrogen bomb, developed by Eward Teller and Stanislaw Ulam
1953	Discovery of the structure of DNA by James Watson and Francis Crick
1954	Patent granted for the process of coating pans with Teflon
	Modern solar cell developed by Daryl Chapin, Calvin Souther Fuller and Gerald Pearson at Bell Laboratories
	Start of the Algerian War
1957	Sputnik 1 launched by the Soviet Union
	LASER invented by Gordon Gould
1958	Harry Coover's Super Glue on the market
1959	Patents filed for the integrated circuit by Jack Kilby and Robert Noyce
	Internal pacemaker invented by Wilson Greatbatch
1960	Commercial halogen lamps with iodine launched by General Electric
1961	First human journey into outer space by Russian astronaut Yuri Gagarin
1962	Silicone breast implant carried out by the Dow Corning Corporation
	Cuban Missile Crisis
1963	Computer mouse invented by Douglas Engelbart and Bill English
1965	Compact disk invented by James Russell
	Technology behind Kevlar® invented by Stephanie Louise Kwolek
	Electronic mail sent through MIT's CTSS system
1967	Pulsars discovered by Jocelyn Bell and Antony Hewish
	Hand-held calculator invented by Texas Instruments
1968	French Revolution of May 1968
	Prague Spring
1969	Artificial heart implanted in a human by Denton Cooley
	Apollo 11 lands humans on the moon
1971	CT-scan carried out

Year	Event
1973	Microprocessor built by Federico Faggin, Ted Hoff and Stanley Mazor
1973	Ethernet invented by Robert Metcalfe and David Boggs at Xerox PARC
	Yom Kippur War
	Oil crisis
1974	Post-it notes invented by Arthur Fry
1975	Commercial implementation of a laser printer (IBM model 3800)
1976	Apple computer for sale
1977	MRI body scan performed by Raymond Damadian
1978	GPS satellite launched
1979	Cell phone publicly demonstrated by Motorola
	Iranian Revolution
1981	Hepatitis-B vaccine invented by Maurice R. Hilleman
	IBM PC introduced
	Scanning tunneling microscope developed by Gerd Karl Binnig and Heinrich Rohrer
	TGV (high-speed train in France) available to the public
1982	Human growth hormone genetically engineered by Genentech
1983	HIV isolated by Luc Montagnier and demonstrated to be the cause of AIDS by Robert Gallo
1984	CD-ROM format specifications published by Philips and Sony
	Macintosh launched by Apple
	Bhopal disaster in India
1985	Windows operating system introduced by Microsoft
1986	Disposable camera, QuickSnap, introduced by Fujifilm
	Russian Mir space station in orbit
	Chernobyl disaster
1987	Fluoxetin (Prozac) marketed by Eli Lilly
1988	Patent for a genetically engineered animal issued to Harvard University researchers
	Philip Leder and Timothy Stewart
1989	Fall of the Berlin Wall
1990	World Wide Web created by Tim Berners-Lee
	Release of Nelson Mandela
1991	Linux version 0.01 launched by Linus Torvalds
	End of the USSR / Start of the Yugoslav Wars
1993	Pentium® processor introduced by Intel
1994	Saquinavir, approved HIV protease inhibitor, manufactured by Hoffmann–La Roche
	Rwandan Genocide
1995	DVD industry standard announced
1996	Birth of Dolly the sheep, the first mammal cloned from an adult somatic cell
1997	El Niño
1998	Toyota releases its first hybrid car
	Google search engine created
2000	GPS precision enhanced for civil and commercial use
2001	Artificial liver invented by Kenneth Matsumura and Alin Foundation
	Self-cleaning glass introduced by PPG Industries
	Launch of the iPod by Apple
	September 11 terrorist attacks
2002	Nanotechnology wearable fabrics invented by Nano-Tex
2003	Complete sequence of the human genome determined
2004	Indian Ocean earthquake and tsunami
	Facebook website created
2005	Partial face transplant on living human
	YouTube website created
	Twitter website created
2008	Start of the Global Financial Crisis
	Election of Barack Obama as the first African American president of the United States
2011	Start of Arab Revolutions
	Tsunami in Japan
	First synthetic organ transplant by Professor Paolo Macchiarini

LET'S DISCUSS IT WITH

FRED GELLI

PRODUCT AND GRAPHIC DESIGNER, FOUNDER AND CREATIVE DIRECTOR OF BRANDING AND DESIGN AGENCY TÁTIL DESIGN

What sort of relationship does man have with nature?

_____ I believe humans have lost their natural connection with the big ecosystem* which is the planet Earth (Gaia). By comparison, people have been on this earth for a very short time, and only learned to write some 10,000 years ago ^{see} p.13.241. Man's intelligence and immaturity have put people in a position of wonder and amazement of their own possibilities, which has led to a loss of the instinctive link with the planet. In nature as well as the ecosystem's logics, competition and cooperation thrive in balance. People, on the other hand, have invented a new drive that radicalised this relationship: greed. But I'm an optimist and I believe that with a little more maturity, our species has a big chance of participating in an harmonic and symbiotic way with Gaia.

> *In nature as well as the ecosystem's logics, competition and cooperation thrive in balance*

What can people learn from nature?

_____ Nature functions according to three principles that guarantee its 'investment' success. Firstly, there is 'optimisation', nature always endeavours to reduce the spending of energy. People have a very different approach, which is maximising, loving waste and extravagance. Secondly, nature always considers closed cycles as bases for productive processes. 'Nothing is lost, nothing is created, everything is transformed!' People consider linear processes, which is absolutely futureless. And lastly, nature considers 'interdependence', where everything in the world is influenced by something and influences something else – everything is connected to everything ^{read} p.167.225. People are 'Cartesian', thinking and acting in a fragmented way. In other words, there is a lot to learn about how nature produces.

_____ Biomimicry* offers an opportunity to take a major creative shortcut. Nature has been there for 4 billion years in which it has been developing strategies and solutions, both physical and chemical. There is a large and precious source of solutions, information and inspiration available to everyone. These available ideas are already complete, ensuring the slightest environmental impact possible, but with high sensorial impact (something all eco solutions should pursue) and, as if that's not enough, they're also 'copyleft'. The connection between biomimicry and sustainability is absolute. There's a flood of biomimicry examples, benchmarks of pure sustainable geniality! It's just a matter of knowing how to mine, because the solutions are all there.

_____ Personally, I love the perspective of pursuing strategic, conceptual and philosophical inspirations, researching how nature deals with a 'briefing'. I also like to expand my horizons, starting with biomimicry which presupposes to mimic nature, to bioinspiration, and also to talk about the 'natural solutions', which includes inspiration by abiotic solutions such as crystals, or processes like atmosphere regulation.

How do you apply biomimicry principles in your work?

Nature is my creative oracle

Biomimicry* was the theme for my graduation project on industrial design. I made it my goal to understand how nature 'packages' things. I studied the planet's atmosphere, fruit peels, and even the uterus as a brilliant package that protects when it needs to protect, and repels when it has to repel the contents. While working on this project 21 years ago, my thoughts were geared towards eco-design, which resulted in the establishment of my design agency Tátil. We were absolute pioneers in the use of recycled materials in packaging and office products. We were constantly disassembling and optimising shapes to guarantee reduction in use of materials and processes. Since then a great deal has happened. Several projects that we undertook were directly inspired by natural solutions, while others were the result of methodology and creative principles completely reasoned by bioinspiration, which is what I like to call biomimetics*. Nature is my creative oracle, where I search for points of view, look to confirm others, and above all, maintain my enchantment for the challenge of creation.

For Natura, the biggest cosmetics company in Brazil and our major client, we have used biomimicry in different approaches. From inspirational sources, to shapes and principles of packaging, and even to strategic inspirations for projects and relationships with communities in the Amazon Rainforest. A lot of these projects are still happening and are being conducted in secrecy. We are currently working on a project in partnership with Janine Benyus' Biomimicry Guild _read_ p.33 on the packaging and transportation of liquids. This project is still in an exploratory research phase. In conjunction with the Guild, our biologists are undertaking an in-depth study of different species which deals with the question: 'How does nature contain liquids?' We have received an incredible report from the Guild listing 30 different potential examples to create packaging for Natura's cosmetics, which is a great source of information and inspiration. We expect that in learning and understanding the species' characteristics, we will discover how nature solves packaging challenges in general and extract some specific solutions to specific problems.

We have also been developing exploratory projects about various themes that function as creative 'provocations' for several of our stockholders. Flowers, for example, have incredible strategies for generating sensory traps _read_ p.117. We made some analogies between the different involvement strategies developed by flowers for their differing 'clients', and the projects we develop on 'experience design'. Flowers can serve as an innovative marketing case. When imagining that Earth has existed for a single year, proportionally flowers would have evolved only about 4 hours ago and would already be an essential part of the planet. When translating this thought into a brand case, this would mean that a new brand could 'entice' the entire world in a very short amount of time. Flowers also invite many others to participate in vegetal reproduction (pollination) such as birds and insects. One could imagine a business model where these others are professionals in various fields who could be made stockholders. Flowers have different strategies for differing 'clients': for moths, the flowers open up at night and are white so as to illuminate in the dark, while for the bats, the flowers are large, resistant and very fragrant. This approach could be applied to one of our clients' stores, creating sensory traps.

There's also a project about how nature 'does business', which has been developed in partnership with FGV (Fundação Getulio Vargas, the largest business school in Brazil). This project is also still 'work in progress'. We are studying ecosystems*, looking at the different types of ecological relationships as benchmarks which include new sustainable business models. We believe that a nature-inspired business is very effective.

Do clients contact you specifically because of your biomimic approach?

_____ An involvement with the theme generates a lot of curiosity and interest. But there are only a few people who are really interested and who also have the intention of acquiring the services of a consulting agency in this area. However, things are starting to change and we already having a biologist on our team. We will shortly be opening a laboratory to conduct regular researches on biomimetics*. This will happen in partnership with some of our clients, and also with research institutions such as the PUC-Rio and the Botanic garden of Rio de Janeiro.

How can creative professionals participate?

_____ The first step for creative professionals in all areas should be to understand the perspective of biomimicry* as a source of inspiration. I have given many lectures in Brazil as well as abroad, and have seen this theme resounding to most people. There is a lack of knowledge and naturally it is of fundamental importance that more courses are opened to bring about the multidisciplinary character of the theme.

FRED GELLI

Fred Gelli graduated in product and graphic design from the PUC-Rio (Pontifícia Universidade Católica do Rio de Janeiro). In the year 1990, when he was still a student, he started the branding and design agency Tátil design de ideias, which he runs today as the founding partner and creative director. In 1999, Gelli became a professor at the PUC-Rio and has been teaching a biomimetics course in the industrial design department since 2008. 'I'm in love with the idea that design is a powerful tool in the big creative challenge that we have ahead of us, which is simply to redesign our occupational logic on this planet.'

LET'S DISCUSS IT WITH

MARINE JACQUES-LEFLAIVE AND EMMANUEL DUPONT

ECODYNAMIC ARCHITECTS, FOUNDERS OF ATELIERZÉROCARBONE ARCHITECTES

What led you to ecology?

_____ M: We come from families who have been working with biodynamics in agriculture for several years. Their acquired knowledge – a way of working with and looking at nature – have been passed on to us. We have assumed the term 'ecodynamic'* in the ecological sense, but above all in the sense of an always dynamic relationship with nature, the materials and the client. There should be a relationship that is continuously on the move. The notion of movement is essential in our architecture. That's a neologism, yet to us it's historical, coming from a family heritage where there's a desire to extend it in construction. To us it's a normal approach to a project, not a special thing but a 'given'. It's part of the basic elements of the project and it's part of the financial aspects. It has nothing to do with fashion or pleasing people, it's part of our very being. We just do it, that's all there is to it.

View of the vineyards in Puligny-Montrachet from la maison du Pot de Fer, designed by AtelierZéroCarbone Architects in 2011.
© AtelierZéroCarbone

As far as your education goes, is this dimension an integral part of it?

_____ M: During our studies there were absolutely no courses on ecology*.

_____ E: That's right, taking an interest in this field was always a personal thing on the part of the students. It was certainly not a 'given'.

_____ M: The school of Architecture taught us other things. We learned to open our minds. We were certainly not given any ecological tools or a global outlook on our relationship with nature. But today, colleges are doing it more and more.

_____ E: That would be because that's where the market is.

_____ M: Yes, part of the market is there now. The ecology trend has opened up opportunities for people who have been interested in the subject for a long time. There is also a downside to the 'trend' aspect, which is that there are people who have a sudden interest, who learn on the job and who don't always do things consistently – as opposed to those who have been involved for a long time and have made it an integral part of their entire approach. But that can't be helped, that's how it works with trends. The pioneers are not necessarily well-known. For example, the French architect Bernard Mainguy and the British architect Bill Dunster – both rather involved and very experienced – dug the ditches and a generation later, gave us the opportunity to work correctly by following in their footsteps. By becoming aware of the possibilities and being convinced of the added value and necessity, it becomes unacceptable to work on projects that don't correspond with these ethics. The pioneers had many problems because they didn't have many opportunities to do exactly what they wanted to do, there was a great financial risk. Nowadays, it's a lot easier.

What do you think of the relationship between man and nature?

M: There's always a link, obviously because we're part of it, but this link seems to have been forgotten.

E: It hasn't been forgotten, we've become distant. I'm quite sure that the world is trying to go in the right direction but we've lost the connection with what has to be done.

M: Society disconnects us completely from nature, from a rhythm of nature, from a relationship with simple things, the sources of wonder. Nature is felt in a subtle, calm and conscious way but doesn't play a major part in our society today where it's all about the extraordinary, the wow! factor. There is an urge to get closer to nature but the journey is certainly going to be long. Man's distance from nature has been quite severe for over 50 years. Personally, we spend a lot of time walking, deciding on designs, discussing ideas and organising our week. It's a very simple thing but it's an interesting time with nature.

Would you say that nature is the best 'industry' there is?

E: I find it odd to say that nature is an industry. It's magnificent, but it's not an industry. It doesn't make any products. It's something that's changing all the time, it's in motion. Nothing is immutable. An industry has a goal: to make a profit and to keep people content. Nature does everything for itself, it doesn't have a specific aim. However, it is incredibly well-organised.

M: That's exactly it, it's fundamentally well-organised.

E: And above all, everything remains to be discovered, we don't really know anything yet.

M: There's infinite wealth and it's completely autonomous. For me, the most pleasing thing about the ecosystem* is that it has taken autonomy to perfection. There's constant movement with slow adaptation.

E: Nature is more than just plants and animals, there's a rhythm, there's the cosmos, the Earth. There are many other more subtle things involved, such as energy.

M: Our relationship with nature, to a large extent, is based on energy. There are plenty of subtle dimensions that exist today that still remain undiscovered, but which influence both the architecture and agriculture just as they influence medicine and man. We should take them into account.

How do you deal with nature and sustainability in your work?

E: Our architectural projects have to function, they have to be consistent in their concepts, in their design and in their spatial organisation. It's a conceptual approach which starts at a very early stage with the client. We are very technical in respect of the materials or energy strategies that we're going to use.

M: We think that a building is a living organism which constantly interacts with the needs of the inhabitants and the environment that it's in. That's the basis of our designs. We work closely with the client and research their way of life, how they feel about it, and what changes in their personal life. So there's a lot of preparatory work and then there's work on the environment in which a house is placed. The house is in effect a skin between the inhabitant and the environment. Our role as architects is to articulate these two objective constraints, these two parameters, to provide something alive in the materials sense, but also on a technical scale. By the word technical we mean simplicity, we're not going to make a gas factory. Our aim is to make something very simple, which approaches nature in the make-up of a wall or a roof, that gets as close as possible to the way nature functions, that's to say naturally. It self-regulates and self-adapts to different climate changes _read_ p.231. The technology that we put in place will either allow the inhabitants, with the aim of full autonomy, or at least medium autonomy, to generate power in situ. This can be achieved by having an autonomous house, like the one we were involved in at the French commune Puligny-Montrachet. This house has transpiring walls and largely works with nature: in the design sense, not only in its composition, in its colours and in its changes, but also at a technical level, because the people who live in it feel very strongly about this. It was actually necessary to screen all the internal electrical wiring so that the inhabitants could feel comfortable about that _see_ Photo p.255. Another example is a design that we're currently working on: a wine cellar in the shape of an egg with an extruded vault. We think that the people who are having this built are portraying the idea of going into a protective egg. The idea of a relationship with the shape of the building appeals to us, the shape that you have in your head and the energy which can influence the place. It's not that we're trying to do it each time but it just happened very naturally. This cellar is going to be above ground because the water table in Burgundy is very high. We are trying to make this a passive above-ground cellar, a rather important objective, because in Burgundy there's a huge consumption of electricity involved in providing cellars with air-conditioning and keeping them cool throughout the year. We're aiming as much as possible for a passive building within our technical capabilities and in the warmer periods solar-powered air-conditioning will cool it down. All the energy needed will always be provided by resources such as wind, wood or solar _read_ p.113.153. To achieve this we're working with a building-energy specialist, a heating engineer and a wood engineer. They are extremely intelligent people who have a special philosophy and are very focused on the objectives instead of the constraints. This notion of constraints and objectives is very important to us. Abroad they talk about objectives and in France we talk about constraints. The idea is always to aim high and to do the utmost with the objectives that the environment imposes on us.

We think that a building is a living organism which constantly interacts with the needs of the inhabitants and the environment that it's in

Do your clients contact you because of your 'sustainable' approach?

_____ M: Most people don't have big budgets but they all want ecological buildings – which are obviously more expensive. There is a price difference between breeze-blocks and glass wool and between wood and natural wood fibres. Using natural products also takes time. Conceptualising projects with international companies does allow us to cut costs. We end up working with foreign products that are not certified in France. This is something which is still novel in France today, except for certain types of highly-specialised projects with rather advanced technical specifications. But we're doing it for all projects and in general things go well. Some clients approach us because they've always dreamed of a bio-something-or-other, and they put their trust in us. There are also those who are extremely passionate and really know what they want. I admit that most people who consult us have a yearning for wood and for a very advanced environmental quality. They are not necessarily looking for certification, which is why they're very interesting for us, because certification causes constraints. It pushes us into a mould that is not necessarily consistent with the life of the inhabitant or the environment.

Certification guides people, it gives them some basic rules, but I think that we're looking for something else, other ways of thinking about buildings, other ways of seeing energy strategies. It therefore gives us great pleasure when people don't necessarily want certification. France is mainly focused on energy consumption. It's possible to make polystyrene buildings with a very low consumption while elsewhere they rather consider things from a progressive perspective. Usually, one ensures a house is well-constructed with sound materials, that it fits the budgetary envelope and is suitable for family life. Some energy-consuming equipment from renewable sources is also possibly installed. Foreign governments propose progressive solutions which have crosswise objectives. You can't build a low-energy consumption polystyrene house with energy-consuming equipment, because the 'lowest' criterion is to have a house made of sound materials that doesn't consume too much water, which gives a feeling of well-being and has a certain percentage of natural light. In France there are no criteria in respect of water, well-being, materials, transport, food, etc. Although there is the HQE (high environmental quality) approach, one only needs to comply with certain points and may disregard the others. That's not of much interest. What is interesting is to work with many 'cursors'. You can't have one cursor at maximum and another at the bottom, with an environmental objective all the cursors should go up simultaneously. This results in a global ecological scene which is extremely interesting. Like nature it's global, a systemic approach where everything is interdependent. The parameters are flexible and there is no single solution. All the notions and the lessons that nature teaches us, form the basis, the ancestral basis that we have to re-appropriate for ourselves. We do it gently, we sometimes fear that countries can take decisions that scare us a bit, but it's a question of time. Nature takes the exact amount of time it needs.

_____ E: It takes time to do it. We are happy when clients have the time, even if they don't have a lot of money, if they have the time then that's ok.

_____ M: We've noticed that time is unbelievably beneficial to a project. This parameter is often neglected. Rhythm is involved in nature. There are seasons and there is a minimum 'gestation' period. It's the same for an architectural project. The problem is that we always have to find a balance between the time which should be taken and the time that must be taken to remain financially viable.

How do you think creative professionals can actually participate in such a sustainable movement?

_____ E: Again you have to make sure that all these ecological concepts are a 'given'. It shouldn't have to be forced.

_____ M: Perhaps creative people should put the ecological question at the forefront. It must be intrinsically linked to the product.

_____ E: I think that's precisely it, but it's a long way off. I think that the day will come when it's absolutely normal to use only renewable resources, to have sustainable things, to take our time, to use sound materials and with a bit of luck, we'll get there.

_____ M: We are in a transitionary period. The connection with nature must be made again, so that it becomes normal and you no longer have to pose this question.

_____ E: Today's generation is really starting to act. In our circle of friends and colleagues, there are plenty of people who are not specifically into ecology*, but who certainly think about these issues.

_____ M: We have a phenomenon where ecologists no longer call themselves ecologists. They're afraid of being labelled, which takes away their integrity. That's extremely painful for sincere, honest people who are trying very hard to do intelligent things, without seeking publicity, without constantly trying to be in the limelight. It's not easy to find the right balance between communicating and yet remaining serene and moderate. You have to guide yourself towards being restrained.

_____ E: And above all you shouldn't be too extremist.

_____ M: Yes, being an extremist ecologist is also a danger. For example, when we are on a building location at an isolated site, we're obliged to take measures for safety reasons, such as extra batteries. This is the first thing that people take offence to, because at a given moment, we're not absolute extremists. Yet we cannot put people in danger. There's always a serene balance to be found. Nothing is bad in small doses, but everything depends on what you do with it, how you use things. What is of importance today, is to go as far as possible within the financial capabilities. That's already a huge step. There are people who are not aware yet of the slightly better materials that are around nowadays . What is important is to guide people towards the possibilities. There's a lot of theory and many publications, but I admit we spend a lot of time exploring different accomplishments, but that's what we enjoy.

Is there something you find especially fascinating in nature?

_____ E: Everything!

_____ M: Nature's consistency and simplicity. It handles a paradox, it is simultaneously violent and gentle, like us. And yet it endures in all its fascinating autonomy. Then there is nature's ability to adapt, to react. In all sorts of ways we are part of nature. We also manage to adapt ourselves, but in a very drastic way. We are in an ecosystem* where we are constrained. There's not much room for personal expression and innovation, no place for different forms of human relationships. We're in a pyramidal hierarchy, which imposes harsh living conditions on many people. Our way of life in Europe today is dependent on poverty in the southern hemisphere. I'm not sure that we are being consistent in terms of nature if we speak of humanity.

_____ E: What fascinates me is the rhythm of the seasons. In Burgundy we're surrounded by vineyards and we're lucky that here in Europe we actually have four seasons. It's very pronounced in Burgundy. It changes all the time and by the same token it comes back every year. It's magic. The vineyards are brilliant in that they truly react to the seasons. It's something which actually gives my life a tempo. I need to take part in the grape harvest every year.

_____ M: It's absolutely essential. To live in this sea of vines which continuously changes in colour, is a stroke of luck for me and I'm very aware of it.

MARINE JACQUES-LEFLAIVE AND EMMANUEL DUPONT

The duo that make-up AtelierZéroCarbone Architectes like to call themselves 'ecodynamic'* architects. Both graduated from the École Spéciale d'Architecture in Paris in 2006. Shortly after graduating, they decided to broaden their horizons and went to London. Marine Jacques-Leflaive spent 4 years working at the ZEDfactory agency on designs for the BedZED community (an eco-village in Wallington, South London). Emmanuel Dupont worked at a Sino-Japanese agency and taught at Oxford Brookes University for 3 years. Today, both are involved in education and do cutting-edge research into the ecological and performance aspects of buildings.

LET'S DISCUSS IT WITH

MATHIEU LEHANNEUR

INDUSTRIAL DESIGNER, SINCE 1974

How do you describe your design approach?

_____ It's very difficult to try to describe an approach. My concern is that from the moment you describe it, even without getting locked into it, it eventually becomes a constraint. I prefer the notion of paying attention to something, rather than having an approach to it. To me this attention and this sensitivity means envisaging human beings as they really are, which is indeed without ever idealising, without ever objectifying and without ever 'ergonomising', but by their contradictory reality, seeing that they are unstable, incoherent, passionate and so disappointing. To see humans as an animal species, neither better nor worse than other animal species, nevertheless a species which deserves one's interest and deserves that one finds answers, in the profound reality of this species.

_____ Human beings are very varied in many respects: with geographic, cultural and economic diversity, but human beings today are not very different from the cavemen. People practically have the same fantasies, the same needs, the same urges, whether sexual, warlike or whatever. There really is no evolution in that sense and therefore there is no real diversity. Most people have a heart that works fairly well and a brain which works fairly well and they're all bombarded with information, from the cave to the megalopolis. The brain operates like a filter, it lets in some information and puts aside the remaining 99.9%. It is governed by stimuli, urges. What interests me is how a designer looks into this living material.

Why do several of your projects interact with the scientific domain?

_____ It's not luck or a desire, it's a necessity. From the moment that one settles on the question of seeing human beings for what they are and generally in an objective quest for truth, it is science which is the discipline most likely to unravel this human being, and attempts to see how it functions in an objective perhaps dispassionate way. I therefore use science as a revealing, deciphering tool. I have no particular fascination with science, I don't project onto it a mission which, in my opinion, it would not necessarily have and which would be a sort of potential for improvement, but it's a decoder. I use it in quite a meticulous way, at precise moments in a project when I'm going to validate hypotheses or oppose them. In fact I only take information when I know that I can do something with it. From the information that is available to me, or at any rate the little that I can understand in the many domains covered, I only take a tiny percentage.

_____ The projects that I've focused on while I've had the VIA Carte Blanche grant, explore the interaction between the human body and it's environment. One of my researches involved the influence of light on the body through the brain's perception. My main contact at that time was an aerospace doctor in the Air Force, who gave me access to his lab, including his tests on human guinea pigs. He was doing research on the capacity for optimising fighter-pilot concentration during missions in wartime. An extremely pragmatic, real thing. The question of light as a potential drug generated by our own bodies interested me. Some of the knowledge acquired during the research, was modified and applied in a project. The result was K, a device that tracks the quantity of daylight a person receives and then emits the additional quantity needed, because lack of daylight can cause low energy.

_____ For project O, I was looking for a way to produce pure oxygen* in houses. For various reasons, 95% of houses have a lack of oxygen. I had not initially planned on arriving at an integration of natural elements. When I searched for elements in the market for the production of pure oxygen, I finally came across spirulina, an organism which appeared in different publications as the best oxygen generator in nature <u>read</u> p.185. Although some experiments were about to be carried out, they were in fields which were quite distant from design. So I contacted two spirulina producers to find out the specific requirements of this species: what would be needed in the way of light to trigger movement and how could I make an optimum use of the 'material'? The result was a device that monitors the oxygen level in the air and optimises it by activating a light, with the spirulina inside triggering photosynthesis*. Dogs and cats are already being domesticated as friendly decorative accessories, but the 'O' device is even more radical. It's a form of instrumentalisation. Nature is not used as a decoration here, but as a component. Where one could speak of an electronic component, this one's a natural component. For a computer a microprocessor is needed, in order to get oxygen, spirulina can be used. So both are used in a similar manner.

Element O, designed by M. Lehanneur
© Véronique Huyghe

*I use science
when I feel that
it provides added
value to the project*

_____ I use science when I feel that it provides added value to the project. That is sometimes necessary to reach my goals. Regarding the different projects mentioned before, I was the one who approached the scientists so that they could provide me with some training in the fields of pharmaceuticals, astrophysics, botany, etc. What is starting to happen, and what is quite encouraging, is that nowadays there's also demand from the opposite direction. The scientific world has developed a need for design in chemistry. In practical terms design allows applications to be discovered for ongoing research. Sometimes, it's not even necessary to wait for research to be completed before starting to think about applications. It's rather interesting to see how, at strategic points in time, the search for applications can slightly modify research. The arrival of design in these fields also constitutes a motivation for researchers, as their work then takes shape. These are significant times.

How do you see the relationships between man and nature?

_____ From the time that people were living in caves, there's not only been an instinctive and inherent desire for domination, but there's also been submission. It's a continuing game: 'I'm submitting to you but I'm going to try and dominate you; I like you, but above all I'm going to try to have power over you'. This is noticeable in the way people relate to nature.

_____ I live in a city, so I don't see nature very much. A city is a sort of degenerate nature. Nature, which isn't necessarily all green, is a construction of things which is not planned by human beings, things in development, things which have a logic to them. Some see it as coming from God, others see it as a result of evolution but in all cases, life as it appears today, is a planned mode of construction, urbanised with an objective. And nature has objectives but they're not always the ones that humans want. Nature is complex and it's difficult for designers to get into this complexity. It develops unbelievable, fascinating strategies and people don't even get close to achieving this complexity. This is where one runs into risks of simplification.

_____ As far as understanding these phenomena at work in nature goes, people are somewhat in the dark. Take a project like the living air purifier 'Andrea' for example, which exploits the filtering properties of plants. As a first approach, I remained in the 'green', thinking that this filtering power of plants resided in their leaves. After some research, I finally realised that the filtering capabilities of plants are in the roots, where there is an exchange system which is invisible to man. This points out one of the problems with designers: they are full of 'green' projects but only 'see' what is before their eyes *, without exploring all the dimensions present in nature.

Andrea, designed by M. Lehanneur
© Véronique Huyghe

Your Local River design is an actual ecosystem. What triggered you to do this project?

_____ This project originated from the human being's connection with food, one of the closest ties between man and nature, since it is linked to survival. 'I feed on you', still constitutes a dominant relationship, but for survival.

_____ The starting point for the project was the question of how people can reconnect with reality. It's about getting back into the ecosystem* from which man has emerged <u>*read*</u> p.167. The Local River helps people to become aware of the interdependence between the species, making them part of it.

Local River, designed by M. Lehanneur
© Véronique Huyghe

The project consists of a tank that can be placed in one's living room and can hold live freshwater fish for consumption. The tank is topped off with vegetable patches, the roots of which purify the water by extracting nutrients from the nitrate-rich dejecta of the fish. The Local River is an extremely basic ecosystem since there are two entities in it – when man intervenes there are three – but otherwise there are only two: fish and plants, which live with an exchange of good, non-aggressive techniques. 'Little fish, I filter your water for you, kind plant that I am, but in exchange I'm going to feed on your excretions'. This is how two things live in harmony, not fraternal but cohabiting.

Having completed this series of projects linked to nature, are you now perceived as a 'green' designer?

_____ In fact, no. Satisfaction lies in the fact that these projects have not been perceived as 'environmentalist' projects, but as odes or tributes to nature. They have been of as much interest to the environmentalist gardener as to the most technoid geek. Each finds something there and that interests me because, without necessarily being at these two extremes, people are on this continuous round-trip, totally connected to nature while nevertheless going off in their 4x4s at the weekend. There's something inconsistent there. Also the clients who approach me don't come asking 'give me some plants, give me some green'. There are of course clients who want to be seen as green, but they're a minority. Even if their problems are very different, the common factor among my clients is that they are interested in the way in which the problems are tackled.

What do you think of initiatives such as the creation of the asknature.org website?

——————— I have to be wary of how I feel about these sites, in exactly the same way that I have to be wary of materials libraries, these are incredible tools if one knows what one is looking for. There is a risk of visiting such a site without any specific idea in mind, thinking of finding something there to get ideas. However, the answers that are provided there are quite simplistic and immediate, such as 'taking some material and making a table out of it'. The first step should be to set an objective and then after outlining what exactly to look for, the sites can be used as a tool. Producing oxygen* is all very well, but how, for what purpose and for whom? These websites are technical resolution tools and the solutions are very context-related.

What is the role of designers in today's context?

——————— I don't feel that I've got a role or a mission. I find all that sort of thing rather pretentious, to feel as an agent with a mission, leading people to another view or in another direction. Designers often say that they want to make things to change behaviour. Who are designers to change anybody's behaviour? Moreover, behaviour is never changed in that sense. I prefer the notion of bringing attention to things rather than having a mission or a role. What a designer can bring to the table, phrased so well by Paola Antonelli, is 'a flexible mind'. Reasoning and the answer, don't necessarily go via a linear way of thinking or development and are not even interested in going that way. There is a difference between Euclidean geometry which proposes that the shortest route is a straight line, and the space-time geometry of astrophysics which proposes that this is not bound to be the case. It is certain that the designer's way of thinking, being that of a creative person in comparison with the scientific world, or with scientific knowledge, or with scientific discipline, is to reason by linking things which were not linked. Thinking around a curve, elliptical thinking which deliberately sets aside some elements of knowledge to attach them to others. This allows the weaving together of things which, on paper, were obviously not able to be woven together. This then allows for creation and if that succeeds, the creation of things which scientific reasoning would not necessarily have led to. In that sense, the designer is not an inventor but is able to relate disparate elements, and perhaps play a role. But as for projects where nature could say 'not bad!', there aren't many of them.

The designer's way of thinking is to reason by linking things which were not linked

MATHIEU LEHANNEUR

Based in Paris, Mathieu Lehanneur heads his own design agency called Since 1974 (which refers to the year he was born). Many of his product designs are related to the world of science such as his Therapeutic Objects in 2001, a number of design proposals for medications from the patient or the illness perspective. In 2006, with the Carte Blanche grant by VIA (Valorization of Innovation in Furnishing), he designed Elements; five items of which the O was the oxygen generator, for example. In the same year, Lehanneur received the Paris Design Grand Prix Award. For his Bel Air project, an air-filtering system based on properties of plants, he received the Best Invention Award from Popular Science in 2008. Several of his projects feature in the permanent collection of the Museum of Modern Art in New York.

What a designer can bring to the table, phrased so well by Paola Antonelli, is 'a flexible mind'

Mathieu Lehanneur

GLOSSARY *

A

Acetylcholine The first neurotransmitter* ever to be identified (around 1914) is a chemical compound playing an essential transmitting role in many neural synapses*. Acetylcholine (ACh) can be found in both human and animal systems. _read_   Neuron and p.159

Action potential In physiology, an action potential describes a furtive rise and decrease of the electrical membrane potential of a cell. The action potential follows a consistent trajectory. Action potentials can be identified on several types of cells, animal cells such as neurons* or muscles cells for instance, as well as plant cells. They play a key role in the circulation of information between cells and, within muscles cells, an action potential triggers the chain of events leading to contraction. _read_   p.81.159

Aerobic metabolism An aerobic metabolism* needs oxygen* to survive, whereas an anaerobic metabolism is able to survive without oxygen. _read_   p.83

Aerodynamic noise Noise created by airflows passing an object (such as an aircraft). _read_   p.181

Aerodynamics In physics, fluid dynamics is a sub-discipline of fluid mechanics that deals with fluid flow – the science of fluids (liquids and gases) in motion. It has several sub-disciplines itself, including aerodynamics (the study of air and other gases in motion) and hydrodynamics* (the study of liquids in motion). Aerodynamics is very useful for analysing and improving the movement of vehicles in air (automobiles, trains, aircraft) and the operation of propulsion systems (gas turbines, airscrews) and also for evaluation of the effects of air flow over static objects such as buildings, or to calculate the performance of wind turbines. A body is said to be aerodynamic when it moves through the air with minimal resistance, by limiting the frictional forces inherent in such movement. _read_   p.21.24.73.99.125

Amino acid They are molecules* whose key elements are carbon, hydrogen, oxygen* and nitrogen. One of their functions in metabolism* is to ensure protein* existence, proteins being linear chains of amino acids. There are more than a hundred different amino acids in existence but only 22 are actually enclosed within the living organism's genome*. Eight amino acids are essential to humans because they cannot be created directly by the human body and is found in food. _read_   p.129

Anisotropic _read_   Isotropic and p.175

Anthropisation The conversion of natural environments by human action. _read_   p.21.31

Aragonite A natural crystal formation of calcium carbonate*. Aragonite can either make up part of a mollusc's shell, or in some cases form the entire shell. Aragonite also appears in caves, on the seabed and in the endoskeleton of corals. _read_   p.213

Automimicry Refers to members of a species trying to resemble other members of the same species. Defenceless males of some bees for example, resemble females and therefore are protected from predators who believe they are equipped with stingers. _read_   p.16

Autotroph Autotroph organisms often are the first link of a food chain, providing organic matter to a whole ecosystem*, as they are able to produce it from inorganic sources such as carbon, for instance. Plants (via photosynthesis*) and some bacteria* are autotroph organisms. They do not need other living organisms to survive. On the contrary, heterotroph* organisms – animals and mushrooms – need organic matter to survive. _read_   p.113

Auxin A chemical that causes and regulates plant growth, also known as plant hormones. Auxins have the ability to induce cell elongation. _read_   p.145

Axon The axon is the thin long extension of a nervous cell. Information (action potentials*) circulate through the whole cell from its dendrites (smaller extensions) to the end of the axon through the cell's nucleus*. Synaptic* zones are located at the end of the axon. _read_   p.159

B

Bacteria Unicellular living organisms which develop very rapidly and exist in very large numbers. The human body for example has more bacteria than number of cells. The majority are harmless, often beneficial. Some, however, are pathogenic and carriers of infectious diseases which can be fatal (cholera, plague, tuberculosis, etc.). Certain bacteria are very useful: to make cheeses, yoghurts or bread, to treat sewage, to replace pesticides or extract metals from mineral ores (the latter process known as biolixiviation). _read_   p.26.30.40.57.61.75.131.137.167.169. 205.207.225

Bio-assisted technology Utilising living organisms or biological processes to acquire or manufacture products, like keeping spirulina to produce oxygen*. _read_   p.40

Biocenose The set of living organisms (animal and plant) constituting a given ecosystem. _read_   Biotope and Ecosystem

Biodegradable A material is biodegradable if it can be degraded by living organisms. Only organic matter (thus containing carbon) can be decomposed back into natural elements by micro-organisms. The time it takes these organisms to break down the material varies, a piece of paper is degraded much quicker than a piece of leather. _read_   p.40.61.71

Biodiversity The degree of variety in living organisms is called biodiversity. Today biodiversity is critically endangered as rates of decline in what is called 'the sixth mass extinction' match or exceed the rates of loss in the five previous mass extinction events in the fossil record. Biodiversity should be ensured and therefore, right now, it should be strongly protected, as it is key to the ecosystems* survival. This book offers a glimpse of what living organisms are able to achieve and, from a selfish, human point of view and self-preservation reflex, biodiversity is essential as a guarantee of keeping an inspirational reservoir for our future developments. _read_   p.10.21.25.30. 39.43.44.48.52

Biofuel Biofuel (solid, liquid or gaseous) is fuel derived from biological material from living or dead organisms, such as vegetable oil-based diesel. _read_   Fossil fuel and p.54.111

Biomimetics _read_   Biomimicry, Bionics and p.15.17.18.19. 22.23.24.25.26.28.31.33.49.54.79.185.252.253

Biomimicry Biomimicry (sometimes known as bionics* and biomimetics*, among other names) is the study and mimicking of nature to solve human problems. This term has been popularised by Janine Benyus after she published her book in 1997, _Biomimicry: Innovation Inspired by Nature._ _read_   Janine Benyus' interview on p.33 and p.9.17.22. 49.59.171.251.252.253.281

Bionics Even if biomimetics*, biomimicry* and bionics all relate to the idea of being inspired by nature, there are slight subtle differences between these words. Bionics is closely linked to the engineering of artificial mechanic or electronic equipments. _read_   p.18.24.33.149.281

Biosphere A planetary system including all the living organisms and the milieus in which they live, thus encompassing all ecosystems*. _read_   p.21.31.44.281

Biotechnology The United Nations Convention on Biological Diversity defines biotechnology as: 'Any technological application that uses biological systems, living organisms, or derivatives thereof, to make or modify products or processes for specific use.' (Source: _Convention on Biological Diversity_, Article 2, Use of Terms, 1992) _read_   p.21.25

Biotope A biological milieu providing a stable environment for a biocenose*. _read_   Ecosystem and p.53.167

Bio-utilisation The use of parts of organisms as raw materials, such as building a house from wood. _read_ p.40.171.185

Blood A liquid tissue which can act conjunctively and is present in the majority of animals. Human blood consists of 55% blood plasma which contains water, glucose*, lipids*, proteins* (among them fibrin* which forms fibres during coagulation), hormones and 45% elements such as red corpuscles containing haemoglobin (responsible for the red colour) which can carry oxygen* and carbon dioxide*; white corpuscles acting for the individual's immune system to destroy infectious agents and platelets (thrombocytes) which are responsible for initiating blood coagulation. Blood transports the oxygen which is indispensable for the functioning and survival of the cells, as well as the carbon dioxide which will be rejected. In man, blood represents about 7% of the body mass. _read_ Carbohydrate, pH, Vasoconstriction and p.26.63.83.85.105.121.143 .177.199.205

Byssus A system of flexible adhesive filaments made from protein*, secreted by mussels to attach themselves to rocks or other mussels. _read_   p.69

C

Calcium carbonate A common chemical compound, which chemical formula involves calcium, carbon and oxygen*, found in rocks. It is one of the main components of sea shells, snails and pearls and is also used in agricultural lime as well as a medicinal calcium supplement. Excessive consumption can however, be hazardous. _read_   p.215

Carbohydrate Carbohydrates are also called saccharides (in short 'sugars') and they play many key roles in living organisms, among other things, being the major source of fuel for metabolism*. There are different types of carbohydrates. For example, blood* sugar is the monosaccharide glucose*, table sugar is the disaccharide sucrose, and milk sugar is the disaccharide lactose. *read* p.18.103.111. 225

Carbon dioxide Carbon dioxide (CO_2) is a chemical compound. It is a colourless, odourless, incombustible gas at standard temperature and pressure, existing within Earth's atmosphere and representing approximately 0.04% of it. Through photosynthesis*, plants (as well as algae and cyanobacteria*) absorb carbon dioxide, sunlight and water to produce carbohydrate* energy for themselves and oxygen* as a waste product. During respiration, though, they emit carbon dioxide, as do all other living things that depend either directly or indirectly on plants for food. Carbon dioxide is also generated as a byproduct of combustion; emitted from volcanoes; and freed from carbonate rocks by dissolution. It is the most important greenhouse gas produced by human activities, primarily through the combustion of fossil fuels*, which means that it keeps some of the Sun's energy from radiating back into space. Its concentration in the Earth's atmosphere has risen by more than 30% since the Industrial Revolution. It is used in food refrigeration, carbonated beverages, inert atmospheres, fire extinguishers and aerosols, for instance. *read* p.37.40.113.185.199.225

Carbon footprint A carbon footprint expresses the impact on the environment of certain products, activities, groups or individuals by measuring the amount of emitted greenhouse gases (often reported as its carbon dioxide* equivalent). *read* p.53

Cell motility A cell's ability to move spontaneously and actively. *read* p.18.26

Cellulose An organic compound made by plants for strength and structure. It is mainly used for the production of paper and textile or as a thickening agent. *read* p.175.231

Chlorophyll A pigment in plants which intercepts light energy, thus triggering the series of reactions that are involved in photosynthesis*. Chlorophyll is also responsible for the green colour of plants. The spectrum of chlorophyll's luminous radiation absorption is such that green is the wavelength least absorbed and therefore the most easily seen by our eyes* when light falls on a plant. *read* Chloroplast and p.113

Chloroplast Chloroplasts are organelles, specialised subunits, found in the cytoplasm of cells in some plants. Among other things, they contain chlorophyll*. *read* p.113

Chromatophore Cells found on the skins of some amphibians, fish, crustaceans or cephalopods. There are various types of chromatophores, producing different colour effects under white light, for example, xanthophores (yellow), erythrophores (red), iridophores* (reflexive and iridescent* effect), leucophores* (white), melanophores (black/brown) and cyanophores (blue). *read* p.93.235

Chromosome Chromosomes are found inside a living organism's cell nucleus*, carrying all the genetic material. A chromosome is made out of DNA* and proteins*. Their number varies depending on the species. For instance, humans have 23 pairs of chromosomes per cell's nucleus, flies have 10 pairs, cows 60 and ferns 1200. *read* p.19.157

Climate refugee A person forced to migrate because of an environmental disaster that is caused by global warming*. *read* p.52.91

Collagen Collagen is a group of proteins* found exclusively in animals, especially in the flesh of mammals, making up to 35% of their whole body protein content. Collagen has a fibrous structure, it is composed of elongated fibrils and can be found in tendons, ligaments, bones, guts, cornea and skin for example. *read* p.69.119

Commensalism A close relationship between two species, where one species benefits and the other is not harmed or helped. *read* Symbiosis and p.223

Composite material A material made out of several types of components. The term often designates semi-finished products made out of a resin matrix and a reinforcement material such as glass, carbon or Kevlar® fibres, but it also refers to any material made out of a 'sandwich' of various layers, bringing resistance to the whole. Composite materials are based on the idea of 1+1 = 3, taking advantage of each constituent quality to create high performance marriages. *read* p.175.177.215

Conchiolin A fibrous protein* forming the basic layer of mollusc shells. The main component of mother-of-pearl, the iridescent* inner layer of some shells. *read* p.213

Copolymer A polymer result of an assembly of two or more different types of monomers. Polymers are plastic materials. The synthetic rubber used to make tyre treads and shoe soles, for instance, is a copolymer made of the monomers butadiene and styrene. *read* p.217

Cryptobiosis Triggered by extreme environmental conditions, the metabolism* of an organism can come to a halt, allowing the organism to survive. This death-like state can last indefinitely. When the conditions allow the metabolism to start again, the organism 'comes back to life'. *read* p.193

D

Deep Ecology A holistic philosophical approach to ecology* that recognises the inherent worth* of all living things and the Earth as a whole. *read* p.45.47

Density The density of a liquid or solid body is the ratio between the density of this body and the density of the reference being pure water at 4 °C at atmospheric pressure, namely 1,000 kg/m³ (62.43 lb/ft³). In the case of gases, the chosen reference is air, at the same temperature and pressure as the relevant gas. A body may be described as heavy when its density exceeds 1 (the reference density of water) and it is therefore not capable of floating on water, for example. *read* p.69.141.165.179

Dermis Collagen-rich* layer of skin that lies between the epidermis* and hypodermis* that holds many nerve ends responsible for the sense of touch and heat. *read* p.205

Dioxygen (O₂) An oxygen* critical-to-life molecule* of gas, constituting 21% of our atmosphere. *read* p.113.199

DNA Abbreviation for deoxyribonucleic acid. It is the carrier of the genetic code in all known organisms. *read* p.19.30.43.157

Domestication Adapting organisms through a process of selection making them more controllable to humans. Examples are the domestication of animals for companionship, domesticating animals for food and labour (livestock) or growing flowers for decoration purposes. *read* p.40

Doppler effect Discovered by the Austrian physicist Christian Doppler (1803–1853), the Doppler effect corresponds to a change in the frequency of waves (such as sound or light) as the source and observer are in motion relative to each other. The faster they come together, the higher the frequency, the faster they move away, the lower the frequency. Doppler effect has many applications: low-earth orbit (LEO) satellites weave towards and away from the Earth for instance, or in reflected radio waves, it is employed in radar to sense the velocity of the object under surveillance. *read* p.101

E

Ecodynamics Ecodynamics aims to relate ecosystems* to evolutionary thermodynamics in order to arrive at satisfactory solutions for sustainable development. *read* p.255.259

Ecology A scientific sub-discipline of biology that studies the interaction between organisms, populations and communities and their relationship to their physical surroundings. *read* p.9.24.31.47.53.167.169.255.258.281.282.284

Ecosophy A neologism, a contraction of 'ecological philosophy'. *read* p.47.284

Ecosystem An area in which a community of organisms interact with their abiotic environment. An ecosystem is the association of a biotope* and its biocenose*. *read* Biosphere and p.18.21.25.30.31.34.47.53.54.167.251.252.256.259.263.281

Elastomer An elastic polymer that is used in the production of car tyres and soles of shoes, among many other things. *read* p.171.205

Elytra A hardened cover protects the wings of certain insects. When the insects take off for flight the cover opens up to reveal and give space to the wings. On some beetles the elytra are fused, rendering them unable to fly. *read* p.147.239

Electromagnetic force A fundamental force that is associated with electric and magnetic fields. This force is responsible for atomic structures, chemical reactions, the attractive and repulsive forces associated with electrical charge and magnetism, and all other electromagnetic phenomena. *read* p.65

Electron Elementary particles carrying a negative electric charge. They can be found in atoms, among neutrons and protons. Their behaviour is still an amazing subject of studies, especially within quantum mechanics*. Electrons are sometimes considered as waves, sometimes as corpuscles. *read* p.37.113.147.157

Electrophysiology Studies the electrical properties of nervous and other bodily activity. For instance, it measures the electrical activities of neurons*, recording the action potentials*. *read* p.30

Emissivity A coefficient which corresponds to the energy emitted by a body in comparison with the energy emitted by the reference 'black body' of physics under the same conditions. The black body in this case is an ideal emitter, which radiates maximum energy whatever the temperature and wavelength considered. The study of the emissivity of materials reveals two main categories: electrically conductive materials generally have low emissivity and electrically insulating materials have high emissivity. The emissivity coefficient is a dimensionless quantity, simply a pure number, with a maximum value of 1 for the reference black body. As a rough guide, metallic silver has an emissivity of about 0.02, while for wood it is 0.90. *read* p.163

Enzyme Enzymes are proteins* that act as catalysts within biochemical reactions. As proteins, they are made out of chains of amino acids*. Their role is essential to life, they operate during digestion, nervous information transmission, hormone synthesis, etc. *read* p.19.111.113.141.169.185

Epidermis The protective top layer of the skin. *read* Dermis, Hypodermis and p.205

Epigenetic factor Something that affects a cell, organ or individual without directly affecting its DNA*. *read* p.17

Ethanol Basically pure alcohol, volatile, flammable and colourless. *read* p.111

Eutrophication Eutrophication takes place when additions of artificial or natural substances, like nitrates or phosphates are made into an aquatic system. The increase of phytoplankton that follows has many negative effects, such as less oxygen* in water, therefore less animals are able to live in such an aquatic environment or, on the contrary, an increase of some species finding the change of conditions to their taste and endangering the existence of others. *read* p.53

Eye An eye can be compared to a video camera connected to a data-processing system. Essentially the eye consists of a cornea, a lens, a pupil and a retina, the latter being connected directly to the brain. The cornea allows surrounding light to enter the eye, the lens changes its curvature to make the adjustments necessary for focusing an image of viewed objects onto the retina, whatever their distance. The closer any objects are to the eye, the more the lens is deformed and the further away the objects are, the more relaxed the lens is towards its resting position. The pupil at the centre of the iris acts like the iris diaphragm in a camera to regulate the amount of light entering the eye, to form an image on the retina. *read* p.9.16.79.81.87.89.97.155.181.235.263

F

Fibrin A fibrous protein* which appears at the moment of blood* coagulation. *read* p.85.205

Fibroin A protein* in silk produced by spiders and silkworms. This material is extremely strong and elastic. *read* Protein and p.217

Formal neuron A formal neuron is a mathematical model simplifying the functioning of a neuron*. Basically, a formal neuron works as a switch: 0 or 1, it conducts information or not. *read* p.25

Formaldehyde Formaldehyde, or methanal, is familiar as formol, a 10% solution of formaldehyde in water. Formaldehyde is a volatile organic compound (VOC) in the family of aldehydes. It has a simple chemical formula, CH_2O. At ambient temperature it is in its inflammable, gaseous state and is evaporated from numerous products: tobacco smoke, candles or incense, various adhesives used in construction materials (plywood panels), furniture or maintenance products. It is classified by the World Health Organisation (WHO) as a carcinogenic compound and is completely banned in some countries. *read* p.69

Fossil fuel Fuel formed by organic remains of prehistoric plants and animals. Examples are coal, petroleum and natural gas. These fuels are non-renewable as the formation of the resources takes millions of years. *read* Biofuel and p.21.31.34.51

Frustule The hard shell of a diatom. *read* p.141

G

Gaia hypothesis The Gaia hypothesis approaches the Earth as a living organism that maintains conditions necessary for its survival, making its physical environment hospitable to the species that inhabit it. *read* p.44

Genome An organism's whole hereditary information encoded in the DNA*. *read* p.19

Gliding / soaring flight On long journeys, it is impossible for a bird to flap its wings continuously, with the risk of tiring very rapidly. It therefore extends motionless wings and uses rising air currents to rest in the air, making subtle changes to their shape for maximum lift*. This type of flight, gliding (or more accurately soaring), is practiced with greater ease by birds with a large wingspan such as the albatross or the majority of birds of prey (eagle, falcon, etc.). *read* p.127

Global warming Increasing average temperature in the atmosphere and on Earth. Among other things, higher temperatures cause the ice caps to melt which results in raised sea levels. The main cause is believed to be greenhouse gas emissions although there is a debate about this. *read* p.31.43.51.52.163

Globalisation Movement of people, goods, ideas and capital across the world, reducing the boundaries between cultures and countries. *read* p.52

Glucose One type of carbohydrate*. *read* p.83.113

Glycogen A long polymer chain of glucose*. It is in fact the storage form of glucose in animals and humans which is analogous to the starch in plants. Glycogen is synthesised and stored mainly in the liver and the muscles. It is an energy reserve that can be quickly mobilised to meet a sudden need for glucose. *read* p.83

Gymnosperms Include conifers such as fir, spruce and pine. The so-called broadleaf trees are angiosperms (Greek *angeion* 'case' and *sperma* 'seed') which have seeds in an ovary. Gymnosperm literally means 'naked seed' (Greek *gymnos* 'naked' and *sperma* 'seed'). In effect, gymnosperms are characterised by the fact that their seeds are not enclosed in a fruit, like the pips in an apple, but are simply located between the bracts of the fruit, between the scales of a pine cone. When male and female pine cones dry out, their bracts open and release the seeds. *read* p.231

H

Heliotropism The movement of plants towards or away from the sun. *read* p.145

Heterotroph Organism incapable of life without the benefit of organic material, in contrast to autotrophs* who can produce organic compounds from sunlight energy. Most living organisms are heterotrophs. *read* p.113

Homochromy The ability of animals to take on the colour of their environment to blend in and go unseen by their predators. *read* p.97

Homotypy Shape resemblance. *read* p.97

Hybridisation In genetics, hybridisation is the process of combining, therefore selecting, different varieties or species of organisms to create a hybrid. *read* p.30

Hydrodynamics Like aerodynamics*, hydrodynamics is a sub-division of fluid dynamics in physics. It is the branch of dynamics which studies the motion produced in fluids by applied forces. *read* p.24.149.153.155.219

Hydrophilia A material is said to be hydrophilic when it absorbs water. *read* Hydrophobia, Super-hydrophobia and p.18.217.239

Hydrophobia A material is said to be hydrophobic, or water-repellent or waterproof, when it repels water (because the material doesn't create hydrogen bonds with the water molecules*). *read* Hydrophilia, Super-hydrophobia and p.18.63.125.203.237.239

Hypodermis Consisting of mostly fat, the hypodermis, a layer beneath the dermis*, attaches the skin to underlying muscles and bones. *read* Epidermis and p.205

I

In vitro From the Latin, translating into 'in glass', which literally designates experiments that are made in a tube, outside the concerned living organism. *read* *In vivo* and p.18.19.169

In vivo Contrary to *in vitro**, *in vivo* designates experiments that are performed within a living organism. *read* p.18

Inflorescence Inflorescence denotes the arrangement of flowers on a plant stem. This arrangement is in fact very complex and much researched. It varies from plant to plant. The pattern created by the distribution of flowers on the stalk resembles a fractal pattern. Inflorescences are defined as determinate or indeterminate. In the case of a determinate inflorescence, the central stem terminates in a flower which matures first. In the case of an indeterminate inflorescence, the stem which ends in a terminal bud can still grow and the flowers open starting from the base upwards. *read* p.63

Infrared light A type of light that humans cannot see. We nevertheless experience it when we feel the heat of the sun on our skin or the warmth of a camp fire. Gamma rays, X-rays, ultraviolet light, microwaves and radio waves are other types of invisible light. All of these rays and waves are the same type of electromagnetic* energy. They are different only because the length of their waves are different. Within visible light, the wavelengths actually determine the colours we see. Infrared wavelengths extend from 780 nm to 1,000,000 nm. Visible light is between 380 nm and 780 nm. *read* p.169

Intrinsic worth A philosophy, also known as intrinsic value, referring to an animal's value as a being in itself, as opposed to its value to other beings. *read* p.45.47.48

Iridescence Iridescence corresponds to a change in the perceived colour of a surface as a function of the viewing angle or the incident light. The elytra (from Greek *elutron* 'sheath'), or wing covers of several species of beetles, as well as the wings of certain butterflies, soap bubbles or oil spreading on water, have this surprising property of revealing several colours 'in one'. Iridescence (Greek *iris* 'rainbow') is also known as goniochromism (Greek *gonio* 'angle' and *chroma* 'colour'). *read* p.73.93.189

Iridophore A type of chromatophore*. *read* p.93

Isotropic A material is isotropic if its mechanical properties are identical in all directions. In general, metals and plastics materials are considered to be isotropic on the macroscopic scale; wood, paper, certain fibre-reinforced composite materials* or honeycomb structures for example, are considered to be anisotropic*. In reality, perfect isotropy doesn't exist, even more so when one considers materials on a microscopic scale. Certain techniques for the fabrication of materials, lamination of metals or extrusion of polymers for example, have a tendency to leave the structure of the material oriented in one direction, inducing anisotropy which has to be borne in mind when these oriented materials come to be reworked.

K

Keratin A fibrous protein present in many living creatures, insoluble in water and forming protective tissues such as epidermis*, fur, hair, nails, horns, beaks or feathers. The keratin molecule* is constructed as a helix, consisting of amino acids* and wound around other keratin molecules by sulphur-based bridges for a consistent, rigid assembly. Keratin is hydrophilic* and is therefore sensitive to moisture and capable of holding up to 40% of its weight in water. It is very strong and also elastic, owing to its twisted structure, which acts like a spring. *read* p.65.133.177

L

Leucophore A type of chromatophore*. *read* p.93

Lift In moving through a fluid (air or water for example), a body is subject to aerodynamic* or hydrodynamic* forces respectively. Two types of forces are identified: drag, parallel to and opposing the direction of movement and lift, which is perpendicular to it. Lift varies according to various factors, among which are air density*, the shape of the moving object and its angle (the angle of 'attack') in relation to the fluid involved, the surface area of the object and its speed in relation to the fluid (or that of the fluid if the object is stationary in moving fluid). Lift is the main force giving aircraft the ability to fly. *read* p.79.89.121.125.153

Lignin A natural polymer, commonly derived from wood. Lignin makes up part of the secondary cell walls of plants, strengthening them and plays a role in the plants' water transport system. Lignin has some similarity to synthetic 'plastics' materials, and is thermo-softening. *read* p.175

Lipids Lipids designate various molecules* that can be found in cells, such as fats, waxes, cholesterol, triglycerides, hormones and fat-soluble vitamins. They help shape, protect and insulate the cells. They also provide an energy source. Lipids are insoluble in water, and account for most of the fat present in the human body. *read* p.18.111

M

Mechanotransduction In order to adapt to its environment, the architecture of bone is continually modified by a process known as apposition and local resorption of bone material. On the microscopic scale it is the osteoblast, osteoclast and osteocyte cells which take part in this bone remodelling phenomenon: in response to external mechanical loading, the network of osteocytes, sensitive to the local bony tissue deformation state, are capable of alerting other specialised cells involved in remodelling (osteoblasts and osteoclasts). The cells thus alerted and stimulated, can then come into play by locally modifying bone density*, causing a change in mechanical properties. _read_ p.211

Metabolism All the physical and chemical reactions in an organism by which its material substance is produced, maintained and destroyed to make energy available. Many metabolic processes are brought about by the action of enzymes*. _read_ p.19.83.129.193.284

Mitosis Mitosis designates the very complex process of separation by a mother cell into two identical cells. The chromosomes* are separated and DNA* is replicated. The two nuclei* have the same number and kind of chromosomes as the parent nucleus, which is different from meiosis, in which the amount of genetic material is halved. It is the process by which the body grows and replaces cells. _read_ p.141

Molecule A group of atoms bonded together, representing the simplest electrically neutral structural unit of an element or compound. _read_ p.18.21.22.26.113.129.133. 141.157.159.169.183.207.225

Monistic philosophy A philosophical view which holds that there is unity in a given field of inquiry, where this is not to be expected. _read_ p.29

Morphogenesis Among other things, the term morphogenesis refers to the natural laws which determine shapes: physical or chemical reactions which allow minerals to have different shapes and colours, the generation of waves in the sea or in deserts under the influence of the wind, processes involved in the development of the shape of an organism during embryogenesis, the relief patterns in the Earth's crust, tissue and organ structures, etc. _read_ p.135.282

N

Nacre Internal surface of the shell of some molluscs, also known as 'mother-of-pearl'. _read_ p.69.213

Nanoprobe An optical device for viewing extremely small objects. _read_ p.18

Nanovector A nanovector basically transports substances from one point to another, on a nanoscale. It is used within the medical field, for instance, to send medication to a precise location in the body. _read_ p.18

Natural selection The main mechanism of evolution, fully explained by Charles Darwin. Organisms that are better adapted to their environment tend to survive and reproduce themselves, continuing their species. _read_ p.15.25.31.35.36.282

Natural Systems Agriculture Mimicking nature by taking prairies as a model to produce food. The idea was developed at The Land Institute in 1977. _read_ p.33

Nature writing Writings of close personal observations of nature, often including philosophical reflections. _read_ p.45

Neurocybernetics Neurocybernetics is the science aiming to understand brain mechanisms and systems on a neuronal* scale. _read_ p.10.25

Neuron Cells conducting the nerve impulses. They consist of a nucleus*, an axon* and several dendrites and are connected to each other via areas of close contact called synapses*. Some estimates consider that the human brain contains more than a 100 billion neurons. _read_ p.25. 26.81.89.93.137.159

Neurotransmitter Chemical substances that are released when a nerve impulse reaches the end of the neuron's* axons*. They are diffused across the synapse*, ensuring the transfer of the impulse to another neuron or to a muscle fibre, for instance. Acetylcholine* was the first neurotransmitter to be identified. _read_ p.159

Nucleotide Molecules* that, when joined together, make up the structural units of DNA*. _read_ p.18.19.157

Nucleus The part of a cell – a membrane-enclosed organelle – which contains all the genetic materia (DNA)*. _read_ p.157

O

Oligomer Low molecular weight polymer, containing relatively few monomer unit <u>*read*</u> p.205

Oligonucleotide A polynucleotide containing only a short sequence of nucleotides*. <u>*read*</u> p.19

Osculum An osculum is an opening in a sponge through which water is expelled. <u>*read*</u> p.223

Osmosis A diffusion phenomenon demonstrated by a material when molecules* of water (or generally a solvent) move through a semi-permeable membrane which separates two liquids whose concentrations of dissolved substances are different. The difference in concentration causes a difference in osmotic pressure and movement of the solvent through the membrane. In the sea, the water is more salty than that in the body of a fish, for example. The animal therefore has a tendency to lose water. Its impermeable skin protects it. It absorbs saltwater via its gills and the mucous membranes in its mouth and the salt is filtered to compensate for water loss. <u>*read*</u> p.83

Oxygen Chemical symbol O, atomic number 8 in the periodic table* of the elements. For us, oxygen is indispensible, representing 86% of the oceanic water mass, 21% of the atmosphere and more than 62% of the human body, and we need to breathe it in constantly. We know oxygen best in its gaseous form, O_2, which is its state under normal conditions of temperature and pressure. <u>*read*</u> p.40. 85.105.111.141.185.199.223.262.264

P

PCM Phase-change materials (PCM) are based on simple physical principles of change of state. In a fusion phase for example, above a certain temperature characteristic of each material, they liquefy by absorbing energy and release it in the form of heat when the temperature falls. There are different types: mineral compounds such as hydrated salts, organic compounds such as paraffins and fatty acids or eutectic compounds (which may be organic or inorganic). PCMs can thus take over from energy-devouring air-conditioning systems. Too warm, PCMs absorb excess heat and help to lower the temperature, too cool, they restore the energy previously absorbed in the form of heat, causing a small rise in temperature. <u>*read*</u> p.227

Periodic table (of the chemical elements) A systematic overview of all 118 chemical elements. The elements are categorised based on their atomic number and grouped in such a way that elements with similar properties are shown close to each other. Besides the atomic numbers, the table also lists the symbols of the elements and sometimes even more detailed information. <u>*read*</u> p.35.51

pH pH is the abbreviation for 'hydrogen potential'. This is a measure of the chemical activity of hydrogen ions in solution. Pure water at 25 ºC is chosen as the reference, as it contains equal quantities of H_3O^+ oxonium ions and HO^- hydroxide ions. Its pH value is 7 and the water is then said to be 'neutral'. The pH value thus gives an indication of the acidity or alkalinity of a solution, namely the concentration of H_3O^+ or HO^- ions. If the pH is higher than 7 (more HO^- ions), the pH is said to be 'alkaline'. If the pH is lower than 7 (more HO^+ ions), the pH is said to be 'acid'. For example, lemon juice has a pH of about 2.5, blood* 7.4, soap 10. <u>*read*</u> p.71

Photochemical reaction Chemical reactions that are caused by absorption of light, whether the light is visible, infrared or ultraviolet. One famous photochemical reaction is the action of sunlight on car exhaust fumes, resulting in the production of ozone. On the other hand, photochemical reactions now help to de-pollute air from exhaust fumes. <u>*read*</u> p.113

Photosynthesis The process of plants and algae converting sunlight, carbon dioxide* and water into glucose* for themselves and oxygen* as a waste product. <u>*read*</u> p.22. 33.34.37.111.113.185.225.262

Photovoltaic cell <u>*read*</u> Solar cell and p.87

Phytoremediation The use of green plants to remove pollutants from the environment is called phytoremediation. Various plants have the ability to clean-up contaminated soils, water or air. They do this by absorbing the contaminants through their roots and then either contain, degrade or eliminate them. <u>*read*</u> p.54

Polycondensation A form of chemical condensation applied for the manufacturing of polymers. <u>*read*</u> p.141

Polysaccharide Polymeric carbohydrate* structures. <u>*read*</u> p.61

Powered flight Naturally, a bird can't provide its propulsion by means of a motor or a jet engine. However, it does so without the need to blow air behind it in order to create propulsive force. Using its pectoral muscles, which form the major part of the musculature of bird wings, it makes the latter move successively up and down, allowing it to push the surrounding air, giving it thrust as a result. _read_ p.125

Protein Proteins are macromolecules made out of amino acid* chains. Proteins, as well as carbohydrates* for instance, are essential parts of organisms and participate in virtually every process within cells. They have various functions, depending on their type and can therefore act as structural components of body tissues such as muscle or hair, be enzymes* or antibodies, etc. _read_ Amino acids and p.18.19.22.30.36.39.69.71.79.83.85.93.111.141.159.185. 205.217

Q

Quantum device An electronic device structure, the properties of which derive from the wave nature of electrons*. (Source: *The National Technology Roadmap for Semiconductors*, 1994). _read_ p.37

Quantum mechanics A mathematical theory that describes behaviour and interaction of matter and energy on the scale of atoms and atomic particles. _read_ p.37.191

R

Radiolaria Most radiolarians are planktonic, and get around by coasting along ocean currents. They create glassy skeletons of often perfect geometric form and symmetry, with a wide variety of shapes, including cone-like and tetrahedral forms. Radiolaria can range anywhere from 30 microns to 2 mm in diameter. They are part of the zoo-plankton, therefore are animals, whereas diatoms are algae. _read_ p.29.223.285

Rare metals (rare earth elements) 17 chemical elements in the periodic table* make up what is called rare earth elements (or rare earth minerals). These mineral reserves are needed for new technologies such as lasers, camera lenses, fluorescent lamps, X-ray tubes and much more. The demand is increasing rapidly and therefore access to all the rare earth elements has become the subject of a

conflict in the WTO between China on the one hand, currently the predominant supplier, and Europe and the United States on the other. _read_ p.51.105

Refraction Any form of wave, whether light, sound or seismic, is subject, among other things, to a phenomenon which makes the path of the light deviate when its speed changes between two mediums. This phenomenon is called refraction. In optics, any medium through which light may pass has a refractive index, which is a function of the wavelength of the light. This allows the speed of propagation (phase speed) of the wavelength in question in the medium to be determined. The higher the refractive index of a material, the lower the speed of propagation of the light. _read_ p.73

Resilience science Study of how ecosystems* adapt, transform or respond to disturbances. _read_ p.36

Restriction enzymes Restriction enzymes are a class of enzymes* being able to cut DNA* molecules* at specific base sequences. _read_ p.19

Riblet effect Sharks can reach high speeds, partly due to the riblets on their skin that are arranged parallel to the swimming direction. _read_ p.155

S

Saline A solution containing salt and water. _read_ p.18. 193

Semi-crystalline polymer A plastic material that has a molecular structure which is both amorphous and crystalline, depending on the areas. _read_ p.205

Sericin Gelatinous protein* that surrounds the fibroin* fibre in silk produced by spiders and silkworms. _read_ p.217

Servo-controlled system A self-regulating feedback system. It is used in the automatic control of machines, and involves a sensing element, an amplifier and a servomotor. _read_ p.145

Silica The main constituent of sand, quartz and other rocks. It is hard and colourless. _read_ p.141.223

Soft chemistry A new promising branch of materials science that differs from conventional solid-state chemistry,

Taking one element out of an ecosystem changes everything radically, with no possibility of recovery

Hervé Naillon

wanting to develop reactions at an ambient temperature in open reaction vessels, just as biological systems do. Glass and ceramics with new properties have thus been developed, inspired by diatom's glass skeleton production. _read_ p.141

Solar cell Solar cells convert sunlight energy into electrical energy. They are also called photovoltaic cells*, although these cells do not necessarily need the sun as a light source. Individual cells are connected and made into solar panels. _read_ p.33.37.87.113

Sol-gel process The fabrication of vitreous materials such as glass without the high-temperature fusion stage that is normally necessary. These processes use solutions containing colloidal inorganic particles (sol) and change them in gel (inorganic solid network swollen with solvent). They are very interesting and promising processes in the sense that they allow glass deposition on materials that would usually not sustain the high working temperatures of glass. They are already in use for protective coatings or to produce thin films and fibres, etc. _read_ p.141

Spectrophotometry Measurement of a material's reflection or transmission properties through the use of a spectrophotometer. _read_ p.147

Spheniscin Antimicrobial substance that plays a part in preserving the stored food in the king penguin's stomach. _read_ p.131

Staphylococcus aureus A bacteria* that is frequently part of the human or animal skin flora. When it enters wounds it can cause minor infections and life-threatening diseases. _read_ p.75.169

Sulphide Sulphide designates mineral compounds in which sulphur is combined with one or more metals. _read_ p.215

Super-hydrophobia A material is super-hydrophobic when it is extremely difficult to wet it. Super-hydrophobia phenomena are complex, and have been studied by the scientists Wenzel and Cassie among others. Observations reveal some surprises: a nano-textured surface can as easily lead to frictionless sliding (the Cassie or 'fakir' effect), as to a highly adhesive surface – water penetrates into the micro-structures and only comes out again with difficulty (the Wenzel effect). _read_ Hydrophilia, Hydrophobia and p.203.237.239

Supramolecular chemistry Supramolecular chemistry is defined as a 'chemistry beyond the molecules*'. It focuses on the chemical systems made up of a certain number of assembled molecules. _read_ p.205

Surface tension An effect within the surface layer of a liquid that causes the layer to behave as an elastic sheet. The molecules* of a material have a tendency to keep together and when close to a different material they try to minimise the contact surface with this material. This is why water forms drops, a sphere being the shape which offers the least contact surface. If, in contact with a material, the surface tension is not high enough to compete with the molecular energy which holds the water molecules* together, the result is that the peripheral molecules are pushed towards the interior of the drop, the water thus retaining its drop form. If on the other hand the surface tension is high, the drop is deformed, the water spreads out. The unit of measurement for surface tension is Newton/metre (N/m). In the industrial domain, surface tension is an important matter. The higher the surface tension, the more easily a material will be printed on or adhered to. _read_ p.22.237

Symbiosis A symbiotic relationship is a close relationship between different species. It can be mutualistic (both species benefit), commensal (one species benefits and the other is not harmed or helped), or parasitic (one species benefits while the other is harmed). _read_ p.31.225

Synapse Space between the pre- and post-synaptic membranes of neurons* which allows a neuron to pass an electrical or chemical signal to another cell. _read_ p.159

Synchrotron radiation A form of electromagnetic* radiation emitted by electrons* going round in a storage ring, at a speed close to that of light (so-called relativistic particles). Synchrotron radiation may range over the entire electromagnetic spectrum from infrared to X-rays and has exceptional qualities of polarisation, coherence and low divergence. It allows the structure and electronic properties of matter to be investigated. _read_ p.213

T

Thermoplastic A type of polymer that becomes 'plastic' (flexible) when heated and hardens when cooled. The process can be repeated, therefore thermoplastics are theoretically recyclable. Our everyday plastics are mostly thermoplastics: polystyrene, polyethylene, polypropylene, acrylic, etc. They are perfect candidates to be processed by injection moulding or extrusion. *read* p.171.175

Transgenesis The process of introducing a foreign DNA* – called a transgene – into a living organism so that the organism will exhibit a new property and transmit that property when reproducing. Due to their simple genetics, bacteria* were the first organisms to be modified in the laboratory. Some transgenic animals are used as experimental models for testing in biomedical researches or to produce human hormones such as insulin, for example. Transgenic plants have also been engineered in order to be more resistant to pests and herbicides, or to increase their nutritional value. There are many ongoing debates on this transgenesis subject. *read* p.30

Turbulence Irregular flow of fluids (liquids or gases) causing the formation of eddies. *read* p.99.121.137

U

Ultrasound A frequency greater than 20 kHz. Like all sound, ultrasound consists of mechanical pressure waves whose speed of propagation depends on the medium they are travelling in. Ultrasound is not audible to people (whose audible frequency range varies from approximately 20 Hz to 20 kHz), but many animals are capable of emitting and/or hearing it. Like the bat, the dolphin uses ultrasound to distinguish obstacles, find food and also to communicate. *read* p.101.227

Urea-formaldehyde A non-transparent resin, made from urea and formaldehyde*. It is used in many adhesives, wood MDF and also for insulation. It is now known that it can cause health problems and is therefore used less and less in production. *read* p.69

V

Van der Waals forces Atoms and molecules are joined together by different types of bonds. The Van der Waals interaction – discovered by Dutch physicist Johannes Diderik van der Waals (1837), who won a Nobel Prize in Physics in 1910 – is a low-intensity electromagnetic

force* of a quantal origin (acting at the inter-molecular level). This is the origin of the astonishing ability of geckos to walk on ceilings and also explains the ability of thermoplastics* to be malleable when warm (a phenomenon related to the appearance–disappearance of Van der Waals forces). *read* p.65

Vasoconstriction Contraction of blood* vessels to decrease blood flow, resulting in minimised blood loss and retained body heat. *read* p.85

Vortex Flow of fluids (liquids or gases) circulating around a centre, a phenomenon that is visible in, for example, hurricanes. *read* p.99.125.137.149.155.181

Z

Zoopharmacognosy Self-medication process of animals through the selection and use of specific plants (Greek *zoo* 'animal', *pharma* 'drug' and *gnosy* 'knowing'). *read* p.33

BIBLIO-
GRAPHY

ABOUT BIOMIMICRY

BOOKS

Janine M. Benyus
Biomimicry: Innovation Inspired by Nature
Harper Perennial, 2002

The reference in the field of biomimetics*. Essential reading.

Dr Gunter Pauli
The Blue Economy - 10 Years, 100 Innovations, 100 Million Jobs
Paradigm Publications, 2010

Dr Gunter Pauli participated in the founding of the Zero Emissions Research Initiative (ZERI). In his book, he challenges the green movement to do better and to do more.

Agnès Guillot and Jean-Arcady Meyer
La bionique: Quand la science imite la nature
Édition Dunod, 2008

Bionics*, a young science born in 1960, today encompasses a vast field of research: technological applications of natural inventions, autonomous robots inspired by animals, artificial hybrids equipped with living parts or hybrid living organisms equipped with artificial parts. This book shows numerous examples in various fields, as well as their fundamental and applied spin-offs: an adhesive which is repositionable *ad infinitum* like the feet of a gecko; houses with ecosystems*; adaptive robots learning by trial and error or evolving from generation to generation; mildew piloting an octopod robot; neuro-prostheses translating thought into movement.

WEBSITES

www.asknature.org

An online inspiration source for the biomimicry community that organises the world's biological literature by function. Following the example set by the Janine Benyus book, asknature.org is the undisputed reference in the field of biomimetics. An extremely fruitful and valuable database packed with inspiration, examples, contacts and exchanges.

www.biomicryinstitute.org

Founded in 2005 by Janine Benyus, the Biomimicry Institute is a non-profit organisation that promotes the study and imitation of na-

ture's remarkably efficient designs, bringing together scientists, engineers, architects and innovators who can use those models to create sustainable technologies. The Biomimicry Institute offers, amongst other things, short-term workshops and two-year certificate courses in biomimicry for professionals.

biomimicry.typepad.com

A blog sponsored by the Biomimicry Institute intended for pointers and commentary on articles relating to biomimicry. Waiting for your comments to be posted.

www.biomimicryguild.com

Founded in 1998, the Biomimicry Guild helps innovators design sustainable products and processes that create conditions conducive to all life.

www.blueeconomy.de

An international community of companies, innovators and scientists, providing open source access to develop, implement and share prosperous business models that strive to improve natural ecosystems* and the quality of life for all.

www.ted.com

TED is a non-profit organisation devoted to 'Ideas Worth Spreading'. It started out in 1984 and offers free online access, amongst other things, to conferences that bring together people from three worlds: technology, entertainment and design.
TEDTalks, *Janine Benyus shares nature's designs*, 2007.
TEDTalks, *Janine Benyus: biomimicry in action*, 2009.
TEDTalks, *Robert Full on engineering and evolution*, 2002.

www.inspire-institut.org

Founded in February 2008 by sustainable development expert Emmanuel Delannoy, the INSPIRE institute (Initiative for Promotion of Industry Reconciled with Ecology And Society) is an 'Association loi 1901' (not-for-profit association). This is a focus for discussion, knowledge-sharing and action in the service of reconciling the economy with the biosphere*. International monitoring, dissemination, training and support.

www.biomimicryeuropa.org

A non-profit international association established in Brussels in 2006, whose aim is to promote innovative solutions directed towards sustainability. Janine Benyus is among the

founders and a member of the board. Hence, Biomimicry Europa intends to develop a strong relationship with the Biomimicry Institute. Gauthier Chapelle, a graduated agricultural engineer and holder of a PhD in biology, is the director and co-founder.

www.zeri.org

Zero Emissions Research and Initiatives (ZERI) is a global network seeking sustainable solutions for society and using nature's design principles as inspiration.

www.moreinspiration.com

Powered by CREAX, this website offers an inspiring overview of innovative products and technologies from all possible domains, including biomimicry.

ABOUT SCIENCE

BOOKS

L'âme au Corps: Arts et Sciences 1793-1993
Catalogue edited by Jean Clair
Grand Palais National Galeries 19 Oct. 1993
– 24 Jan. 1994. National Museums Union.
Gallimard / Electa

The catalogue of the exhibition *L'âme au Corps – Arts et Sciences 1793-1993*, which was held in the National Galleries of the Grand Palais from October 1993 to the end of January 1994 on the occasion of the bicentenary of the Louvre Museum, the Natural History Museum and the National Conservatoire of Arts and Crafts. The aim of this event was to present to the public the courses of action which are inextricably involved in shaping our imagination and our thinking, tackling the relationships linking the arts and sciences in our time. In this book of more than 500 pages, divided into eight chapters, we look at the themes closely related to bio-inspired approaches. 'Machine man', 'electric man' and 'prosthetic man' are some of the domains presented in this well-documented, well-illustrated book.

D'Arcy Wentworth Thompson,
On Growth and Form: The Complete Revised Edition
Dover Publications, 1992

This book was a major scientific work, published for the first time in 1917. The work of D'Arcy Thompson (1860–1948) revealed an interdisciplinary approach that was ahead of its time, relating the laws of nature and the principles of physics in a very relevant way. The author, who shared Darwin's evolutionary ideas, uses reasoning from mathematics and physics to describe natural forms of plants and animals. The examples he gives constitute a very valuable range of sources of inspiration for biomimetics* applications.

V. Fleury, J.F. Gouyet, M. Leonetti
Branching in Nature: Dynamics and Morphogenesis of Branching Structures, from Cell to River Networks
Springer and EDP Sciences, 2001

This book is a compilation of lectures on the theme of: 'Branching in Nature – Dynamics and Morphogenesis of Branching Structures, from Cells to River Networks' which were given in the Les Houches School of Physics (France), in 1999. The event, which brought together scientists from many varied disciplines – mathematicians, physicists, chemists, crystallographers, botanists, biologists, neurobiologists, geologists, microbiologists and geographers – allowed interdisciplinary discussion on the concepts and laws which govern the development of branching structures. This debate led to an acknowledgement of the existence of universal laws governing the morphogenesis of branching structures and their interest for the construction of artificial systems.

Philippe de la Cortadière
Histoire des Sciences: de l'Antiquité à nos jours
Éditions Tallandier, 2004

This composite publication, with six parts devoted respectively to mathematics, physics, astronomy, chemistry, earth sciences and life sciences, explains the major episodes in the development of these disciplines over the course of the centuries. This historical analysis is completed by a glimpse of the research advances in each field and their potential applications.

Dictionnaire culturel des sciences
Édition du Seuil / Regard, 2001
Edited by Nicolas Witkowski

A compendium of thousands of articles, this 'Cultural Dictionary of the Sciences' deals with all scientific disciplines, taking account of the diversity of civilisations, interspersed with aspects of these linked to the sciences proper and also their relationships with art, literature, cinema, sociology, myth, politics, history, religions, humour, ethics, economy, poetry and popularisation. A well-researched publication which brings to life some lost links between science and culture.

Dictionnaire d'histoire et de philosophie des sciences
Presses Universitaires de France, 1999
Edited by Dominique Lecourt

This book gathers together 900 keywords defined in a context which systematically unites philosophical thoughts in a historic survey of scientific investigation. Concepts, laws, names, correlations bringing an enlightened view of different ways of thinking in all the scientific disciplines and their historical development. The natural laws which are the foundations of the biomimetics* approach are particularly well described.

Grand Dictionnaire de Philosophie
Larousse et CNRS Editions, 2003
Edited by Michel Blay

This 'Complete Dictionary of Philosophy' is a collection of the work by 200 authors, with 1,100 entries and 70 essays. It offers an account of progress in the development of the fundamental notions and main operating concepts in philosophical discussion. Among other things, it refers with meticulous detail to the history of ideas, notably to the links between philosophy and the different scientific disciplines. The knowledge accumulated, the influencing factors, the current situation of ideas and questions, the nature of debates and social issues all constitute excellent guides as part of the presentation of each item. A particularly useful and well-researched tool for conceptual analysis of the evolution of ideas relating to mimicry, biomimetics* and bio-inspired methodology.

Charles Darwin
The origin of species: by means of natural selection or the preservation of favoured races in the struggle for life
John Murray, 1859

This is Charles Darwin's *magnum opus*, the fundamental text of modern biology. The first edition, 1,250 copies, was sold out in one day. This publication, dedicated to the theory of natural selection* in species, was going to initiate lively controversy, which is still getting the advocates of creationist theories worked-up about it today. Apart from his interest in the development of concepts in biology, Darwin's work, which for the most part results from very acute observations, undoubtedly provides remarkable descriptions of the 'ins and outs' of evolutionist theory. The various descriptions of the evolution of animal species are still sources of inspiration for many applications of biomimetics.

Jill Bailey
The Way Nature Works
Macmillan, 1992

The perfect book to gain a good understanding of nature and the way it functions. A team of scientists tries to answer a series of simple questions about nature: for example, how birds fly or how sedimentary rocks are formed.

WEBSITES

iopscience.iop.org

IOPscience is a platform for IOP-hosted journal, magazine and website content. It incorporates some of the most innovative technologies and publishes a *Bioinspiration & Biomimetics* journal (both online and in print).

www.cnrs.fr

The French National Centre for Scientific Research, a valuable information source on the latest scientific developments.

www.nature.com

Nature Publishing Group (NPG) is a publisher of high-impact scientific and medical information in print and online. NPG publishes journals, online databases, and services in the fields of life sciences, physical sciences, chemical and applied sciences and clinical medicine. An essential reference source in scientific publication.

ABOUT ECOLOGY

BOOKS

Rachel Carson
Silent Spring
Houghton Mifflin, 1962

Rachel Carson, a biologist, was contacted by a friend who was worried when she noticed a reduction in the number of birds in the area where she lived. After several years of research, Rachel Carson highlighted the fact that not only birds, but also other animals, were being poisoned by pesticides. Her book gave birth to the ecological movement.

Catherine Larrère
Les philosophies de l'environnement
Presses Universitaires de France, 1997

Environmental questions, especially in Anglo-Saxon countries, are often about the relationships between mankind and nature. A new

Focusing on only one solution is never a good thing, people should consider a diversity of options

Catherine Larrère

aesthetic was developing, which was shaking up anthropocentrism, with the intention of no longer regarding nature as just simply a 'reservoir of resources'. This book deals with the different themes associated with this philosophical thinking, for example intrinsic value, wilderness and animal well-being.

Catherine Larrère and Raphaël Larrère
Du bon usage de la nature:
Pour une philosophie de l'environnement
Aubier - Collection Alto, 1997

Catherine and Raphaël Larrère postulate milestones for a new vision of nature. A nature mankind could be part of without shame, that he could keep in a decent state to be his home, for now and for future generations. Beyond opposition between naturalism and humanism, they call for good, eco-centred use of nature.

Hicham-Stéphane Afeissa, John Baird Callicott, Catherine Larrère, Augustin Berque, Dale Jamieson et al.
Écosophies: La philosophie à l'épreuve
de l'écologie
Éditions MF, 2009

A book which brings together the reflections of several American and French thinkers on topical issues in ecological* philosophy.

Arne Naess
Ecology, Community and Lifestyle:
Outline of an Ecosophy
Cambridge University Press, 1989

David Rothenberg's translation of *Okologi, Samfunn og Livsstil* by Arne Naess. A philosophical reference book which questions the relationship between man and nature.

William McDonough
and Michael Braungart
Cradle to Cradle, Remaking the Way
We Make Things
North Point Press, 2002

American architect William McDonough and German chemist Michael Braungart's book defends hitherto unpublished theories in the field of ecology, not based on a reduction of consumption but rather on a revisiting of industrial processes. A biomimetic* model where everything must be re-used, returned to the soil as biological, non-toxic nutriment or recycled 'technical' nutriment *ad infinitum*. No waste, one of the watchwords. This holistic approach applies to every type of system (social, economic, architectural, etc.). It relies on a vision of human activities as combined me-

tabolisms*, potentially healthy and vigorous if they are fed by a controlled flow of materials, organic and synthetic nutriments.

Design et développement durable:
Il y aura l'âge des choses légères
Victoires éditions, 2003
Edited by Thierry Kazazian

Scenarios for transformation of our consumer society into a user society capable of satisfying our needs and our desires in a sustainable manner. A manifesto uniting design and futurology, this book is a force for proposal of business strategies aiming to offer a better quality of life for all, while building the basis of a 'light' economy.

Elizabeth Pastore-Reiss, Hervé Naillon, Ed.
Le marketing éthique: Les sens
du commerce
Village Mondial, 2002

For an ethical approach to marketing, built around Plato's three fundamentals: goodness, beauty and truth.

WEBSITES

www.treehugger.com

A media outlet dedicated to driving sustainability mainstream. Green news, solutions, and product information.

www.ted.com
TEDTalks, *New thinking on the climate crisis*, Al Gore, 2008.

DESIGN AND ART

BOOKS

Victor Papanek
Design for the Real World, Human Ecology
and Social Change
Academy Chicago Publishers, 2005

A completely revised second edition of Design for the Real World. A classic, translated into twenty-three languages. For a sensible and responsible design.

Angeli Sachs
Nature Design: From inspiration
to innovation
With essays by Barry Bergdoll, Dario Gambon and Philip Ursprung, edited by Museum für Gestaltung Zürich, Switzerland, Lars Müller Publishers, 2007

Nature Design is a concise book which presents 'models from nature' concepts and their novel applications in the domain of techniques used not only in design, but also in the expression of bio-inspired forms in the fields of architecture, landscape, photography, scientific research and art. Apart from a historical analysis the book presents many examples of applications and produces the key elements for careful reasoning on the subject of innovation meeting environmental constraints.

Sylvia Barbero, Brunella Cozzo
and Paola Tamborrini
Ecodesign
h.f.ullmann, 2009

Ecodesign is a directory of 340 examples of the use of biomaterials and sophisticated technologies inspired by nature. This recently published compilation shows, in a relevant manner, some current applications resulting from a bio-inspired approach. From a wedding dress made from starch to toys made from maize, one discovers here the actual process of attractive and original ecological design which is environmentally friendly.

Peter Pearce
Structure in Nature is a Strategy
for Design
The MIT Press, 1980

'Systems can be envisaged which consist of some minimum inventory of component types which can be alternatively combined to yield a great diversity of efficient structural form.' Peter Pearce.

Theodore A. Cook
The Curves of Life
Dover Publications, 1979

An exploration of the spiral, or helix, and its mathematical expression through The Golden Ratio.

WEBSITES

www.moma.org/interactives/exhibitions/
2008/elasticmind/index.html

An exhibition staged by the New York Museum of Modern Art in 2008, commissioned by Paola Antonnelli and an internet site with content as inspiring as the interface.

www.ted.com
TEDTalks, *The power and beauty of organic design*, Ross Lovegrove, 2005.
TEDTalks, *Design and an elastic mind*, Paola Antonelli, 2008.

ABOUT MATERIALS

MATERIAL LIBRARY / WEBSITE

matériO / www.materio.com

matériO is an European network of information centres on materials and innovative products with five physical showrooms and an extensive online database. Established in 2001 in Paris, it provides its members with a large selection of specific, reproducible and obtainable materials, key elements in the creation process. This organisation's ambition is to forge links between creative people of diverse backgrounds – including architecture, industrial design, scenography, fashion design, publishing, or fine arts – and manufacturers, engineers or researchers. For the past few years, matériO has taken a special interest in the subject of biomimicry. Many 'biomimetic' materials are indexed within the current materials libraries and were featured in an exhibition in Paris in 2010.

www.biopolymer.net

Online resources for a better environment. Links to materials, as well as institutions and certifications.

extranet.kingston.ac.uk/rematerialise

A material library built by Kingston University, UK, housing materials which either use less non renewable resources or come from renewable resources.

LITERATURE

André Dhôtel
Rhétorique fabuleuse
Garnier, 1983
(Reprinted. Le temps qu'il fait, 1990)

An absolutely delightful poetical and philosophical journey, formidably relevant and intelligent. An essential read.

PLEASING TO THE EYE

BOOKS

Ernst Haeckel
Art Forms in Nature
Dover Publications, 1974

Olaf Breidbach, Irenaeus Eibl-Eibesfeldt and Richard Hartmann
Art Forms in Nature: Prints of Ernst Haeckel
Prestel, illustrated edition, 1998

Olaf Breidbach
*Art Forms from the Ocean:
The Radiolarian Prints of Ernst Haeckel*
Prestel, 2005

Ernst Haeckel's fascinating plates, worthy of continuous rediscovery.

Hans Christian Adam
Karl Blossfeldt
Taschen, 2001

A virtuoso photographer who encourages us to see the world of vegetation in a fresh light.

WEBSITES

www.les-petites-dalles.org/Caralp/Radio-laires.html

A source of beautiful images of radiolarian* glass skeletons.

www.subblue.com/projects

Tom Beddard's work on fractals. Well worth a look.

www.silkesieler.de

Silke Sieler is a motion graphics designer based in Hamburg, Germany. Warm signal is a short abstract movie dealing with nature and maritime creatures, metamorphosis and transformation – it connects art and science.

matsysdesign.com

Established in 2004 by Andrew Kudless, Matsys is a design studio that explores the emergent relationships between architecture, engineering, biology and computation.

www.kokkugia.com

Kokkugia is a progressive architecture and urban design practice exploring generative design methodologies developed from the complex self-organising behaviour of biological, social and material systems.

www.sciencephoto.com

A store of specialised scientific photographs.

phototheque.cnrs.fr

CNRS (the French National Centre for Scientific Research) photo library.

CREDITS

Publisher Frame Publishers

Direction Élodie Ternaux (matériO)

Contributing authors
Élodie Ternaux, Michèle Ternaux, Jean-Pierre Ternaux

Production Sarah de Boer-Schultz

Illustrations Dépli Design Studio
(Benjamin Gomez and Myriam Hathout)

Graphic design Général Design/MAJi
(Maroussia Jannelle with Morgane Rébulard)

Translation and editing TransL Vertaalbureau
(Clive Pygott and Liz van Gerrevink)

Prepress Edward de Nijs

Printing D'Print

Iconography Florence Massin

Special thanks to
**Janine Benyus, Fred Gelli, Hervé Naillon,
Catherine Larrère, Mathieu Lehanneur,
Marine Jacques-Leflaive, Emmanuel Dupont,
Estella Anderson, Patty Borneman**

Trade distribution USA and Canada
Consortium Book Sales & Distribution, LLC.
34 Thirteenth Avenue NE, Suite 101
Minneapolis, MN 55413-1007
T +1 612 746 2600
T +1 800 283 3572 (orders)
F +1 612 746 2606

Distribution rest of world
Frame Publishers
Laan der Hesperiden 68
1076 DX Amsterdam
The Netherlands
www.frameweb.com
distribution@frameweb.com

ISBN: 978-90-77174-48-7

© 2012 Frame Publishers, Amsterdam, 2012

Whilst every effort has been made to ensure accuracy, Frame Publishers does not under any circumstances accept responsibility for errors or omissions. Any mistakes or inaccuracies will be corrected in case of subsequent editions upon notification to the publisher.

The Koninklijke Bibliotheek lists this publication in the Nederlandse Bibliografie: detailed bibliographic information is available on the internet at http://picarta.pica.nl

Printed on acid-free paper produced from chlorine-free pulp. TCF ∞
Printed in China

987654321

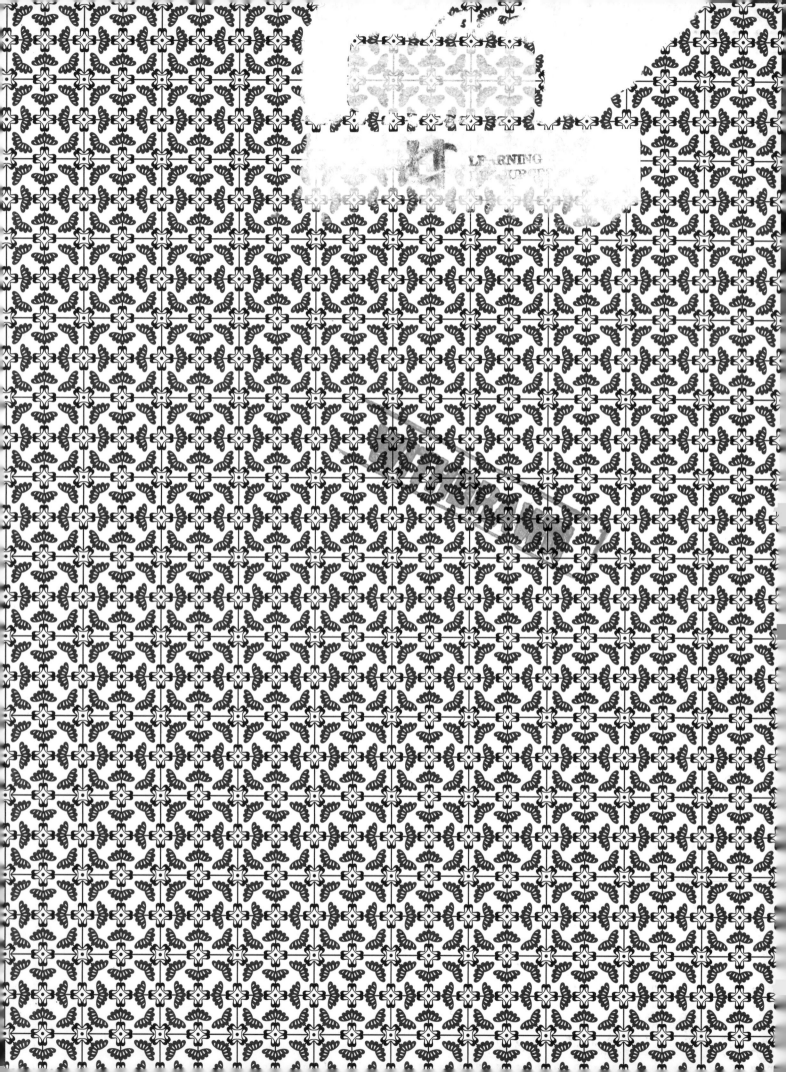